CW00446561

Change and Continuity in Applied Linguistics

Selected papers from the
Annual Meeting of the British Association for Applied Linguistics
held at the University of Edinburgh, September 1999

Edited by
Hugh Trappes-Lomax

Advisory Board: Srikant Sarangi, Celia Roberts and Gunther Kress

BRITISH ASSOCIATION FOR APPLIED LINGUISTICS
in association with
MULTILINGUAL MATTERS LTD
Clevedon • Buffalo • Toronto • Sydney

British Library Cataloguing in Publication Data

A CIP catalogue record for this book is available from the British Library.

ISBN 1-85359-526-8 (pbk)

Multilingual Matters Ltd
UK: Frankfurt Lodge, Clevedon Hall, Victoria Road, Clevedon, England BS21 7HH.
USA: UTP, 2250 Military Road, Tonawanda, NY 14150, USA.
Canada: UTP, 5201 Dufferin Street, North York, Ontario, M3H 5T8, Canada.
Australia: PO Box 586, Artamon NSW 2064, Australia.

Typeset by Wayside Books, Clevedon.
Printed and bound in Great Britain by Short Run Press Ltd.

Contents

Introduction
Hugh Trappes-Lomax, University of Edinburgh   iv

1   Changing views of language in Applied Linguistics
    Gillian Brown, University of Cambridge   1
2   Society, education and language: the last 2,000 (and the next 20?)
    years of language teaching
    Michael Stubbs, University of Trier   15
3   The secret life of grammar-translation
    Malcolm J. Benson, Hiroshima Shudo University   35
4   Changing views of language learning
    Susan Gass, Michigan State University   51
5   Change and continuity in second language acquisition research
    Florence Myles, University of Southampton   68
6   Rethinking interactive models of reading
    Martin Gill, Åbo Akademi University, Finland   82
7   Continuity and change in views of society in Applied Linguistics
    Ben Rampton, King's College, London   97
8   Talking disability: the quiet revolution in language change
    Mairian Corker, University of Central Lancashire 115
9   Critical discourse method of field: tracking the ideological shift in
    Australian Labor governments 1983–1986
    Bernard McKenna, Queensland University of Technology 131
10   'Risk is the mobilising dynamic of a society bent on change':
    how metaphors help to stabilise the developing discourse of the
    learning society, and how they don't
    Alison Piper, University of Southampton and Charmian Kenner,
    Institute of Education, University of London 151
11   The role of idioms in negotiating workplace encounters
    Almut Josepha Koester, University of Nottingham 169
12   Looking at changes from the learner's point of view: an analysis of
    group interaction patterns in cross-cultural settings
    Tan Bee Tin, University College Chichester 184

Contributors 205

Introduction

HUGH TRAPPES-LOMAX
University of Edinburgh

The papers in this volume are a selection from those presented at the BAAL Annual Conference held at the University of Edinburgh in September 1999. Caught up in fin-de-millennium excitement, the organisers had originally proposed a 'where are we now?' theme with the title 'Applied Linguistics – the State of the Art', but when this was critically analysed as implicitly static and non-scientific it was altered to 'Change and Continuity in Applied Linguistics'. The four plenary speakers (Brown, Gass, Rampton and Stubbs) were invited to focus on one of four sub-themes: changing views in Applied Linguistics of, respectively, *language, learning, society* and *teaching*.

To picture the 'state' of an academic 'art', or to distinguish one 'art' from another and from previous states of itself, we may usefully borrow from Swales' (1990) approach to the characterisation of a genre:

> ... a set of communicative *purposes* ... recognised by the *expert members* of the parent discourse community [thereby constituting] the *rationale* for the genre. ... In addition to purpose, [we can see] patterns of similarity in terms of *structure, style, content* and intended *audience*. If all high probability expectations are realised, the exemplar will be viewed as *prototypical* [my emphases].

Substituting 'academic purposes' for communicative purposes, 'academic community' for discourse community, and 'academic discipline' for genre, we see by analogy that the rationale for the existence of an academic discipline is constituted by its agreed set of purposes (what are these?); and that recognition of the discipline is helped by knowing its

- structure (the fields that are recognised within the discipline, the relationships between these and with related disciplines)

- style (e.g. rationalism vs. empiricism, qualitative vs. quantitative approaches, objectivism vs. subjectivism)

- content (the nature of the data) and

- intended audience (if no longer just educationalists, especially language teachers, who?).

Within the present selection of papers, all these issues are extensively debated, explicitly or implicitly. In introducing them, I shall avoid any attempt at summary and instead will try to highlight what have seemed to me, in editing them, the most pervasive themes.

A Pluri-centred Field?

In periods of change, it may be particularly difficult for members to agree on what is prototypical. The origins of (modern) Applied Linguistics in the effort to give academic foundations to the practical study of languages (to borrow a phrase from Henry Sweet) are, as yet, not entirely lost in the mists of time, but it is open to question whether the original linguistics-fed, pedagogy-focused types of activity are still perceived by most applied linguists, or at least BAAL members, as prototypical, or whether indeed there is a prototypical Applied Linguistics any more. Applied Linguistics must be seen as a broad church (Brown), a pluri-centred field (Rampton), or perhaps, like SLA, as a multiplicity of spokes in search of a hub (Gass).

These pleasantly archaic, even bucolic, images tend, however, to obscure the conflicting risks of fragmentation and isolationism, of which the former seems more real at present than the latter. To avoid mere anarchy we need a centre of some sort, which can hold. (As Brown points out, following Davies, the case for this is stronger if by 'we' is meant specifically people who call themselves applied linguists, rather than, more generally, all those – educationalists, socio-logists, engineers, etc. – who might participate in an Applied Linguistics confer-ence.) If this centre cannot, for many people, be the concept of linguistics applied (see, for example, Davies, 1999), we must probably look for it in some formulation along the lines of Brumfit's (quoted by Brown) 'theoretical and empirical investigation of real-world problems in which language is a central issue'. Brown is surely right to describe the range of issues opened up by such a definition as unconstrained. How are we to agree when language is 'central'?

Language Teaching/Learning/Education

Seven of the 12 papers in this volume are concerned, more or less directly, with language teaching and learning, or more generally with language in educa-tion, three of these adopting a historical approach, at least in part.

Brown approaches her topic – changing views of language in Applied Linguistics – via a historical perspective on articulatory phonetics and linguistics in relation to the teaching of, respectively, pronunciation and grammar; she notes a shift away from teaching formal aspects of language in native-speaking countries like Britain - but less so in other parts of the world (with which, she says, the West should not allow itself to get too out of step).

Brown's account is of a 'young' discipline with a short – essentially 20th-century – history. Both Stubbs and Benson take a far longer – two-millennium – view, Stubbs addressing what he calls the 2000-year-old problem of the place of language teaching in general education, Benson focusing on one particular methodology – grammar and translation – by which language teaching has been delivered over much of this period. Their histories are political and social as much as linguistic and pedagogic. Benson notes, for example, how grammar and translation in the Renaissance period 'carried forward all the traditions that had been established in Roman education: (a) the model of a better society whose symbolic foundation was the study of grammar; (b) urbanized, normative, conservative, and often elitist attitudes; and (c) a focus on literature'. Stubbs describes how 'language across the curriculum' became, in the '70s, '80s and '90s, a political football, reactionary in its demand for explicit knowledge about language, according to the left, and too politically involved in questions of language and social class, according to the right.

Local Conditions

One notable similarity between all three of these papers is the importance attached by their authors to local conditions and the ways in which these are relevant to

- locally appropriate styles of Applied Linguistics (Brown);

- problems of description of language variation and the selection of varieties to be taught: Brown shows how this problem has increased as a result of 'data overload' from corpus resources; Stubbs illustrates the point with examples from Scotland (the story of Scots) and Germany (a story of improper German);

- favoured methodologies: Benson points out that that the 'concept of a single method or approach to language teaching, a model suitable for any people in any country at any time, is likely to run into local attitudes that find it inimical to their pedagogic and social requirements' and observes in particular that 'communicative methodologies may not succeed in FL contexts where the social characteristics associated with grammar-translation still pertain; that is, contexts in which conservatism, elitism, nationalism, desire for control, respect for regularity, and a liking for literature are to be found'.

This theme is developed also by Gill (on interactive models of reading), who writes that 'past attempts to impose idealised versions of "our" reading behaviour on those with different practices, expecting to reproduce in these new settings the cultural and intellectual value they have for us, now appear naïve'; and Bee Tin (on group interaction patterns in cross-cultural settings), who concludes that how group work 'works' might not be the same for different contexts and different learning groups, and that it is important to relate change

> not only to the teacher's ideology and belief but more importantly to the students', especially when the changes are originated and promoted by a professional or institutional community (including researchers, practitioners, policy makers, etc.) whose socio-cultural and educational background is not the same as the students'.

The 'Neglected Situation'

First recognised as neglected by Goffman, the situatedness that gives meaning to interaction, experience, performance, practice, learning, is a central theme of Rampton's paper (on changing views of society in Applied Linguistics) and also in three papers which confront the 'fault line that runs through much work in Applied Linguistics and is responsible for a good deal of institutional schizophrenia and mutual incomprehension' (Gill), namely that between cognitive and social practice approaches. In his critique of interactive models of reading, Gill argues that to cross this fault line to an 'integrated, contextually responsive approach to reading' – i.e. one which takes account of situated practice – we should 'not even try to set out from where we are now'. In contrast, Gass and Myles, from their different American and European starting points and perspectives, argue for inclusivity. In Gass's words,

> stemming from these seemingly opposing views [...] is an interest in the ways internal factors (such as those represented by a UG approach to SLA) and external factors (such as those represented by an input/interactionist or variationist approach to SLA) might work *together* to account for learning [my emphasis].

Myles argues that what we are witnessing is not just 'togetherness' – a readiness for dialogue – but a change: a greater willingness to accept and to take seriously a functionalist approach.

'Discursive, Social and Applied Linguistic Analysis'

Where for Gass, investigating acquisition, a 'sociolinguistic bent' is an option, favoured by some researchers but not by all, for Rampton that bent, especially in the guise of micro-ethnographic analysis, and accompanied by 'some kind of reverence for the complexity and plenitude of situated interaction', is the most basic requirement in pursuing the 'massive agenda for discursive, social and applied linguistic analysis'. Rampton points to a movement in the social sciences where,

> instead of trying to define the core features of any social group or institution, the focus has turned to the flows of people, knowledge, texts and objects across social and geographical space, to the production and policing of boundaries of inclusion and exclusion, and to experiences of indeterminacy and ambivalence.

Such an observation fits easily enough with the aims and methods of critical language study, with which we are increasingly familiar, if not universally at ease, but Rampton extends it to the domain of the Applied Linguistics of language teaching, asking:

> What happens if anti-essentialism moves in, and we start to wonder whether feelings of group belonging aren't themselves socially constructed in the here-and-now? The answer, of course, is that the applied linguistics of other-language teaching-&-learning starts to look a bit different. It is hard to think of any other area of language study which is as centrally concerned with fluidity, marginality and transition.

This is an intriguingly radical view – language teaching has always been in the business of idealisation, if that is what is meant by essentialism – of a perceived trend in a traditionally core part of the discipline of Applied Linguistics. Here – recalling the 'real-world problems in which language is a central issue' view of the bounds of our discipline – we clearly do have problems, which are real-world, and in which language is indisputably central. The audience for any empirical or theoretical research findings is not hard to seek either.

In four other papers, all empirical studies of situated practice, issues relating to (one or more of) the above – 'real world', 'problem', 'centrality of language', 'audience' – are perhaps less clear-cut and therefore, in a 'where are we now?' collection such as this one, all the more interesting. Face-to-face office communication (Koester), recent British and EU literature on lifelong learning (Piper and Kenner), classroom interaction involving deaf participants (Corker) and a sample of Australian political documents from the '80s (McKenna) are the ix

situations in which the 'practice' of language is problematised and evaluated in a more (e.g. McKenna) or less (e.g. Koester) 'critical' way. Rampton writes of how, methodologically, social science 'gives up its dreams of being a legislator, a "healer of prejudices" and an "umpire of truth", and instead, the best it can do is operate as a translator and interpreter'. In their essentially qualitative approach to their data (albeit supported, in the case of two of the papers – those of Koester and Piper & Kenner – by corpus-quantitative techniques) and their concern with the macro significance of micro-environments (particular idioms and metaphors at particular times and in particular places) we do see a style of language study which is closely similar to that of translators or interpreters, making plain what was hidden, what was 'not transparent for the people involved' (Piper and Kenner, quoting Fairclough). But one can also detect, I think, the 'healer of prejudices', for example in Corker's articulation of the distinction between the discourses of impairment and disablement, and even the 'umpire of truth', for example in McKenna's exposé of 'flexibility discourse':

> applied to the labour force, *flexibility* implies downward movement, or diminution. Applied to capital, it implies the neo-classical assumption that capital is free to maximise production or profits or markets.

The analysis, McKenna points out, 'works on the assumption that there are traces of the social in the text. By analysing text, the social is made evident'. Leaving aside issues of subjectivity and objectivity (see the paper by Stubbs), this clearly foregrounds the social and/or political and backgrounds the linguistic, and is therefore part of that movement of Applied Linguistics identified by, for example, Rampton (1995) and Brumfit (1997), from the pedagogic, the linguistic and psycholinguistic to the sociolinguistic, from the study of language to the study of language practices. Such an analysis may be highly illuminating – but where, we may reasonably ask, is the Applied Linguistic hub of which this is a spoke?

However we may feel inclined to answer this question – and we may not feel so inclined at all if we agree with Rampton (1997, discussed in Davies 1999) that Applied Linguistics is an 'open field' – it is worth remembering, as Stubbs points out, that such a tendency is nothing new:

> Current emphases on language and power seem modern, in a period post-Foucault, but they were also central in work by Plato and Aristotle, who placed an analysis of political speeches at the centre of their training programmes. Language study for the Greeks had political and ethical goals, and perhaps post-modernist views are not as new as they sometimes seem.

Applied Linguistics is (no doubt properly) concerned with the 'ceaseless battle [within the communicative sphere] between … the centripetal tendency towards integration and the centrifugal forces towards usurpation and new formations' (Bakhtin quoted in the paper by McKenna). It is, however, also part of the battlefield.

References

Brumfit, C. (1997) How applied linguistics is the same as other science. *International Journal of Applied Linguistics* 7, 1.

Davies, A. (1999) *An Introduction to Applied Linguistics.* Edinburgh: Edinburgh University Press.

Rampton, B. (1995) Politics and change in research in applied linguistics. *Applied Linguistics* 16, 2.

Swales, J. M. (1990) *Genre Analysis.* Cambridge: Cambridge University Press.

1 Changing Views of Language in Applied Linguistics

GILLIAN BROWN
Research Centre for English and Applied Linguistics, University of Cambridge

Abstract

I begin by examining some of the cycles of fashion in teaching and research in Applied Linguistics during the 20th century, looking particularly at cycles based on input from linguistic theory and pondering on how far we can extrapolate from those cycles into future changes in our views on language. I move on to consider current challenges to the notion of Applied Linguistics as it was perceived in its early years: first, from the mass of information now pouring in from computer corpora showing that variety in language is much more subtle and dependent on far more intermingled varieties than earlier accounts had supposed, which raises issues with respect, for instance, to the notion of 'standard English' and the constructing of a teaching syllabus; secondly from the number of other disciplines which offer a variety of different views on the nature of language, and lead to the apparent fragmentation of Applied Linguistics. This fragmentation raises the question of whether there is a widely agreed heartland in Applied Linguistics, and whether this involves language and, specifically, whether it involves a linguistically informed view of language.

Interpreting the Title

I should first explain how I have interpreted the title offered to me, since the more I worked on this paper, the more all parts of the title seemed capable of multiple interpretations. I take the 'changing views' part to refer to how views have changed in the past, as well as to how they appear to be currently changing and are likely to continue to change. With respect to the issue of change, it seems to me helpful to consider how the relatively young discipline of Applied Linguistics has developed so far, and to try to identify how it is developing, the

1

nature of the recurrent patterns or cycles of activity which we can perceive in its short history.

The next part of the title can also be interpreted in a number of ways. For example, we can understand it as referring to the way in which different aspects of language have come into focus at different times in Applied Linguistics, and that is certainly part of what I understand the title to mean. But we could also understand it as implying a shift of view from that which assumed that language was the focus of Applied Linguistics to one which challenges the central position of the study of language in Applied Linguistics, and I intend to address that issue too.

Finally, still on the title, there is the issue of just what is to be understood by the term Applied Linguistics, and this issue will arise at several points in the paper.

A Historical Perspective

I am going to approach the topic by beginning with a historical perspective.

However you conceptualise Applied Linguistics today, it is hard to deny that, as a discipline, it evolved from beginnings in the teaching of foreign languages, particularly English as a foreign language. And it began to evolve, beginning about a hundred years ago, from the application of the linguistic knowledge of the time to issues in language teaching. It is, I shall assert, this aspect which has been, and still is, understood by most applied linguists in non-English speaking countries around the world as constituting the mainspring of Applied Linguistics; though no-one would deny that some individual applied linguists also devote their attention to a much wider range of enquiry and of application, and may derive their theoretical underpinning from disciplines such as education, sociology, cognitive psychology or even engineering, as well as (or rather than) from linguistics.

Perhaps the most widely known early contribution to the beginning of Applied Linguistics in Britain was made between 1900 and 1950 in the area of pronunciation teaching by Daniel Jones (and later by his pupils) at University College London. His description of the sounds of English first published in book form in 1909 (Jones, 1909) followed in the footsteps of 19th-century giants like Alexander Ellis and Henry Sweet. Daniel Jones built on their work to produce the first internationally popular and principled description of English aimed at foreign learners and their teachers. It was possible for him to produce a more principled description of English because of the prior development of the linguistic discipline of articulatory phonetics.

Articulatory phonetics and pronunciation teaching

Articulatory phonetics was the first area of modern linguistics to be systematised, by which I mean that an unprecedentedly exhaustive and principled taxonomy of sound types was created, with a terminology which was, for a while, used throughout much of the world, encapsulated in *The Principles of the IPA*, the work of the International Phonetic Association. It is true that nowadays some aspects of that late 19th and very early 20th century work are open to criticism, but the significance of this work at the time can hardly be overemphasised. It enabled the establishment of articulatory phonetics as an international academic discipline.

Once articulatory phonetics was established as a discipline, it became possible to attempt to teach foreign students the consonant and vowel sounds of, for instance, English, by more than a simple process of imitation. It became possible to identify progress in their acquisition, as the student moved from sounds which might initially have been quite distant from the target to sounds which, in some features at least, approximated the target more closely. The pronunciation teacher could now sensitise the student to the configuration and placing of lips and tongue, and guide the student towards a more successful articulation of the target consonant or vowel. The development of articulatory phonetics as a linguistic discipline meant, in fact, that the teacher could begin to teach in a positive way rather than simply by providing a model.

One outcome of this professionalisation of pronunciation teaching through the application of linguistic theory was that, with the passing of time, an increasing proportion of time was spent in courses for foreign students on teaching them how to pronounce the target language, and, as postgraduate Diplomas for applied linguists developed in the late 1950s and 1960s, a remarkable proportion of time was dedicated to the teaching of articulatory phonetics, not only in University College London, where Daniel Jones and his colleagues had carried on a lone crusade throughout the first decades of the century, but also later in the other centres where Applied Linguistics in Britain next developed, first in Leeds, and then, in the late 1950s, in Edinburgh as well.

By the 1960s, the place of pronunciation teaching was deemed by many applied linguists to be ludicrously over-emphasised. By then the study of many other aspects of language was being developed in a systematic way and these offered new and different prospects of exploration. This perception of overemphasis on pronunciation led to a reaction, a swing of the pendulum, so great that pronunciation is today largely ignored in many Applied Linguistics courses and courses for EFL teachers in Britain, and indeed in North America as well. The programme for the last BAAL meeting of the millennium exemplifies this trend.

We should note, however, that in many countries of the world, for instance in Scandinavia, in Eastern Europe, South America and the Far East, pronunciation is seen by each succeeding generation of local teacher trainers and applied linguists as a crucial and central part of the syllabus of foreign language teaching. Getting the pronunciation of the target L2 to a standard which David Abercrombie, first Professor of Phonetics in the University of Edinburgh, specified as one of 'comfortable intelligibility' is still taken to be a crucial aspect of the learning of a second or foreign language in many countries overseas. So we may perceive a, perhaps temporary, divergence of interest between many applied linguists in Britain, who find pronunciation teaching outmoded and peripheral, and those who teach Applied Linguistics overseas, who may be variably enthusiastic about it but nonetheless see it as an essential and continuing part of the curriculum.

Historical perspective: linguistics and teaching grammar

The cycle which I have suggested we can perceive in the rise and fall of EFL pronunciation teaching within Britain seems to me perceptible in other spheres of the relationship between linguistics (or cognate theoretical disciplines) and English Language teaching.

Almost simultaneously with the linguistic development of phonetics (and, eventually, phonology), came the development of systematic approaches to syntax by linguists such as Otto Jespersen, Paul Christopherson, Harold Palmer and, somewhat later, Charles C. Fries in the 1940s working in the USA. With the break-away from Latin-based syntactic descriptions and the gradual development of structuralist models of language, a new approach to teaching grammar became available. The methodology which developed from a structuralist approach with its insistence on the paradigmatic dimension interacting with the syntagmatic dimension, naturally led to a slot and filler approach to the teaching of grammar, and for 20 odd years grammar was extensively taught on the basis of this approach. And, as in the case of pronunciation, so with syntax. In the late 1950s and 1960s there was an explosion of pedagogical grammars, as well as grammatically based textbooks which more or less overtly taught grammar, sometimes disguised in little dialogues like 'the Brown family at breakfast', which drilled particular grammatical structures. As in pronunciation, the emphasis was on form, and on getting the form correct. As had been the case with pronunciation, a considerable proportion of time was devoted to grammar in any Applied Linguistics diploma course of the time, and, just as happened with pronunciation, there was an eventual reaction against the dominance of this type of teaching, both for students and intending teachers, and, again, this gave rise to a rather similar outcome. Nowadays there are Masters courses in Applied Linguistics and Masters courses for EFL teachers in Britain and in North America which contain little or no direct teaching of English grammar.

We observe once again that, in spite of a shift away from teaching formal aspects of language in native-speaking countries like Britain, there still exists a conviction among applied linguists, teacher trainers and government ministries in many countries around the world that you need to teach details of the formal standard language which is your target language. Again, then, in this aspect of language teaching, we appear to see a difference in the focus of interest between some of those who teach Applied Linguistics in countries where English is the L1, like Britain, and many of those who teach Applied Linguistics overseas, particularly in countries relatively remote from those where English is natively spoken, countries like those in Eastern Europe, India and the Far East.

Forms and Using Forms: Recycling the cycle

The revolutionary achievement of the last 40 years in both Applied Linguistics and language teaching has been the recognition that a sound knowledge of the forms of a foreign language will not, alone, guarantee your ability to communicate effectively in that language, even at a receptive level. Already in the early 1960s, it was beginning to be acknowledged that, however well you might be able to pronounce the target language, if you had not had the opportunity of extended listening to native speakers talking, you were likely to have severe difficulties with listening comprehension. Similarly, however well you constructed sentence patterns in isolation, you needed to observe how they were used in discourse for different purposes and for different audiences in order to use this range of sentence types effectively and to understand the effect of their use by native speakers and writers. The advent of mass tourism during the 1960s exposed with brutal clarity the failure of traditional academic foreign language courses to prepare the majority of their students to communicate at a quite basic level in the foreign language which they had studied daily for five or more years at school. It was this revelation, as much as any theoretical development, which jolted the profession into thinking about other aspects of language used in communication. New areas of study flooded into Applied Linguistics during the 1960s.

Just as pronunciation and formal grammar had their heyday and then diminished in importance (at least for some applied linguists), so this happened with other paradigms created by the new areas of study. Thus, for example, contrastive linguistics enjoyed a brief time in the sun during the 1960s and 1970s but then retreated to its footholds in Eastern Europe. The functional approach deriving from speech act theory enjoyed a heyday in the 1970s and early 1980s and then faded in general from the focus of attention, though some adherents continue to explore its value. What seems to happen, in cycles which manifest increasing rapidity of occurrence, is that a different aspect of language form or use is brought to the fore, is flavour of the year or decade, and then disappears from the general focus of attention, typically, however, maintaining a relatively small band of adherents, sometimes centred in a single institution, sometimes scattered more thinly over several locations.

Applied Linguists and Applied Linguistics

The effect of these rapid cycles is, on the one hand, valuable in drawing attention to different aspects of language, to different patterns of acquisition and to different uses in society which may have been overlooked hitherto. But on the other hand, the effect may be damaging in that, with the proliferation of foci of interest, it becomes more difficult to discern where the heartland of Applied Linguistics lies, if indeed there still is a heartland which would be generally acknowledged in Applied Linguistics.

I believe there would have been fairly general agreement about what constituted the centre of the discipline up until the mid 1970s. Indeed, the four volume *Edinburgh Course in Applied Linguistics*, published in the early 1970s and widely used as a model course around the world, was predicated on such an assumption. But since then, the rapidly increasing fragmentation of interests makes such a centre harder to perceive.

The fragmentation which invests Applied Linguistics is of course common in other applied disciplines which seek to apply their expertise to real-world problems, rather than sit in the ivory towers of theory. Within such disciplines new types of real-world problem constantly arise, each demanding a different approach to be adopted, each challenging some existing theoretical assumptions. Yet in disciplines as diverse as Applied Mathematics, Applied Economics and Applied Psychology, even though, within each discipline, the area has become so deeply fragmented that people within the same discipline attend different conferences, read different journals, and adhere passionately to quite different theories, at least they have shared an extended undergraduate education where some concepts at least are common – in mathematics, or in economics or in psychology.

Applied linguists, on the other hand, are often drawn from initial disciplines as diverse as modern foreign languages, ancient classical languages, literature, education, speech therapy, linguistics, psychology, social anthropology, philosophy, translation studies, communication studies, even from physics, computing and engineering – you could no doubt add many more. Their formal education in Applied Linguistics often consists only of a brief nine-month course. It is hardly surprising then to find this particular applied academic area is particularly prone to fragmentation. You may regard such fragmentation with dismay, particularly when it gives rise to unedifying disagreements about whether or not what one scholar is doing is or is not 'really' Applied Linguistics, or you may regard it as an immensely valuable asset, arising from the particularly rich and fertile environment which is brought about by the confluence of people from such diverse backgrounds and with such diverse interests.

It seems to me actually quite hard to insist that any study remotely concerned with language is not properly considered part of Applied Linguistics if you look at the institutional history of Applied Linguistics. At the second AILA congress, held in 1969, there were already 14 separate specialist sections ranging over a wide variety of what would usually be thought of as other disciplines, including papers on communications engineering, computational linguistics, neurolinguistics, stylistics, experimental phonetics, lexicography, translation theory, cognitive psychology, sociology, the political implications of language planning and theoretical linguistics, as well as papers on what would more readily be recognised as directly applied linguistic concerns with second language teaching and learning (see, for instance, Perren & Trim (eds), 1971). The 1999 AILA congress held in Tokyo included an even greater variety of papers from other disciplines, some of whose connection with language seemed to be remote. It seems that the broad definition of Applied Linguistics as practised by the AILA committee must make it impossible to exclude any paper written by anyone in the social sciences or in computational engineering which is, however remotely, concerned with language, culture, society or cognition.

However, you might, as Alan Davies helpfully suggested at the 1999 AILA Congress, want to draw a distinction between 'Applied Linguistics', which nowadays apparently sees itself as a super-discipline which embraces many other disparate disciplines, and 'applied linguists'. It is clear that many people who give papers at Applied Linguistics conferences do not think of themselves as applied linguists, and would be astonished to be so described – because they think of themselves professionally as engineers, sociologists, psychologists, educationalists, neurologists or whatever. But there do exist, as we know, people who think of themselves professionally as applied linguists, and those of us who provide Masters courses which purport to educate applied linguists have a professional interest in what such an education consists of. For us, it seems important to be able to identify a common core in the discipline – a common core which will be recognised not only in countries where English is the L1, but which will be recognised around the world. I believe that that common core would be widely agreed to include, at least, some systematic study of language, a point I shall return to.

Challenges to Applied Linguistics

For Applied Linguistics as an academic discipline today, fighting for survival in an increasingly competitive environment within and between universities both in Britain and overseas, there exist new challenges, quite apart from the daily challenges of funding and survival, which seem to me to derive from two major factors. Both of these factors will, I believe, be with us for many years to come, and both will have an effect on the changing views of language within Applied Linguistics, and indeed, on the future of Applied Linguistics as an academic discipline.

Data overload

The first major factor, which seems to me on the one hand exhilarating and on the other potentially quite problematic for Applied Linguistics, derives from data overload. I refer here to the amount of data currently available to us which informs us about language and, particularly, about its variety: on the vast differences between some written and spoken forms of language, differences which multiply as you look at the uses of language in different genres, in different standards and dialects, and in different social contexts with their different sociological and cognitive implications, as well as in the different types of patterns of first and second language acquisition in different settings. You can, no doubt, add to this list of factors affecting variability. A huge amount of relatively new information is being increasingly made available by the explosion in the late 1990s of computer corpora of enormous dimensions, an explosion which we must suppose will continue to grow exponentially.

It is an effect which I suspect may not be going to be affected by cycles of fashion in the way that pronunciation teaching and grammar teaching were, because the technology itself and the output of data will be constantly updated and changing and the types of analyses offered us will be continually refined. The basic effect of enormous amounts of data being made available to us is not going to go away.

This data overload does, I believe, affect applied linguists working in a country in which their own L1 (let's suppose it's English) is the majority language, rather differently from those working in countries where the target language is not widely spoken or used. An applied linguist working on his or her own language can hardly ignore the extraordinary amount of variation which is now drawn to our attention, with different parameters criss-crossing each other in an immensely complex way as you take into account variety due to dialect, genre, the gender of the speaker, the relative power of speaker–hearer, the number of speakers and hearers interacting, and so on. We are now told, for example by Biber, Johansson, Leech, Conrad & Finegan (1999), that there is a written genre, fiction, which in many grammatical and lexical respects resembles spoken conversation far more than it does another written genre, academic prose. This makes the easy spoken/written distinction which some of us have relied on for years look increasingly flaky. Now that this sort of information is available, the extraction of a pedagogical model of English grammar, of the identification of a 'standard' language based on 'the written form of the language', is seen by many applied linguists as becoming increasingly problematic.

Given this amazing richness of variety, the question arises whether or not it makes any sense to continue to attempt to teach foreign students a single standard of language pronunciation or a single standard of grammar for the target language. If you decide not to attempt this, the problems do not go away but merely transpose themselves into different sorts of familiar problems. You immediately encounter a difficult range of questions concerned with the structure of the syllabus: what consistent model of the language, in form or use, can be offered to the beginning and early intermediate student? where are the examples of language which the beginning student is exposed to supposed to come from, and why might some be more appropriately chosen than others? what are the principles of selection to be? can we identify which language samples are more likely than others to promote rapid and efficient learning of whatever it is we want to teach among at least some types of student?

The problems, and the excitement, which arise for applied linguists working on their own mother tongue in their country of origin may be rather different from those experienced in other countries, but these other countries differ, it seems to me, among themselves. In those countries nearest to Britain in continental Europe and Scandinavia, where many speakers achieve an impressive, almost native-speaker-like aptitude in English, and applied linguists there also have ready access to computers and to immense corpora, the issues are not so very different from those in Britain. However the teaching decisions may be more clear cut for them, in spite of developments which may lead to a reassessment of the model of English that their students are offered. We appear to be seeing the emergence of a view in some of these countries that the model of English which should be taught is the local educated form of English grammar and choice of lexis, with the local educated form of pronunciation. However, as I understand it, it is still believed that a *single* model of forms of English should be explicitly taught – and the effect of replacing a British or American model with, say, an educated German model is perhaps not likely to change current practice significantly, at least until new more complete linguistic descriptions are produced. We shall then see whether the outcome is very different from the outcome at the moment, where the effective model for most students will be, as it has always been, their own teachers. These teachers will generally be educated L2 speakers of English, who most of the time, in using English, produce a form of English very close to what we must still recognise as an L1 standard form. Of course they may not produce the characteristic distribution of particular features in different genres which is now being revealed to us in L1 usage. However, this seems unlikely to give rise to difficulties of comprehension by native speakers since it will probably give rise to only minor problems very like those experienced in working out what is meant by the speaker of an L1 dialect which is slightly different from your own.

The issue for countries which lie further away from native sources and have much more narrowly restricted access to computers and to large corpora must surely be different. The question of a sudden explosive overload of data on varieties does not, at the moment, necessarily have a great deal of relevance for them. It is true that, in some parts of the more distant world, there is an increasing desire to teach the local educated form of English, but again, this does not raise quite the same tangle of issues as coping with the interacting parameters which affect variety in the L1. Indeed, one can only reiterate that the local teacher of English has always been the most powerful model of English for students, and suggest that all that is happening here is that a pre-existing situation is now being recognised by teachers and applied linguists. When, or whether, this situation will be fully ratified by governments and testing agencies remains to be seen.

Information overload

The second challenge which I see as influencing the way Applied Linguistics develops is the plethora of information now available from every remotely relevant subject area. Just as we now have unprecedented availability of data in terms of computer corpora and their attendant analyses, so we also have unprecedented availability of information in books, journals, web-sites and papers at conferences, all of which seem to be increasing startlingly in numbers month by month, if not week by week. Most applied linguists read in other areas besides linguistics and what an individual selects from all this material from other disciplines such as cognitive psychology, philosophy of language, education, sociology, social anthropology, politics, artificial intelligence, communications engineering or literary criticism may often determine his or her general approach within Applied Linguistics. Each of us has to select from the mass of material available, even in our own area of specialisation. Each of us feels guilty at knowing that we can't possibly access all the mass of relevant material that we know is available out there, and we can only guess at how much is there that we haven't even heard of. None of us can possibly read all the relevant literature, attend all the relevant conferences or belong to all the relevant organisations, even in our own specialist fields. The effect of the selection that each of us makes from this wealth of information seems likely to lead to even greater fragmentation of interests among applied linguists, hence to be more divisive than unifying.

Once again we should note that this massive availability of information depends to a great extent on which country you live in. The plethora of opportunity to interact with so many different disciplines which is available to applied linguists in Western Europe, for instance, is simply not available to most of those working in the third world or even to many who are working in eastern and southern Europe. The diversification of interests of many L1 applied linguists working in their relatively well-funded country of origin may appear self-indulgent or even bizarre to those struggling with basic issues of language teaching in highly traditional curricula and in much less fortunate material circumstances.

The Place of Linguistics in Applied Linguistics

From these contextualising excursions, I now circle back to my topic, to the issue of changing views of language in Applied Linguistics, this time more challengingly focussing on changing views of the place of a linguistic approach to language in Applied Linguistics. There are those who suggest that the heartland of Applied Linguistics, if it is concerned with language learning and language teaching, should lie not in linguistics but in other disciplines such as education, cultural studies, sociology or cognitive psychology. Chris Brumfitt (in 1991 and again in 1995/6) has defined Applied Linguistics as concerned with 'the theoretical and empirical investigation of real-world problems in which language is a central issue'. This certainly encompasses a swathe of interests, and practitioners might appropriately call on a range of theories from different disciplines in confronting such an unconstrained range of potential issues.

As I suggested earlier, it seems clear that the discipline of Applied Linguistics has grown into a very broad church. But even if we focus only on professional applied linguists, we find some applied linguists who do not see linguistics as providing them in any way with adequate theories for the exploration of their interests. I suspect that a majority of applied linguists would take a less extreme view but might nonetheless believe that linguistic theory alone could not give an adequate view of the phenomena that interest them, just as many modern-day theoretical linguists themselves appeal to theories deriving from cognate disciplines to underpin their own approach. In this sense, then, I think there may be a change of view which permeates much of Applied Linguistics: that whereas for most people the teaching and learning of language remains at the core, linguistics is no longer regarded, if it really ever was, as the sole purveyor of relevant theory.

But I think there is a better, and less contentious, way of thinking about the issue of the relationship between linguistics and Applied Linguistics, and that is to avoid the big question altogether and to ask a much more focused question: do there remain any central and active areas of Applied Linguistics which are still heavily influenced by linguistic approaches to language? And the answer to that more focussed question must obviously be 'yes'. All of the following areas, for instance, depend to some degree on input from linguistic theory: pedagogical grammars, reference grammars, corpus linguistics, contrastive linguistics, psycholinguistics, sociolinguistics, language assessment, pronunciation teaching, lexicography, applied pragmatics – in which I include for instance aspects of discourse analysis, translation studies and stylistics – to mention only some obvious ones. All these areas rely crucially, though not exclusively, on linguistic input for the theory which underlies their descriptions and analyses.

And there is a further area which perhaps exemplifies even more clearly the close interaction of a particular current linguistic theory with applied linguistic investigation. It is an area which is now growing rapidly in this country, though it is much more strongly established in North America and Europe, and that is the area called by its adherents Second Language Acquisition research. (I personally think it has adopted an unfortunately pre-emptive title, given that this relatively new area takes no systematic account of research in traditional areas of second language acquisition, let alone in that area of second language research known as Interlanguage, inaugurated in the late 1960s by Pit Corder and Larry Selinker in Edinburgh.)

However, in the area which calls itself Second Language Acquisition research, there is no doubt that a current theory of linguistics, Chomskyan Minimalism, is crucial to the enterprise. And, in contrast to the view put forward by Pit Corder in 1973 that applied linguists only work with other people's theories, there is no doubt today that those who work in Second Language Acquisition believe that they are contributing significantly to the development of the linguistic and cognitive theories underlying their work. No-one in this field believes that those who study and speculate on patterns of development (or indeed of non-development) in second language acquisition are somehow only worker bees who collect data and have no intellectual existence independently of the theoretical queen bee. Second Language Acquisition is recognised as a successful independent theoretical area, solidly within Applied Linguistics, with its own international journals, its own international conferences, its own AILA committee, and so on. It is one area, among many other areas, within Applied Linguistics which relies on a particular linguistic theory to provide the under-pinning for part at least of its field of enquiry.

Conclusion

In 1973, in his book *Introducing Applied Linguistics*, Pit Corder remarked 'I am enough of a purist to believe that "applied linguistics" presupposes "linguistics"; that one cannot apply what one does not possess' (1973: 7). My own inclination would be to agree with him, and to suggest that you need at least a basis in linguistics to work and research in Applied Linguistics, always remembering however that a linguistically informed approach may be necessary but is not sufficient for undertaking work in Applied Linguistics.

However, if you insist that what you are doing certainly comes within the remit of Applied Linguistics but is exclusively dependent on theories derived from disciplines other than linguistics, my response would be that Applied Linguistics is now such an all-embracing discipline that it can certainly accommodate both our views. But in any case, I would insist that we must both acknowledge that a linguistically informed approach to language is fundamental in such central areas of Applied Linguistics as I listed previously above. These are areas which are widespread around the world, found in dozens of departments of English and of Applied Linguistics. They cannot be dismissed as moribund relics of the past since they are demonstrably alive and well, and are growing and developing year by year.

And finally I would say to those who argue against the centrality of language study in Applied Linguistics that it is important for those of us who work in relatively privileged institutions, in relatively privileged countries of Western Europe or North America, to remember the conditions under which most applied linguists across the world are working in Russia, in China, in India, in Africa, in South America or around the Pacific rim. In many countries what applied linguists can do is tightly constrained by their own institutions or by the Ministry of Education, who typically take a highly traditional view of applied linguistics as the handmaiden of a traditional type of language teaching. It would, in my view, be a tragic mistake for Applied Linguistics in the western industrialised world to allow itself to get too far out of step with Applied Linguistics in other parts of the world. We should remember that the vast majority of practising applied linguists who concern themselves with teacher training and with practical aspects of language teaching have never doubted that linguistically informed language study lies at the heart of Applied Linguistics.

References

Allen, J. P. B. and Corder, S. P. (eds) (1973/4) *The Edinburgh Course in Applied Linguistics* (Vols 1–4). Oxford: Oxford University Press.
Biber, D., Johansson, S., Leech, G., Conrad, S. and Finegan, E. (1999) *Longman Grammar of Spoken and Written English*. Longman, Pearson Education.

Brumfitt, C. (1995/6) Theoretical practice: Applied linguistics as pure and practical science. *AILA Review* 12, 18–30.

Corder, S. P. (1973) *Introducing Applied Linguistics*. Penguin Education.

International Phonetic Association (1888) *Principles of the International Phonetic Association. Being a description of the International Phonetic Alphabet and the manner of using it*. London: University College London.

Jones, D. (1909) *The Pronunciation of English*. Cambridge: Cambridge University Press.

Perren, G. E. and Trim, J. L. M. (eds) (1971) *Applications of Linguistics*. Cambridge: Cambridge University Press.

2 Society, Education and Language: The last 2,000 (and the next 20?) years of language teaching

University of Trier

Abstract

In *Introducing Applied Linguistics* (1973), Pit Corder emphasizes the 'total language teaching operation', which I will discuss here under three headings:

SOCIETY

Language teaching is carried out against different cultural backgrounds, and therefore cannot avoid questions of value. An understanding of the present may require substantial factual knowledge of the past. This is illustrated with cases from Scotland and Germany.

EDUCATION

A 2,000-year-old problem is the place of language teaching in a general education. The Trivium and the Quadrivium gave educational priority to a thorough training in language study. Recent attempts to develop school programmes of 'language across the curriculum' have been a mixture of educational success and political fiasco.

LANGUAGE

The empiricist–rationalist controversy also has a 2,000-year history. A recent period of mentalism in linguistics has been followed by developments in technology which have led to a renaissance of empiricism. The findings of corpus linguistics have major long-term implications for both linguistic theory and language teaching, though the short-term applications are currently less clear.

Introduction

For the Pit Corder lecture at the BAAL conference in Edinburgh in 1999, the organizers asked me to talk about continuity and change in applied linguistics, with particular reference to language teaching. This was a pretty tall order, because the whole topic has a very long history: one influential book is entitled *25 Centuries of Language Teaching* (Kelly, 1969). In addition, as Pit Corder (1973) repeatedly emphasizes in his book *Introducing Applied Linguistics*, we have to keep in mind what he calls the 'total language teaching operation'. This includes:

(1)   the social and political context of language planning

(2)   the organization of the curriculum and the syllabus

(3)   and language description (including statistical facts).

I will not survey a 2,000-year history, but I will refer frequently to questions which go back a very long time, and which will probably never be definitively answered, but which require to be reconsidered by each generation as new research methods become available. I will argue throughout for appropriate modes of empirical research. In post-modernist views of academic work, grand theories are out of fashion, but it would be unfortunate if this means abandoning attempts to define the place of language teaching in a general education, and attempts to describe a language as a system.

Society: Local conditions

My first main topic concerns the historical and cultural background to language teaching. I grew up and lived in Scotland for over 20 years, and I have now been living in Germany for ten years. So I will start from some points about society, education and language in Scotland and Germany, and I will start from a point which has been much cited recently. This is the principle that language teachers must pay attention to local conditions, rather than taking a set of ideas, and then 'shooting off to various parts of the world and implementing programmes' (Widdowson, quoted in Phillipson, 1992: 260).

The Scottish case

The local conditions principle has often been ignored in the past in teaching English in Scotland. I did the whole of my schooling in Glasgow. In English lessons, it was acceptable to study Robert Burns, occasionally, but it was not acceptable to speak his language in the classroom, or even in the playground. We learned virtually nothing of other Scots literature. We studied William

Shakespeare, but not William Dunbar, and very little Scottish history either. Scottish history was not compulsory in the school history curriculum in Scotland until 1990 (Lynch, 1992: xv).

It has long been common for Scots to be made ashamed of their own language. My mother was born in Scotland, of Scottish parents, and lived in Glasgow for the whole of her life. When she worked as a secretary in the 1940s, she took elocution lessons in order to try and get rid of her lower-middle-class language habits. There was nothing out of the ordinary about this: it puts her in the same tradition as David Hume (1711–76), who was so ashamed of his Scotticisms that he had a list of them on his desk, so as to better avoid them in his writing. Indeed, it is said that he died confessing not his sins, but his Scotticisms (McCrum *et al.,* 1986: 151; Kay, 1993: 85, 88, 91; Jones, 1995: 48).

I don't think many Scots nowadays would make the mistake of ignoring history and culture in a study of language. It is very clear how the historical shift in the political power base of Gaelic, Scots and English is still visible in the geographical, social and functional distribution of these languages in contemporary Scotland.

Up until the 1200s, there was a Celtic line of kings in Scotland. The last of the Celtic line died in 1286, but even before this date, members of the royal family were Anglo-Norman educated. In 1306, after an interregnum, the power passed to the Bruce family. Robert the Bruce was a Gaelic-speaking Celtic king, but was also descended from an Anglo-Norman family (Lynch, 1992: xiv, 96). He sent a despatch to the Pope declaring Scotland's independence in 1320, and he is still one of the major icons of Scottish nationalism. In 1406, the throne passed to the Stewart family, with a line of succession from James I to James V, and via Mary Queen of Scots to James VI. James IV (reigned 1488–1513) was Scotland's last Gaelic-speaking king, though he learned Gaelic as a second language (MacKinnon, 1991: 35). Now came the high point of Scots, as one of the languages of the court and of a spectacular period of literature, including writing by William Dunbar (1460?–1520?), the court poet to James IV. (Kinsley (ed.), 1979.) In 1603, there was the Union of the Crowns, James VI moved to England, the power base moved again, this time to London, and Scots lost prestige in the face of English. The tragic events after the Jacobite Rebellion of 1745 led to the destruction of highland society and the further decline of Gaelic.

What is still visible is the synchronic variation which is the result of these diachronic changes: this 1,000-year historical shift from Gaelic to Scots to English. Gaelic became the language of the rural working class in the extreme north-west highlands, and Scots became the language of the urban and rural working class in the lowlands. The death of Scots has been frequently announced, and has not yet happened, but by the 20th century it had sadly fallen in prestige. By the early

1900s, as far as the dominant English-speaking class was concerned, it was little more than a source of comic characters and music hall jokes: from William Wallace in the 1200s to Oor Wullie in the 1900s.

Amongst the major challenges for Scottish education, as devolution starts to have an effect, will be to develop appropriate self-images – versions of Scots history, literature and language – which are more interesting than the junk which is sold to tourists. There are images of Scotland which are fit for shortbread tins, but not for the nation's education system (McCrone *et al.*, 1995). Part of this challenge will be whether Scotland – and also England – can develop forms of regionalism, which do not turn into the nastier forms of nationalism. Of central importance will be the attitude taken to the Scots language in schools. Here is a statement from the Head of English in a school in Ayrshire (from *The (Glasgow) Herald*, cited by Kay, 1993: 21–2):

> Scots ... still has a gey ruch road tae travel, for it's a road fu o the dubs an mires o neglect an abuse, as well as bein paved wi prejudice. We hae tae begin wi the varieties o demotic speech weans bring tae the schuil that are vital expressions o their ain an their community's identity, but if the schuil disnae respect an value the speech o aa oor weans, we will continue tae discriminate against weans that stey close tae their roots. If oor uniquely Scottish educational system cannae learn hou tae cope wi educatin oor weans in the native languages o Scotland, sae that Scots an Scots English complement ane anither, Scottish teachers will continue tae fail Scottish culture as they hae duin owre lang.
>
> [weans = 'wee ones' = bairns = children]

The linguistic status of this text is unclear: it has been constructed to make a point, and in any case there is no single variety of Scottish English, no fully accepted standardized spelling system, and no codified linguistic norm. But there is no doubt about the function of the text in signalling Scottish identity. Its language is also quite close to Anglo-English. If I was to cite a variety of Scots which is further from English, most readers would require a translation: see the texts in MacCallum & Purves (eds) (1995). For other examples of texts in Scots and different views on the Scots language, see McClure *et al.* (1980), McClure (1988), Kay (1993), Macafee (1994, 1997), Jones (1995) and Skelton (1999). A very readable sociolinguistic introduction to the place of Gaelic in Scottish identity is MacKinnon (1991).

A German case

Here is a different case of local conditions. In a secondary school near where I live in Germany, around half the pupils are native speakers of Russian. They are children of *Aussiedler*, people who moved out of Germany at some time over the last 200 years or so, but whose families have maintained to some extent German language and culture, and who have right of residence in Germany. The children usually have grandparents who speak German, the parents may or may not speak German, and German has only sometimes been passed on to children of the current generation. Where it has been passed on, it may be an archaic variety from the 18th or 19th century.

In one case recently, four young men arrived in the school from Kazakhstan. (They were cousins: two pairs of brothers.) They had native competence in Russian, which had been their language of formal education, and was what they spoke with the other pupils; and they had learned some Kazakhi, which had been an obligatory foreign language in their school in Kazakhstan. When they arrived in the school in Germany, they scored zero in a German-language entrance test, were placed in the beginners' group, and it was assumed for several weeks that they spoke no German. Then one of the teachers realised that they knew vocabulary which had not been taught in class. The teacher, who comes from south Germany, also realised that they were using archaic forms of Swabian, a southern German dialect. It turned out that this was their mother tongue, in the sense of the language they used at home, on the farm, back in Kazakhstan.

Probably, before they arrived in the school, they had never had to write standard German, which was the language of the entrance test, and they would have had to read only archaic forms used in the Lutheran bible. Or perhaps it had just been made clear to them that their variety of German was not worth speaking. When their competence in Swabian was pointed out to other teachers, who spoke only High German, the teachers argued that it wasn't 'proper' German anyway. Luckily, the head teacher comes from Swabia, and he took some objection to this line of argument.

In this German case, 'local conditions' means that German is taught to a group of young people who may not feel at home in any country, and against a background of rapidly changing use of German across the generations, and a set of complex attitudes to language, ethnicity and nationality. Language teaching in Europe may increasingly have to take into account the role of international politics, as Howatt (1997: 263) has recently pointed out. Within the European Union, there is now large-scale immigration from the east and south, and a new consciousness of regional and national identity.

Conclusions: Society

The concept of 'local conditions' is probably too vague to support much theoretical weight, but it usefully emphasizes that even major facts of history and culture are often ignored. These Scottish and German cases show several things about the relation between language teaching and the politics of regionalism. Language learners always have their own ideas about their history and culture, which may not be at all evident to outsiders, and this means that no single set of language teaching prescriptions can be mechanically applied in all circumstances.

My comments on these Scottish and German cases have been partly personal, and in such areas it is impossible to separate fact and value. But this does not mean that questions of empirical validity can be ignored, and my comments depend on bodies of historical knowledge. I did not receive such historical knowledge at school. Nor did my mother: like David Hume, she had been told that good Scots was bad English (though she was never entirely convinced). So, there are implications here for both teacher training and school curricula. Tolerance of language diversity and bidialectalism are not new concepts, but they are still valid.

Education: Language across the curriculum

These Scottish and German cases also strongly imply that language education should be a unified enterprise. Some TESOL traditions distinguish sharply between mother tongue and second or foreign language teaching, but the British tradition of applied linguistics from the 1960s onwards (e.g. Halliday, McIntosh & Strevens, 1964) has usually regarded mother tongue teaching and foreign language teaching as part of a general language education. This leads to my second main topic, which is the relation between language teaching, language education and a broader curriculum.

Views on how modern foreign languages or mother tongues should be taught are not separate from changing views on the curriculum in general. The major curriculum models listed below are ideal types, but recognisable in concrete forms. They variously emphasize cultural heritage (this is classical humanism), student-centred discovery learning, critical cultural analysis, and measurable practical skills:

classical humanist	knowledge-centred	elitist?
progressivist	student-centred	romantic?
reconstructionist	society-centred	democratic?
technocratic	skills-centred	measurable?

Schools cannot teach everything: as Raymond Williams (1961) puts it, they have to make a 'selection from the culture', and different decisions are made at different historical periods as to how language study fits in with other subjects on the curriculum. Again, I will not attempt to survey different views of language teaching. I will just note that, in the last 30 years, two communicative aims have been particularly influential: practical language skills, communicative competence in that sense; and inter-cultural competence, learning about other societies with tolerance of their cultural values. In practice, neither of these aims is likely to be found in a pure form. Since the 1960s, a general consensus has grown up around a broadly communicative philosophy, and this general shift away from humanistic views of language teaching, to practical communicative aims, has made it more difficult to locate language teaching in a broader curriculum (Davies, 1991: 55).

The point I will concentrate on is one made by Hawkins (1984) in his rationale for the language awareness movement. He points out that even when different languages are taught within a single school – classical languages, English as a mother tongue, French as a foreign language, ethnic minority languages – the languages are typically taught in isolation from each other and fragmented into different traditions. This fragmentation may be an unavoidable consequence of the local conditions principle.

Another source of fragmentation is the unresolved relation between know-ledge about language and use of language. Attempts to integrate language system and language use have also long been central to British linguistics, and Halliday (1978: 4) makes this link via the 2,000-year-old distinction between grammar, logic and rhetoric. The reference is to a model of language developed by the ancient Greeks.

The Trivium and the Quadrivium

This is also the model of language which underlies the classical humanist curriculum which has come down to us, over 2,000 years, from Plato, via the medieval universities. For all kinds of reasons, this model of education is no longer acceptable. But it is worth while looking briefly at the ideal form of a curriculum which has its origins in Greek training in what would nowadays be called 'critical language awareness', and which has been the most influential curriculum in the western world. In the version which was used in the design of the first European universities from around 1200, there was a clear view of the place of language education in the seven liberal arts: a view which put the WORD first, and the WORLD second. This view is outlined below:

First the WORD, the inner

    TRIVIUM: linguistically oriented studies

    grammar: grammatical competence

    logic, rhetoric: communicative competence.

Then the WORLD, the outer

QUADRIVIUM: mathematically oriented studies

arithmetic, astronomy, geometry, music.

Whatever one thinks of how the Trivium later became trivialized, it certainly embodied a powerful theory of the relation between language and the mental and material world, and it had a clear view of the place of language in an ambitious programme of education. The Trivium consisted of grammar, logic and rhetoric: not only the language system independent of context (grammar), but also language use, persuasion and style (logic and rhetoric).

These forms of knowledge, concerned with the Word, were distinguished from other forms of knowledge, concerned with the World. This was the division and specialization between the Trivium and the Quadrivium. The Trivium came first: students first had to learn the principles of language and logic, and only then did they apply these principles to an understanding of the material world. First, the principles of consciousness, then their applications. First the inner, then the outer. I am here quoting a brilliant analysis of this curriculum by Bernstein (1996).

Now, this all embodies a simple and elegant view of the content and sequencing of education, with a particularly coherent theory of the place of languages in the curriculum. However, I am not going to argue that we should re-introduce the Trivium. First, the sequencing – theory before practice – would not find much favour nowadays. And second, there has to be room for new subjects and new subject combinations. In any case, the problem is rather that we still have the Trivium – or are still trying to get rid of it. The division between Trivium and Quadrivium still underlies the way in which faculties and subjects are organized in universities. Indeed the division between language-oriented studies and mathematics-oriented studies has been causing trouble ever since. I return to this language-mathematics split below.

We clearly cannot re-introduce the seven liberal arts (which involved their own fragmentation). But they do embody a serious, elegant and ambitious programme which integrates linguistic education into a general education, and it is important not to lose sight of this purpose. 'Language across the curriculum' is a slightly dated phrase, but a valuable aim. From the 1970s to the 1990s, particularly in the UK and Australia, substantial attempts were made to introduce programmes variously referred to as 'language across the curriculum', 'knowledge about language', and 'teaching about genre'. These programmes had initial educational success, sometimes quite spectacular, which was followed by political defeat and fiasco. The programmes were attacked from the progressive left for being reactionary: by this was meant that they demanded explicit knowledge about language. And they were attacked from the conservative right for being too political: by this was meant that they addressed questions of language and social class.

When I was involved in this debate, as a member of the Cox Committee (DES, 1989; Stubbs, 1989), I found it unnerving to be told, at the same time, by the right wing that I was too far left, and by the left wing that I was too far right. It was only much later that I began to realise what was going on. Cameron (1995) and Martin (1997) have now provided very good analyses of this dilemma: unfortunately too late to save the Cox Committee from committing various blunders due to political naivety. However, it is important to learn from such mistakes.

Conclusions: Education

My main point here is that people have been trying for 2,000 years to find a way of integrating language teaching into a general education. Very impressive curricular proposals have been made, but recent educational and political muddles show that the problem is far from solved.

One relation of all this to the Trivium is fairly straightforward: grammar, rhetoric and logic have been hopelessly fragmented. First, rhetoric has acquired a pejorative meaning, often little different from 'propaganda'. In Britain, it has often disappeared completely as a school or university subject. In the USA, it has been turned into 'Freshman Composition': what Bradbury (1976) satirises as 'a course in existential awareness and the accurate use of the comma'. Second, grammar has often been detached from its rhetorical functions. In turn, it has also often disappeared, so that many English teachers have not been taught grammar themselves. And third, logic was one of the language-oriented subjects of the Trivium, but in the 20th century, logic has drifted away from language study, and become more closely aligned to mathematics (Seuren, 1998: 300). This has led to a deepening split between linguistic subjects and mathematical subjects. One result here is that different approaches to semantics now seem to have very little to do with each other: formal semantics is inspired by logic, but empirical semantics uses ethnographic or corpus data.

Language: Technology and description

I will relate these points about grammar, rhetoric and logic to my third main topic, which concerns the renaissance in empirical linguistics made possible by new technologies.

Linguistics and Applied Linguistics

Linguistics has its origins in different areas of applied language study. The first attempts to look at language systematically must have been triggered by the development of various writing systems. As Trim (1988: 3) points out, this 'extraordinary achievement of applied linguistics is the beginning of history', in the sense that it created the possibility of recording historical events.

Linguistics also has its origins in precisely the set of ideas which led to the Trivium and Quadrivium. Current emphases on language and power seem modern, in a period post-Foucault, but they were also central in work by Plato and Aristotle, who placed an analysis of political speeches at the centre of their training programmes. Language study for the Greeks had political and ethical goals, and perhaps post-modernist views are not as new as they sometimes seem.

However, there were different views in Greek thought about the relation of practice and theory. One view was that grammar should be the empirical study of the actual usage of the poets and prose writers. Another view held that the study would have higher esteem if it was based on logical and psychological principles (Robins, 1988: 464–5). We are still living with this empiricist–rationalist controversy.

Technology and language teaching

So, these ideas also have a 2,000-year history. In the past 100 years, another major origin of linguistic ideas has been technology. In his *History of English Language Teaching*, Howatt (1984: 177) points to the parallels between two such occasions: in the 1880s, the image of phonetics was 'a mixture of advanced technology (the telephone, ... the phonograph, and so on) and of pure phonological science'; and in the 1950s, a similar situation was brought about by the invention of the tape-recorder: a mixture of language labs and structural linguistics.

On some occasions, innovations in teaching have followed contemporary linguistic theory: for example, semantic units (in a notional syllabus) and pragmatic units (in a communicative syllabus) were certainly helped along by concepts such as speech act and communicative competence. (Though some innovations in ELT came first: see Channell, 1998 on the history of pragmatics and ELT.) On other occasions, innovations in language teaching have followed technology, and have received their theoretical justification post hoc. For example, audio-lingual drills seem to have followed from an opportunity provided by language labs, and to have been justified after the event by theories of habit formation.

Howatt published his book in 1984 just a few years before a third such case, where a huge technological advance has affected language description, and where applied linguistic concerns have led to substantial theoretical advances. There are rather striking parallels between new technology, new techniques of linguistic description, and proposals for new syllabus designs in the 1880s, 1950s and 1990s:

1880s	TECHNOLOGY:	telephone, phonograph
	TECHNIQUES:	broad and narrow transcription
	THEORY:	phoneme theory
	SYLLABUS:	Reform Movement
1950s	TECHNOLOGY:	tape recorders, language labs
	TECHNIQUES:	immediate constituent analysis
	THEORY:	structuralist linguistics
	SYLLABUS:	audio-lingual method
1990s	TECHNOLOGY:	computers plus corpora
	TECHNIQUES:	collocational analysis
	THEORY:	lexico-grammar
	SYLLABUS:	lexical-syllabus

The obvious contemporary case of the effect of technology is the use of computational techniques in the preparation of major dictionaries and grammars. In 1995, four major English monolingual dictionaries were published (by CUP, OUP, Longman and Cobuild) which were all based on large corpora. They were made possible by three things which are intimately and productively related:

- the technology which provides the data on language use

- the commercial pressures for new teaching materials

- the associated descriptive progress in linguistics.

However, the phenomenal growth in language teaching materials and the extent to which commercial pressures shape the language teaching profession are hotly debated. So, more generally, is the appropriate relation between technology, data, commerce and teaching practice.

Lexico-grammar

A remarkable feature of Corder's book, *Introducing Applied Linguistics*, is that it discusses two topics which were rediscovered by corpus linguists only some 15 years after the book was published. First, Corder (1973: 212–3) emphasizes the importance of quantitative findings about language use. Second, he discusses (1973: 315–7) what he calls a 'lexical syllabus' (cf. the title of Willis, 1990), in which we select the lexical material which is to be taught, and then find the grammatical framework within which to teach it:

> There is no logical dependency either way between the lexico-semantic system and the syntax. ... [T]he two interpenetrate to such an extent that the distinction between them is beginning to lose its significance.
>
> (Corder, 1973: 316)

Corder is here stating the finding which has now been very thoroughly documented by corpus linguistics.

Here is a single example which shows the relation between lexis, grammar and pragmatics. The word *proper* has important cultural meanings, and is used frequently in discussing language in education. Scots has frequently been condemned as 'not proper English'. In the aftermath of the Cox Report in 1989, Prince Charles made a much quoted statement about education. As *The Daily Telegraph* (28 June 1989) put it, he 'launched a scathing attack on standards of English teaching'.

> We've got to produce people who can write PROPER English. It's a fundamental problem. All the people I have in my office, they can't speak English PROPERLY, they can't write English PROPERLY.

Such statements can only 'strike a chord' or 'ring a bell', as we say, if they fit into wider ways of talking and therefore into wider cultural schemas.

Lexical patterns often seem obvious once they have been pointed out, but the patterns I am about to illustrate are not explicitly recorded even in recent corpus-based dictionaries (CIDE, 1995; COBUILD, 1995; LDOCE, 1995; OALD 1995). The examples in the dictionaries confirm my data, but the underlying principles are not given. The main pattern is that *proper* typically co-occurs with

- negatives, such as *no, not, never, can't*
- words such as *fail, need, without*
- words which imply warnings and criticisms.

This pattern can be seen in these attested examples:

(1)   *no* time yet for a *proper* examination of the map

(2)   put forward *without proper* consideration of your needs

(3)   the crying *need* is for a *proper* international airport

(4)   two out of five people *lack* a *proper* job

(5)   *failed* to give it a *proper* look

(6)   *hinders proper* training

(7)   *totally outside proper* democratic control

(8)   *unless proper care* be taken to improve it

(9)   My family tell me that I should stop dreaming and get myself a *proper* job.

Example 8 is taken from the *OED*: it dates from 1745. Example 9 is taken from Francis *et al.* (1998: 366).

The basic semantic pattern is very simple, and can be shown with a few such examples. It is a common misunderstanding that corpus linguistics is concerned with collocations in the sense of (semi-)fixed phrases. This is not so. The basic finding concerns the frequency of abstract semantic frames with typical but variable lexis. Here I can give only this isolated example, but corpus work has now shown that all of the most frequent words in English are involved in semantic frames of this kind. Such co-occurrence patterns are given in the very substantial descriptive work by Francis *et al.* (1996, 1998).

In summary, such corpus data show that words occur in typical lexical and syntactic patterns, and often with predictable evaluative connotations. It is from descriptions of large corpora that many radical ideas about the nature of the language system are currently arising. First, it turns out that language is organized much more intricately than previously suspected: not only in well-defined sub-parts, seen as either *langue* or competence, but also in *parole* or performance, especially in the co-selection of lexis and grammar. Second, native speakers have only very poor intuitions about many pragmatic aspects of language. If they had better intuitions, then these pragmatic aspects would be recorded in dictionaries, but they often aren't.

Corpus study shows up patterns which are not visible in single examples. (See Channell, 1998 for a good statement of this argument and for other examples.) It is this point about repetitions which is crucial. Corpus linguistics is based on methods of observation which make repetitions visible, and the fact of repetition makes quantitative methods essential. The crucial shift is from studying what is possible to studying what is probable.

Quantitative and empirical methods

The major tool in corpus linguistics is the concordance, and there is nothing new about using concordances to study meanings. In second-hand bookshops in Edinburgh and St Andrews, I recently bought two concordances published in the 1700s. One is a concordance, from 1790, 'to the remarkable words made use of by Shakespeare; calculated to point out the different meanings to which the words are applied' (Ayscough, 1790). The other is 'A Complete Concordance to the Holy Scriptures ... or a Dictionary and Alphabetical Index to the Bible ... very useful to all Christians who seriously read and study the inspired writings' (Cruden 1833, 10th edn; 1st edn 1737). So, one of the basic principles of corpus linguistics has long been common-place: meaning is use, in the sense that words acquire meanings through their repeated collocations. Large corpora allow the frequency and typicality of such collocations to be empirically observed.

At the BAAL conference, I gave my lecture just next to the David Hume Tower in Edinburgh University, and a painting of Hume looked down on us during our coffee breaks in a room in the Tower. So, it seemed appropriate to quote his recommendation of quantitative empirical methods. He recommended that when we read a book, we should ask:

> 'Does it contain any abstract reasoning concerning quantity or number?'
> No. 'Does it contain any experimental reasoning concerning matter of fact
> and existence?' No. 'Commit it then to the flames, for it can contain
> nothing but sophistry and illusion.'.   (Hume, 1748)

Chomskyans may consider this a little extreme, but it makes a useful point about quantification and observational methods.

Technology, observation and quantification

An emphasis on continuity in applied linguistics may seem to imply that there are no new ideas under the sun. But the change brought about by computer technology is a change due to the speed with which very large amounts of data can be processed. What is, logically speaking, a quantitative change is so large that it is experienced as a qualitative change which allows new observations and reveals new patterns.

The computer technology which is now available for language description has two rather different aspects: it involves new observational techniques, and it is quantitative. As Sinclair (1991: 100) says: 'the language looks rather different when you look at a lot of it at once'. One thing is very clear: technology increases our powers of observation. And the development of the natural sciences was only possible due to the development of observational instruments, especially the invention of the lens, and hence of the telescope, the microscope and the camera. These instruments have revealed patterns which were not visible to the naked eye. People could observe things that no-one had seen before, because they were too far away, or too small, or moved too quickly (Banfield, 1987: 265–7). The ability to freeze images in time also made them publicly accessible to different observers. A large corpus with search software is analogous to these observational devices: concordance software can reveal patterns invisible to the naked eye.

It is sometimes objected that corpus methods over-emphasize some aspects of language use, such as collocations. This may be true, but the whole point of an observational tool is to emphasize something. We don't normally complain that microscopes over-emphasize tiny little things, that telescopes only allow us to study far-away things, or that x-rays give too much prominence to the insides of things (Partington, 1998: 144). And we don't normally criticize a stethoscope because it cannot be used as a periscope.

I am quite well aware that you don't become a scientist just by putting on a white coat and looking down a microscope (and that technology is not the same as science). But it remains true that the development of science would have been impossible without observational technologies. I am also well aware of the criticism that patterns may be created by the observational technology itself. This criticism was made of Galileo's work (Lakatos, 1970: 98, 107). In 1610 Galileo claimed he could observe, with his new telescope, mountains on the moon and satellites round Jupiter, and that these observations refuted the claim that heavenly bodies were perfect crystal spheres. His critics pointed out that his observations depended on an optical theory of the telescope, which he did not have.

What computer-assisted corpus methods make visible is repetitions. We can bring together, in a corpus, utterances which have been produced at different times by different speakers, and we can observe, in concordance lines, the characteristic patterns which recur. The study of recurrent patterns requires the quantification of observations, and it is really rather surprising that approaches to language study could ever have been developed which dismiss out of hand the idea of observing things and of counting how often they occur.

This perspective has not been entirely lost in language teaching. Everybody takes some account of numerical matters in teaching a language: at least in the early stages, language teaching has to concentrate on a core vocabulary, frequent grammatical patterns and so on. Detailed statistical findings have been available here from the 1920s onwards in work by Harold Palmer, Michael West, Edward Thorndike and others. What is particularly odd is the neglect of quantitative work in linguistic theory. Much linguistic description contains no statements of proportions. It is as if chemists knew about the different structure of iron and gold, but had no idea that iron is pretty common and gold is very rare. Or as if geographers knew how to compare countries in all kinds of ways, but had never noticed that Canada is rather bigger than Luxembourg (Kennedy, 1992: 339, 341).

Conclusions: Language

My main point about language description and technology is as follows. Debates about the appropriate relation of empiricism and rationalism have been going on for 2,000 years. Some questions – even if they are 2,000 years old –

will keep recurring, because they concern central intellectual problems. They will never receive a definitive solution, because they are not small technical puzzles, but 'great and apparently insoluble riddles' (Brumfit, 1997: 27 quoting Popper). But these questions have to be reformulated in different ways for each generation. They won't be solved by corpus methods, but corpus methods provide a new angle on them.

Corpus findings have also led to a major debate over the appropriate relation between underlying research and teaching practice. Corpora are not teaching materials: they can be used to provide concordances and other quantitative information, and this can help in the design of teaching materials. Spolsky (1970) distinguishes between implications and applications, and I am absolutely sure that recent advances in language description have major long-term implications for linguistic theory. As Corder pointed out, there will have to be a radically revised division of labour between vocabulary and grammar, but it will take time before we know exactly how this will work out. I am also sure that the findings have major implications for language teaching, in new discoveries about the units of language production and comprehension, and the cultural significance of these units. The shorter-term applications are still being debated.

Conclusions

I have discussed two questions which were formulated very explicitly 2,000 years ago, when language study had its origins in very pragmatic work on persuasion and textual interpretation, and when it had a clear ethical purpose. Both questions concern unavoidable dualisms. The first concerns the relation between words and the world:

> Can we state sufficiently clearly how the teaching of individual languages fits into a broader language education and into a general education?

The second concerns the relation between empiricism and rationalism:

> What are the appropriate methods, in both broadly social and more narrowly linguistic research, of integrating quantitative and qualitative knowledge?

In Applied Linguistics journals, the balance between subjectivity and objectivity is currently the topic of a very sharp debate, triggered by a post-modernist loss of confidence in long-standing core criteria for academic work. These relativist positions have, in their turn, been sharply criticized (by, for example, Rampton, 1995; Widdowson, 1995a,b; Davies, 1996, 1999; Gregg, Long *et al.*, 1997; Brumfit, 1997). Post-modernist arguments have certainly shown that truth and objectivity are much more problematic than is often assumed. But doubts have also been cast on whether serious post-modernist argument can be reliably distinguished from parody, and indeed whether a brilliant hoax can be distinguished from a bad joke (Fish, 1996). I am referring mainly to the Alan Sokal case (Sokal, 1996 and much more), but one recent review of an Applied Linguistics book has asked whether the book was intended as a 'spoof' (Davies, 1996 on Phillipson, 1992).[1]

There does seem to be a paradox at the centre of Foucault's arguments that all knowledge is a tool of the will to power, and that truth is 'produced within discourses which in themselves are neither true nor false' (Foucault, 1980: 118). Even if you are intent on demystifying culture, and exposing the conceptual undergrowth of the social sciences, you still need criteria which show that your analysis is better than the unreflecting assumptions which are taken for granted by the rest of us (Merquior, 1985: 147–9).

Each generation has to consider the new forms of empiricism which arise. I cannot do better here than to quote Davies (1991: 60) from an article in which he assesses Corder's work:

> Renewal of our connection with data is as important as an understanding of what count as data.

New forms of data have to be carefully assessed and interpreted, but it would be absurd to ignore them. I have come down clearly on the side of empirical methods, and I have given examples of the need for bodies of historical knowledge, new methods of observation, and new kinds of publicly accessible data.

A last comment. There is no neutral technology of observation. As Young (1971) put it:

all facts are theory-laden

and all theories are value-laden

therefore all facts are value-laden.

That's logic ... Nevertheless, some facts are based on publicly-accessible empirical evidence. The post-modernists among you may argue that I don't realise the implications of my own text. But I can reply that, in order to study intertextuality, we need both historical knowledge and corpus methods. That's rhetoric ...

Acknowledgements

This is a revised version of the Pit Corder Lecture given in Edinburgh in September 1999. At the BAAL conference Mike Breen chaired a discussion of the lecture: the main discussants were Ros Mitchell and Peter Skehan, and I am grateful to them and to other participants for comments and criticisms. I am also very grateful to: Joanna Channell for detailed and constructive criticisms of an early draft; Fiona Christie, Gabi Keck, Werner Schäfer and Jürgen Strauss for comments on later drafts; and colleagues at Cobuild in Birmingham for access to the Bank of English.

Note

1. Davies (1999) also expresses severe reservations of post-modernist positions in Applied Linguistics. It is well beyond my remit here, but it would be a fascinating exercise to compare two books, with very similar titles, by the first two professors of Applied Linguistics at the University of Edinburgh: Corder (1973) and Davies (1999).

References

Ayscough, S. (1790) *An Index to the Remarkable Passages and Words Made Use of by Shakespeare*. London: Stockdale.

Banfield, A. (1987) Describing the unobserved: Events grouped around an empty centre. In N. Fabb *et al.* (eds) *The Linguistics of Writing*. Manchester: Manchester University Press.

Bernstein, B. B. (1996) Thoughts on the trivium and quadrivium. In *Pedagogy, Symbolic Control and Identity* (pp. 82–8). London: Taylor & Francis.

Bradbury, M. (1976) *Who Do You Think You Are?* London: Secker & Warburg.

Brumfit, C. (1997) Theoretical practice: Applied linguistics as pure and practical science. *AILA Review* 12, 18–30.

Cameron, D. (1995) *Verbal Hygiene*. London: Routledge.

Channell, J. (1998) The systematic teaching of communicative value: Fifty years of pragmatics in ELT. Plenary lecture to IATEFL conference.

CIDE (1995) *Cambridge International Dictionary of English*. P. Procter (ed.). Cambridge: Cambridge University Press.

COBUILD (1995) *Collins COBUILD English Dictionary*. J. Sinclair (ed.). London: Harper Collins.

Corder, S. P. (1973) *Introducing Applied Linguistics*. Harmondsworth: Penguin.

Cruden, A. (1833) *A Complete Concordance to the Holy Scriptures* (10th edn). London: Tegg.

Davies, A. (1991) British applied linguistics: The contribution of S. Pit Corder. In R. Phillipson *et al.* (eds) *Foreign/Second Language Pedagogy* (pp. 52–60). Clevedon: Multilingual Matters.

Davies, A. (1996) Ironising the myth of linguicism. *Journal of Multilingual and Multicultural Development* 17 (6), 485–96.

Davies, A. (1999) *An Introduction to Applied Linguistics*. Edinburgh: Edinburgh University Press.

DES (1989) *English for ages 5 to 16. The Cox Report.* London: DES and Welsh Office.

Fish, S. (1996) Professor Sokal's bad joke. *The New York Times* 21 May 1996.

Foucault, M. (1980) *Power/Knowledge*. C. Gordon (ed.). Brighton: Harvester.

Francis, G., Hunston, S. and Manning, E. (1996, 1998) *Collins Cobuild Grammar Patterns* (Vol. 1: Verbs; Vol. 2: Nouns and Adjectives). London: Harper Collins.

Gregg, K., Long, M., Jordan, G. and Beretta, A. (1997) Rationality and its discontents in SLA. *Applied Linguistics* 18 (4), 538–58.

Halliday, M. A. K., McIntosh, A. and Strevens, P. (1964) *The Linguistic Sciences and Language Teaching*. London: Longman.

Halliday, M. A. K. (1978) *Language as Social Semiotic*. London: Arnold.

Hawkins, E. (1984) *Awareness of Language*. Cambridge: Cambridge University Press.

Howatt, A. P. R. (1984) *A History of English Language Teaching*. Oxford: Oxford University Press.

Howatt, A. P. R. (1997) Talking shop: Transformation and change in ELT. *ELT Journal* 51 (3), 263–8.

Hume, D. (1748) *An Enquiry Concerning Human Understanding*. Edinburgh.

Jones, C. (1995) *A Language Suppressed: The pronunciation of the Scots language in the 18th century*. Edinburgh: John Donald.

Kay, B. (1993) *Scots: The Mither Tongue* (2nd edn). Darvel, Ayrshire: Alloway.

Kelly, L. G. (1969) *25 Centuries of Language Teaching*. MA: Newbury House.

Kennedy, G. (1992) Preferred ways of putting things with implications for language teaching. In J. Svartvik (ed.) *Directions in Corpus Linguistics* (pp. 335–73). Berlin: Mouton de Gruyter.

Kinsley, J. (ed.) (1979) *The Poems of William Dunbar*. Oxford: Clarendon.

Lakatos, I. (1970) Falsification and the methodology of scientific research programmes. In I. Lakatos and A. Musgrave (eds) *Criticism and the Growth of Knowledge* (pp. 91–196). London: Cambridge University Press.

LDOCE (1995) *Longman Dictionary of Contemporary English* (3rd edn) D. Summers (ed.). London: Longman.

Lynch, M. (1992) *Scotland: A New History* (Revised edn). London: Pimlico.

Macafee, C. (1994) *Traditional Dialect in the Modern World: A Glasgow case study*. Frankfurt: Lang.

Macafee, C. (1997) The case for Scots in the 2001 Census. (WWW.) http://www.abdn. ac.uk/~src045/whatson/case.htm. (Accessed 5 November 1999.)

MacCallum, N. R. and Purves, D. (eds) (1995) *Mak it New: An anthology of twenty-one years of writing in Lallans*. Edinburgh: Mercat.

MacKinnon, K. (1991) *Gaelic: A past and future prospect*. Edinburgh: Saltire.

Martin, J. (1997) Linguistics and the consumer: The practice of theory. *Linguistics and Education* 9 (4), 411–48.

McClure, J. D. (1988) *Why Scots Matters*. Edinburgh: Saltire.

McClure, J. D., Aitken, A. J. and Low, J. T. (1980) *The Scots Language: Planning for modern usage*. Edinburgh: Ramsey Head.

McCrone, D., Morris, A. and Kiely, R. (1995) *Scotland – the Brand*. Edinburgh: Edinburgh University Press.

McCrum, R., Cran, W. and MacNeil, R. (1986) *The Story of English* (Revised edn). London: Faber.

Merquior, J. G. (1985) *Foucault*. London: Fontana.

OALD (1995) *Oxford Advanced Learner's Dictionary* (5th edn) J. Crowther (ed.). Oxford: Oxford University Press.

Partington, A. (1998) *Patterns and Meanings*. Amsterdam: Benjamins.

Phillipson, R. (1992) *Linguistic Imperialism*. Oxford: Oxford University Press.

Rampton, B. (1995) Politics and change in applied linguistics. *Applied Linguistics* 16 (2), 233–56.

Robins, R. H. (1988) Appendix: History of linguistics. In F. Newmeyer (ed.) *Linguistics: The Cambridge Survey* (Vol. 1) (pp. 462–84). Cambridge: Cambridge University Press.

Seuren, P. A. M. (1998) *Western Linguistics*. Oxford: Blackwell.

Sinclair, J. (1991) *Corpus, Concordance, Collocation*. Oxford: Oxford University Press.

Skelton, C. (1999) A comparative study of the present status of Lowland Scots and Swiss German. Unpublished MSc thesis. University of Edinburgh.

Sokal, A. (1996) Transgressing the boundaries: An afterword. *Dissent* 43 (4), 93–9.

Spolsky, B. (1970) Linguistics in language pedagogy: Applications or implications? In J. E. Alatis (ed.) *Linguistics and the Teaching of Standard English to Speakers of Other Languages or Dialects* (pp. 143–55). Washington DC: Georgetown University Press.

Stubbs, M. (1989) The state of English in the English state: Reflections on the Cox Report. *Language and Education* 3 (4), 235–50.

Trim, J. (1988) Applied linguistics in society. In P. Grunwell (ed.) *Applied Linguistics in Society. British Studies in Applied Linguistics* 3 (pp. 3–15). London: CILT.

Widdowson, H. G. (1995a) Discourse analysis: A critical view. *Language and Literature* 4 (3), 157–72.

Widdowson, H. G. (1995b) Review of Fairclough discourse and social change. *Applied Linguistics* 16 (4), 510–16.

Williams, R. (1961) *The Long Revolution*. Harmondsworth: Penguin.

Willis, J. D. (1990) *The Lexical Syllabus*. London: Collins.

Young, R. B. (1971) Evolutionary biology and ideology. *Science Studies* 1, 177–206.

3 The Secret Life of Grammar-Translation

MALCOLM J. BENSON
Hiroshima Shudo University

Abstract

Grammar-translation, the method of teaching a language by the intensive study of its grammar and the application of that grammar to the translation of texts, is here examined in its historical context. Beginning with the bilingual experiences of Roman schoolboys, this language teaching method has been associated with social constructs such as authority, elitism, conservatism, and the search for superior models of living. These, and other, constructs made it attractive at certain periods of language teaching history, and comprise its 'secret' life. They in part explain why, despite the pressure of alternative methods, it continues to flourish in certain contexts today.

Introduction

The term 'grammar-translation' has been very unfortunate for language teaching. Not only has it cast an undeserved shadow over grammar and over translation, it has also had the effect of cutting off sensible discussion on what grammar-translation, the method, was really about. In this paper I would like to re-open the topic of grammar-translation, not in any attempt to advocate its re-introduction into language teaching, but to offer some ideas about a methodology that has been in use for rather more than two millennia, and as such should concern language teachers today.

Richards *et al.*'s (1992) definition of the 'Grammar-Translation Method' provides a suitable starting point: 'a method of foreign or second language teaching which makes use of translation and grammar study as the main teaching and learning activities'. The words *its main teaching and learning activities* challenge the historian of language teaching to pinpoint those periods in which grammar and translation played a *dominant* part in language teaching pedagogy. The result is a focus on three educational eras:

(1) Roman education, in which the foundational concepts of grammar and, to a lesser extent translation, were laid out.

(2) Reformation–Renaissance education, when classical methods, including the study of grammar and in particular the practice of translation were revived.

(3) Nineteenth-century education, when the classical model of studying grammar and doing translation (by its critics hyphenated into 'grammar-translation') was adapted to modern language teaching.

The initial thrust was Roman, when the study of grammar was the necessary prerequisite for the study of rhetoric, and associations and connections were established that were to affect the whole course of Western education. Later, during the Reformation–Renaissance, changes such as the rise of printing and the demise of Latin as a *lingua franca* caused renewed interest in grammar and translation, particularly to satisfy the humanist desire to translate the classics into the vernaculars. Finally, in the 19th century, the hyphenated version of grammar-translation emerges, subsequently called a 'method' but in reality both a continuation of the traditional way of teaching languages, and a travesty of it as well. This period deserves particular attention because it makes understandable the eagerness with which the Reform Movement of the 1880s was greeted.

Grammar-Translation in the Roman Context: Foundations

Roman education was bilingual Greek/Latin from about the second century BC (Caravolas, 1994). The fact that Cicero did regular translations out of Greek, that his writings contain a lot of Greek, and that orators were expected to deliver occasional orations in Greek, draws attention to the bilingual needs of educated Romans (Gwynne, 1926). These needs sprang from the Roman view of Greek civilization as a superior entity, whether in philosophy, literature, medicine, or science. The young child learned elementary Greek together with his first language, Latin, from his nurse or from a slave-tutor (*paedagogus*), as Quintilian sets it out. At the age of about seven the student proceeded to the school run by a *grammaticus*, a teacher of literature and languages, though often more accurately just a grammar teacher. Specifically, the *grammaticus* taught 'the art of speaking correctly and the interpretation of the poets'. Grand as this sounds, the student actually began with the sound systems of Latin and Greek, presented formally and contrastively. The eight parts of speech – following Aristarchus and Palaemon – came next, and with these came declensions and conjugations, as Quintilian (I, 4, 22) says: *Nomina declinare et verba in primus pueri sciant* (Boys should begin by learning to decline nouns and conjugate verbs.).

In grammar, the Roman grammarians – Donatus, Servius, Priscien – did work that followed the Greek model set out by Dionysius Thrax. By the middle of the 1st century AD grammar had attained a prominent position in Roman life, and this continued even more strongly in the 2nd century. Declensions and conjugations were formally set out, possibly by Palaemon, and two enduring features of grammatical explanation make their appearance: barbarisms and solecisms. These were, as Taylor (1995) says, to feature strongly in future grammatical thought and teaching.

The Roman student progressed from his grammatical studies in Latin and Greek to the reading of Greek classics. In due course, once a Latin literature had been established, it was quickly adopted by *grammatici*. Two important themes were evident in the adoption of Roman literature as the model to be followed: the literature theme itself, and the nationalist theme. The literature theme was to develop into being the virtual definition of western education; that is, western education at this point took a turn towards literature, with the word 'educated' being until very recently understood as referring to a person who had an easy familiarity with the classics.

The nationalist theme is more diffuse, but should not be neglected as it reappears in subsequent eras. Greek and Roman education had been directed specifically towards public service to the state, which was regarded as the noblest vocation a man could have. Grammar and, to a lesser extent, translation, was therefore the first step towards a life of public service, and grammar itself was characterized by a drive towards rules and regularity. Neither Greeks nor Romans had any interest in a multilingual–multicultural world, holding outsiders as barbarians, and outside intrusions into their respective languages as barbarisms. The discipline imposed on and by language from early schooling onwards bore a symbolic – and perhaps actual – relationship with the discipline required for the expansion of the Empire.

As well as establishing a connection between grammar and literature, and between grammar and nationalism, several other connections were also set in place.

One – perhaps obvious – was the connection between this kind of education and urban surroundings. The great cities of the Roman world, and later the Renaissance and 19th-century worlds, were home to books and libraries, printing presses and schools, and later cathedrals and universities. These urban environments usually focused narrowly on literacy, to the exclusion of other areas such as physical and musical education (Atherton, 1998). Non-urban matters were either sentimentalized or neglected entirely. Even the language to be used by Quintilian's ideal orator was to be different from the language of uneducated people. The result was that an urban elite was isolated and differentiated from the bulk of the population.

This divisive aspect of education was unfortunate, as it not only confirmed the elite status of the grammar-educated boy, but also confirmed in him the idea that authority – in this sense the admiration and emulation of the past – was fundamental to the educational process, and therefore to life. Whatever was old was good. Unlike his uneducated cousin, who probably wished to move as rapidly as possible towards a better, more modern future, the grammar boy was immediately oriented towards the past. He began to pay homage – via translation, imitation, and emulation – to the great authorities of the past. This became another pillar of classical study.

'Authority' may also be taken in the sense of a rule, or set of rules. The achievement of the Roman grammarians – based on Greek models, as seen above – in reducing a mass of linguistic data to a fixed set of rules was seen as significant. Of course rules brought about exceptions and deviations, and it was the function of the grammar teacher to separate the 'proper' use of words from the unacceptable (Atherton, 1998: 238). He could range through the ancient authors detecting barbarisms or solecisms, or simply insisting on his authoritative judgments:

> The grammarian was, first, the guardian of the language, *custos Latini sermonis*, in a phrase of Seneca, or 'guardian of articulate utterance' in the description of Augustine. He was to protect the language against corruption, to preserve its coherence, and to act as an agent of control.
>
> (Kaster, 1988: 17)

By the time of Quintilian, in the first century AD, the tension between rules and ordinary usage (*consuetudo*) was already a well developed topic that exercised the minds of grammar teachers, then as now. There was also a further complication: that the great authors themselves, the very subject of pupils' study, often broke the rules. These departures from the norm had to be explained by the *grammaticus* somehow or other. Atherton (1998) contends that the pupils took part in a linguistic progression, which might be briefly set out in three steps: (a) the initial separation of the pupils from the mass of their friends whose language was 'intrinsically flawed and irregular', (b) progression to an understanding of the rules and control over them, and (c) an awareness that there could be 'departures from rules' provided these departures were legitimized by 'the authority of literary status, age, or 'good' usage, and classified by the grammarian's expertise' Atherton, 1998: 242). Rules, the keeping of them, and the departing from them, were therefore central to the teaching of language. This provided the Roman child with a paradigm of life itself. Quintilian's ideal orator, 'a good man skilled at speaking' (*vir bonus dicendi peritus*), was therefore as much a moral ideal as a linguistic one. The education that would make him both morally good and oratorically able can therefore be seen as an essentially conservative one, and it was this view of life that was transmitted to pupils who were likely to occupy important positions in society.

To sum up, Roman education established connections between grammar and translation leading to literary sophistication on the one hand, and ideals of education that were derivative, urbanized, normative, and fundamentally conservative on the other. Atherton (1998) sums it all up as 'the *merits* of regularity' (239). Many of these terms apply to the teaching of language in the Reformation–Renaissance period, and to the 19th century as well. Possibly they also have explanatory power regarding the enduring quality of grammar-translation today.

The Reformation–Renaissance: Rebuilding the fabric

Continuity and change

Translation and grammar re-emerged as major activities in classrooms during the period from the 15th to 17th centuries. During these years the thirst for education, as symbolized by the founding and re-founding of schools, took language pedagogy into secular areas such as history, literature and astronomy. In the classroom, humanist thinking led to a new interest in re-aligning education with the cultural ideals of the classics, particularly as expressed by Cicero and Quintilian. Both had drawn inspiration from Greek ideals of oratory and education, and wished to replicate these ideals in Rome, particularly with a view to producing the perfect orator. This 'leadership' question was now faced by Renaissance humanists, who sought a programme of instruction that would produce what Grafton & Jardine (1986) have called a 'structuring framework' that would produce the 'key figures the society needs' (220). The classical world, broadly defined, appeared to offer just such a structuring framework, and it was assumed that emulating this model would also produce the key figures needed for leadership.

As in the classical world, the perfect leader would have to be a man of words, and once again Quintilian's *vir bonus dicendi peritus* was invoked. At the very least the good man would know Latin, and since humanist thinking linked the study of the three sacred languages with the correct interpretation of the Bible, now both Greek and Hebrew were added. After all, Erasmus had written: 'Our first care must be to learn the three languages, Latin, Greek, and Hebrew, for it is plain that the mystery of all Scripture is revealed in them' (in Rummel, 1995: 112). All the humanists concurred on the need for language study, regardless of whether they approached it from a religious standpoint like Luther, or from a linguistic–philosophical standpoint, like Melanchthon, or from an international humanistic perspective, like Erasmus. Further, the humanists practiced what they preached: they wrote grammars and made collections of colloquies for students, for example the *Regulae grammaticales* of Guarino Guarini and the colloquies of Erasmus and Vives.

Schools – the prime loci in which humanist ideals would be worked out – redoubled their efforts to provide a solid grammatical base for the new learning. When Henry VIII re-founded Canterbury Grammar School in 1541 the curriculum for the first year students was set out:

> In the First Class they shall learn thoroughly by heart the rudiments in English; they shall learn to put together the parts of speech; and to turn a short phrase of English into Latin; they shall run through Cato's verses, Aesop's Fables, and some Familiar Colloquies.   (Leach, 1911: 467)

Learning 'the rudiments in English' meant learning by heart the basic rules of Latin: what a noun was, what a verb was, and so forth. The innovation of using English in the beginning stages of Latin grammar shows that teachers were more aware than before of the value of the vernacular, and took the opportunity to educate the pupil in his own language while introducing the new one (Charlton, 1965). English, in fact, had been seen in grammatical texts from the early 15th century, a point which could be taken as the origin of the pedagogical grammar movement: the desire to simplify the initial learning of grammar. Turning 'a short phrase of English into Latin' became known to generations of schoolboys as 'making Latins' or 'vulgars', or 'Englishes', in which the usher/schoolmaster gave the pupils some simple English phrases for translation into Latin.

The actual business of learning Latin, Greek, and occasionally Hebrew is well documented (Latin: Watson, 1916 and Charlton, 1965; Greek: Grafton & Jardine, 1986; Hebrew: Jones, 1983). It was based on the 'traditional' version inherited from the Romans, but with two significant changes. The first of these was that the content of instruction – Latin – had changed, because by the 9th century it had 'irrevocably narrowed down to liturgy and the written word' (Auerbach, 1965: 121). Thereafter, the teaching situation was a foreign language one, with the exception that the students studying it were, for the most part, familiar with its sounds from their religious training (Murphy, 1980). There were no native speakers, with the result that spoken Latin in the Reformation–Renaissance period developed strongly accented forms that were sometimes incomprehensible internationally. Despite this, pupils everywhere were taught to speak Latin, though the 'narrowing' of the language placed greater emphasis on the written forms such as the grammar and literature, and promoted further written forms such as dictionaries.

Specific classroom innovations regarding grammar and translation at this time were very few, the only one of note being the 'double translation' usually associated with Roger Ascham (1570). In fact the method had a far earlier provenance, since Vives in 1531 had suggested double translation as an effective classroom method, as can be seen in the advice offered below:

Therefore, as soon as they have learnt syntax, let the pupils translate from the mother tongue into Latin, and then back again into the mother tongue. Let them begin with short passages, which can be gradually increased in length day by day.   (in Watson, 1913: 113–4)

Ascham suggested the other way round, first from Latin into English, and later back again:

The master first helps the child construe and parse a passage from Sturm's edition of Cicero's letters; the child then translates the passage into English on his own in a paper book; the master then takes from him the textbook; after an hour, the child then translates his own English back into Latin in another paper book; then the master lays the textbook, Ciceronian 'original' alongside the child's effort, and without chiding, gently shows him where Cicero would have used a different word, or syntactical arrangement.

(in Boutcher, 1998: 130)

But double translation did not require any major shift of emphasis or methodology. The humanist definition of grammar was still very much as Quintilian had it, and still linked speaking, writing and the reading of literature (e.g. Cicero, Virgil, Terence, and Caesar) into a holistic language and culture program. The old grammars of Donatus and Priscian were available at the beginning of this period, and by the end there were many vernacular grammars available to the schoolteacher. Following Hoole's (1660) outline, the pupil began with three years of grammatical instruction with the usher, or junior master. In the first year he was introduced to Latin grammar, learned basic vocabulary, and held simple conversations (pairwork); by year two he was translating Latins, speaking and writing in Latin, and reading elementary material; in the third year he reviewed and improved on everything done earlier, did Biblical translations both ways, read *Aesop's Fables*, studied Comenius' *Janua Linguarum*, and read more widely, particularly from religious texts. At that point the pupil's grasp of Latin grammar – particularly the speaking and writing appropriate to that level – was assumed to be adequate to the task of starting on serious literary work with the master, including translation and writing. Greek also started in the fourth year, and possibly Hebrew in the sixth. Only the evidently modern arrivals – Biblical texts and Comenius and the study of Hebrew – were different from what a Roman schoolboy had experienced.

The impact of printing

The second of the major changes in the Reformation–Renaissance time was the printing press. The outpouring of books at this period meant that a well equipped humanist school had a library of 250–300 books, including 'classical authors, grammars, vocabularies, dictionaries, fables, dialogues, rhetoric, oratory, letters, phrases, anthologies' (Watson, 1916: 110). The students themselves now owned copies of the books, and were no longer dependent on the medieval *lectura*, the word-for-word dictation of the textbook. Further, standardization of the lines and pages of a classical work made 'many of the old forms of teaching ... obsolete' (Nauert, 1995: 53). It also altered the nature of classroom activity, since the need to rely on memory was decreased, though by no means eliminated. More generally, the attention of a whole new audience was directed towards the written word (Eisenstein, 1983).

The increasing number of vernacular translations of the classics also had the effect of altering the status of the schoolmaster, who was no longer the sole authority on a text, and increased the opportunity to do translation as a class-room activity, since available printed authorities existed and could be referred to. One result was that the literary connection – that is, the progression from basic grammar-translation work to the study of literary texts – received a boost from the printing revolution. Translations in the vernaculars also brought the ideals of classical civilization into school systems all over Europe. The Graeco–Roman world was identified with western civilization, and emerging nation-states vied to show themselves heirs to this rich 'background'.

Translation into the vernacular had the effect of bringing the classics into the ambit of the local language, and transferring its 'ownership' into a local context. This began when the pupil first encountered Latin in vernacular translation:

Amo/as/at	I love
Doceo/ces/cet	I teach
Lego/gis/git	I rede
Audio/is/it	I here

(John Stanbridge, *c.* 1520; in Charlton, 1965: 107)

From this grammatical beginning the pupil advanced to translation of the classics, which in turn were repositioned into a vernacular context. This rendered the classics a subject of study, where previously they had been part of the lived reality of life. And since this process occurred in every country, the effect was to compartmentalize Europe in a way that had been impossible when all educated people understood one language and acknowledged one Church (Eisenstein, 1983).

Unfortunately the new liberal atmosphere engendered by the printing revolution was not universally popular. It threatened the stability of society, and reactions took the form of controls being placed on what should be taught and learned. Roman education had experienced this earlier when grammar teachers had to be licensed by the Emperor, particularly whenever moral, religious, or political norms appeared to be threatened. In England, grammar itself came under state control in 1540, when Henry VIII mandated Lily's grammar for use throughout all schools. Strict moral requirements were placed on grammar teachers. This made linguistically able grammar teachers hard to find, resulting in a generally low standard of accomplishment in the very area in which they professed to be expert. Often the requirement asked for a morally sound person who also knew grammar, rather than the other way round. The result of such employment criteria was that poor teaching and flogging became associated with grammar teaching at this time, though both had been in evidence in Roman education, and both were to reappear in the 19th century also. Talented teachers like Ascham, Brinsley and Hoole looked for innovative ways to help the weak teacher and to make the learning of grammar more enjoyable. Thus double translation, authentic dialogues, the regular use of the L1, and other suggestions were set out in methodology books. But school traditions died hard, and new ideas spread slowly. Despite the generalized criticism of grammar-translation 'tyranny' from writers like Milton and Locke, and the emergence of a 'naturalistic' school favoring direct methods, untalented grammar teachers continued to turn to the familiar grammar book and the cane.

We have seen that grammar and translation in the Renaissance period carried forward all the traditions that had been established in Roman education: (a) the model of a better society whose symbolic foundation was the study of grammar; (b) urbanized, normative, conservative, and often elitist attitudes; and (c) a focus on literature. To these were added social and religious agendas that used education to rework the medieval world into a new, secular form. Grammar was standardized across Europe by means of generally accepted texts. Hebrew was added to Latin and Greek in an already crowded language curriculum, though certainly Latin had undergone a narrowing in the intervening years.

The 19th Century: Preoccupation with grammar

Education in the 19th century regained some of the prominence that it had enjoyed during the Reformation and Renaissance. In Britain, although it underpinned an expanding Empire, education was not yet seen as a whole, but was rather applied differentially to the lower, middle and upper classes. While Victorian Hellenism was flourishing in elite schools, the three Rs were struggling to establish themselves at the opposite end. In between, the middle classes aspired upwards, longing to demonstrate their ability to give their sons a classical education which, since it lacked any practical outcome, could only be seen as training for high office. Fundamental to whatever aspirations a 19th-century person had was grammar, in its full and ancient meaning of the ability to speak and write correctly, and, for the best, to have some Latin tags to embellish their parliamentary speeches. It is not surprising, therefore, to discover that over 856 grammars were issued in Britain in the course of the 19th century (Michael, 1991).

The way in which classics was taught in the top schools was to some extent responsible for this popular outburst of enthusiasm for grammar, though a more general factor was at work too. That general factor was the increasing interest in psychology. What became known as 'faculty psychology' gripped the Victorian mind, combining as it did the areas of will, judgment, imagination, reason, understanding, and morality. For example, it was the teacher's job to see that,

> the will was strengthened, the judgment improved, the imagination warmed or excited, the reason developed, the understanding enlarged, or the moral powers exercised. The most important of all his teaching responsibilities was stimulating the memory. From this followed the heavy emphasis on rote learning, particularly at the lower levels of education.
>
> (Rothblatt, 1976: 130)

The classical languages, in theory at least, accomplished everything that faculty psychology demanded, and the voices that argued that the same could be achieved through, say, the study of science, were barely heard. It seemed, again in theory, that there was no form of mental training that would not be enhanced by a classical education.

Attempts to break with this dominant paradigm were hampered by the fact that Latin grammatical terminology had become so rooted in the minds of language teachers that even when faced with a language without any inflections they still attempted to apply the same rules to it:

	Nom.	Voc.	Acc.	Gen.	Dat.	Abl.
Singular						
Masculine	wise	wise	wise	wise	wise	wise
Feminine	wise	wise	wise	wise	wise	wise
Neuter	wise	wise	wise	wise	wise	wise
Plural						
Masculine	wise	wise	wise	wise	wise	wise
Feminine	wise	wise	wise	wise	wise	wise
Neuter	wise	wise	wise	wise	wise	wise

(J. Sterling, *A Short View of English Grammar*, 1735, in Michael, 1987: 319)

Figure 1 Classical terminology applied to English Grammar

The absurdity seen in Figure 1 arose because until the end of the 18th century teachers 'were rarely able to conceptualize the differences in method between studying your own language and learning a foreign one' (Michael 1987: 318). What had happened was that the innovators of the 16th and 17th centuries – who admittedly had worked within the classical paradigm – were either forgotten or disregarded, even though many of their ideas were equally applicable to modern language teaching – one thinks here of Comenius' illustrations. The result was that no separate methodological strand had developed to cope with the living modern languages. As Adamson (1964) says:

> It must not be forgotten that the schools had no traditional method of teaching a modern language and that the teachers not unnaturally followed in the main the procedure employed in teaching Latin and Greek. The general scheme included grammar (which meant much learning by heart), translation and the reading of French classical authors of the seventeenth century; and two hours a week sufficed for these things. Conversation in the foreign tongue was only exceptionally employed in special classes for the purpose; the aim was not speech or writing, but ability to read.   (241)

Inadequate conceptualization of an appropriate methodology was therefore a major restraint on the development of language teaching at this time. But there were also forces *within* language teaching itself that tended towards acceptance of the classical model. One of these arose because the lowly status of modern languages in the curriculum led to another absurdity: the unnecessary complicating of the foreign language in an attempt to give it equal status with the classics. This was particularly ironic given that the original aim of grammar-translation was to make language teaching easier for the student (Howatt, 1984). The result was that mid-19th century students were faced with tasks of quite amazing complexity (Figure 2).

---

379. It has been observed, (No. 357) that the conjunction *que*, used before the indicative mood, coming after the verb, expressing an act of the mind in the affirmative form, is never to be omitted in French. This shows that that conjunction does not *in itself* govern the subjunctive mood, as is erroneously thought by most learners; but there are, however, several cases in which *que* requires that mood after it. They are when *que* is used instead, or in the sense, of the following conjunctions: *à moins que, avant que, sans que, jusqu'à ce que, quoi-que, soit que,* which are themselves always followed by the subjunctive.

Examples.

J'attendrai *que* la pluie soit passée.   I shall wait until the rain be over.
(*jusqu'à ce que*)

Je ne sortirai pas *que* vous ne m'ayez   I shall not leave the house before
payé.   you pay me.
(*avant que*)

Exercise.

1. Give me your letter *that* I may send it to the post-office.

2. He says that he will not marry *until* he has a profession.

3. He cannot play, but he hurts himself.

(1) *Que* for *afin que*; to send, *envoyer*.

(2) To marry, *se marier, que* for *avant que ne*; profession, *état*, m.

(3) Cannot, *il ne saurait, que* for *sans que -ne*.

(de Lévizac's *Grammar of the French Tongue*, J. C. Tarver (ed.), 1840: 430)

Figure 2 Grammar Rule No. 379

The order of presentation shown in Figure 2 is maintained throughout all 520 pages of the text proper: rule, examples and exercises. This focus on rules, the neglect of speaking, the constant translation, the amazing variety of discrete sentences, and in particular the lack of more general human goals, indeed represented a low point in language teaching.

Grammar-translation was also seen by teachers as fitting in neatly with the new competitive exams from about 1850. The oral inadequacies of weak language teachers could now be covered up in the hunt for grammatically correct forms, while the exams themselves acquired spurious validity in view of the clearly right or wrong answers that examinees produced. When the first Oxford Local Examinations were established in 1858, the Latin paper – now one of the optional subjects – was predictable: (a) a passage for translation from Caesar's *Gallic Wars*, Books I–III, with questions on the parsing and the historical and geographical allusions, (b) an easy passage for translation from another, 'unseen' book , and (c) a passage of English for translation into Latin (with Latin words supplied). However, the French paper was essentially the same: (a) a passage for translation from Voltaire's *Histoire de Charles XII*, and another passage for translation from a French newspaper, and (b) English sentences for translation into French. The German paper was similar, using Schiller's *Revolt of The Netherlands* as the book for translation (Roach, 1971).

However, even if grammar-translation had advocates both inside and outside the language teaching profession, it was inevitably subject to advancing social forces. One of these appeared in the form of a rejection of the essentially male approach to language teaching, as embodied in grammar-translation of the classics. The rise of mass schooling in the mid-19th century was at odds with values that sought to promote 'active leadership, valour in the service of the state and prudence in the handling of public affairs' (Bayley & Ronish, 1992: 364). Classrooms in which communication was neglected and in which attempts at conversation were actively ridiculed no longer had any appeal outside their original context. In particular, such a methodology seemed inappropriate to the large numbers of girls now entering educational systems. Similarly, the methodology that led to an appreciation of literary masterpieces did not sit well with an aspiring middle class that increasingly sought utilitarian outcomes from the education its children received.

Specific themes traditionally connected with grammar and translation, for example conservatism, control, regularity, admiration of a distant past and of literature, now, at the end of the 19th century, were seen as inadequate for modern language teaching. Most had not survived the transition from the classics to the modern languages. By the 1880s and 1890s advances in phonetics had provided a fresh opportunity for language teachers to overthrow what had come to look like a bad experiment.

Conclusion: Lessons to be learned?

If 19th-century grammar-translation should now be seen as an experiment that went wrong as far as the modern languages were concerned, its wholescale overthrow might also be seen as having been detrimental to language teaching. The eagerness to introduce 'scientific', 'direct' methodologies, far from introducing an exciting new paradigm, instead ushered in an era of insecurity and doubt that was not resolved until after World War II. A representative figure here is Harold Palmer, whose early enthusiasm for phonetics and direct teaching suffered badly when he was confronted by the realities of institutional language teaching in Japan (Smith, 1999). Fortunately his tremendous energy then took him into new and productive areas such as vocabulary control and collocations, but these 'new' areas in many ways represented a *return* to the tenets of the older grammar-translation model.

More recently, Communicative Language Teaching, the current paradigm, has suffered reverses in FL contexts where the social characteristics associated with grammar-translation still pertain; that is, contexts in which conservatism, elitism, nationalism, desire for control, respect for regularity, and a liking for literature are to be found. In such contexts the overall language teaching goals tend to favour reading proficiency over other skills. On the other hand, communicative approaches appear to flourish in progressive, open, democratic, socially pliable contexts. These may be sweeping generalizations, but they are of sufficient validity to suggest that the concept of a single method or approach to language teaching, a model suitable for any people in any country at any time, is likely to run into local attitudes that find it inimical to their pedagogic and social requirements.

There may be three further lessons from this study of grammar-translation, one from each era dealt with in this paper. In Roman education, the evidence from Quintilian indicates that grammar and translation work was part of the preparation for the more advanced study of rhetoric. It was a *progymnasmata*, or preparatory exercise, sometimes dealing with basic grammatical problems, and at other times reaching as high as the more elementary aspects of rhetoric, such as 'narrative'. The aim of these exercises was clear: to provide both a practical linguistic basis and a deeper theoretical understanding of grammar (Morgan, 1998). This formalizing aspect of grammar in relation to the essentially L1 situation of the times – even though two languages were involved – is still the accepted model, and contemporary L1 and L2 writing instruction still depend on a foundation of classical rhetoric. Further, the Roman program of studies is interesting because it had all the elements of a discipline, in the sense that it produced specific, recognizable results. Such was the power of this discipline that it established the basic educational method and value system for Western education, down to very recent times.

In the Renaissance–Reformation period new factors were present: the printing press focused attention on the written word; education became more controlled; the need for good translations was fundamental to the humanist enterprise; and vernacular teaching was on the rise, displacing the traditional classical approach. The schoolboy still did a lot of grammar and even more translation, though the grammar was now 'pedagogical' in the sense that it was for an L2 learner. The translation, too, was as much to improve the student's English as it was to broaden his mind with classical wisdom. In keeping with Renaissance ideals, language learners were now seen as having individual differences, an idea which had not been a consideration in Roman times.

The 19th century saw the classical grammar-translation model – now much impoverished even where most vigorously followed – applied to modern languages, principally to cover up a methodological vacuum. Various factors, such as the demands of examinations, the indifferent skills of teachers, and a social ethos that valued discipline and competitiveness, all combined to make grammar-translation appear appropriate. These factors, as can be seen, have little to do with language learning. They comprise the secret life of grammar-translation, and help to explain why this, the oldest language teaching method of them all, is still prominent in large parts of the world today.

References

Adamson, J. W. (1964) *English Education 1789–1902*. Cambridge: Cambridge University Press.

Ascham, R. (1570) *The Scholemaster.* London: John Daye.

Atherton, C. (1998) Children, animals, slaves and grammar. In Y. L. Too and N. Livingstone (eds) *Pedagogy and Power* (pp. 214–44). Cambridge: Cambridge University Press.

Auerbach, E. (1965) *Literary Language and its Public in Late Latin Antiquity and the Middle Ages.* London: Routledge and Kegan Paul.

Bayley, S. and Ronish, D. Y. (1992) Gender, modern languages and the curriculum in Victorian England. *History of Education* 21, 363–82.

Boutcher, W. (1998) Pilgrimage to Parnassus: Local intellectual traditions, humanist education and the cultural geography of sixteenth-century England. In Y. L. Too and N. Livingstone (eds) *Pedagogy and Power* (pp. 110–47). Cambridge: Cambridge University Press.

Caravolas, J-A. (1994) *Précis D'Histoire 1, 1450–1700.* Montréal: Les Presses de l'Université de Montréal.

Charlton, K. (1965) *Education in Renaissance England.* London: Routledge and Kegan Paul.

Eisenstein, E. (1983) *The Printing Revolution in Early Modern Europe.* Cambridge: Cambridge University Press.

Grafton, A. and Jardine, L. (1986) *From Humanism to the Humanities.* London: Duckworth.

Gwynn, A. (1926) *Roman Education from Cicero to Quintilian.* Oxford: Clarendon Press.

Hoole, C. (1660) *New Discovery of the Old Art of Teaching School.* London: Andrew Crook.

Howatt, A. P. R. (1984) *A History of English Language Teaching.* Oxford: Oxford University Press.

Jones, G. L. (1983) *The Discovery of Hebrew in Tudor England: A third language.* Manchester: Manchester University Press.

Kaster, R. K. (1988) *Guardians of Language: The grammarian and society in late antiquity.* CA: University of California Press.

Leach, A. F. (1911) *Educational Charters and Documents 598 to 1909.* Cambridge: Cambridge University Press.

Michael, I. (1991) More than enough English grammars. In G. Leitner (ed.) *English Traditional Grammars: An international perspective* (pp. 11–26). Amsterdam: John Benjamins.

Michael, I. (1987) *The Teaching of English.* Cambridge: Cambridge University Press.

Morgan, T. (1998). *Literate Education in the Hellenistic and Roman Worlds.* Cambridge: Cambridge University Press.

Murphy, J. J. (1980) The teaching of Latin as a second language in the 12th century. *Historiographia Linguistica* 7, 1/2, 159–75.

Nauert, C. G. Jr (1995) *Humanism and the Culture of Renaissance Europe.* Cambridge: Cambridge University Press.

Quintilian, (1920) *Institutio Oratoria* (Loeb Classical Library, H. E. Butler, ed.). London: Heinemann.

Richards, J. C., Platt, J. and Platt, H. (1992) *Longman Dictionary of Language Teaching and Applied Linguistics.* London: Longman.

Roach, J. (1971) *Public Examinations in England 1850–1900.* Cambridge: Cambridge University Press.

Rothblatt, S. (1976) *Tradition and Change in English Liberal Education.* London: Faber and Faber.

Rummel, E. (1995) *The Humanist–Scholastic Debate.* Cambridge, MA: Harvard University Press.

Smith, R. C. (1999) *The Writings of Harold E. Palmer: An overview.* Tokyo: Hon-no-Tomosha.

Tarver, J. C. (ed.) (1840) *A Theoretical and Practical Grammar of the French Tongue* (21st edn) (J. P. V. L. de Lévizac, 1799). London: Longman.

Taylor, D. J. (1995) Roman language science in the early empire. In E. F. K. Koerner and R. E. Asher (eds) *Concise History of the Language Sciences* (pp. 107–10). Oxford: Pergamon.

Watson, F. (1916) *The Old Grammar Schools.* London: Frank Cass.

Watson, F. (1913) *De Tradendis Disciplinis* (The Transmission of Knowledge, Trans. F. Watson as *Vives: On Education*). Cambridge: Cambridge University Press.

4 Changing Views of Language Learning

SUSAN GASS
Michigan State University

Abstract

This paper focuses on the field of SLA and its evolution over the past 30 years or so. I consider the field's relationship with other disciplines, particularly language teaching. In attempting to understand today's SLA world, I also weigh various challenges to the field – notably challenges and controversies within the discipline itself and challenges and controversies that can be thought of as external. In the case of the former, the focus is on the concept of attention and its role in the mediation of differing views of acquisition. In the case of the latter, I argue that we need to be clear on what is and is not within the scope of the discipline. I close with a discussion of the relationship of SLA and language teaching, a starting point for the field itself. However, the relationship is now considered from a different perspective with an emphasis on the basics of acquisition and not on pedagogy. Finally, I discuss the uniqueness of our field and the niche that we have carved for ourselves with regard to more general issues of learning and language knowledge.

Introduction

This paper deals with changing views of language learning. This necessitates to some extent looking at the history of the field, making it particularly appropriate and particularly meaningful to write this paper for the BAAL conference held in Edinburgh. This is so because in thinking about the history of the field, many of the early researchers had their start in Edinburgh working with Pit Corder. Dating the beginnings of the field of SLA is not an easy task, so in this paper I take as an arbitrary date the late 60s[1] when Corder wrote his 1967 paper in which he argued that learners' errors were important not just in telling us what

51

pedagogical intervention was necessary, but in what they revealed of an internal linguistic system. One must also think of the early 1970s when Selinker gave the name of interlanguage to the phenomenon that we were studying. This is not intended to diminish the work of those who preceded this time – namely the work of Lado (1957), Fries (1945), Nemser (1961), and so forth because their work set the foundation for what was to come. So, in the mid-1960s to early 1970s the foundations were laid for the flourishing and diverse field that is with us to day.

We begin this excursion by commenting on the diversity that has been and that perhaps even more so exists today in the field. I include different research traditions and consequently different views on the scope of the field of SLA.

In thinking about changing views of language learning and trying to under-stand the present, we begin by looking at the present in the context of the past. So we will take a small peek backwards and focus on the roots of the field, wobbly roots at that, and reflect on how we have emerged into the position that we as a field occupy today, a position of emerging strength.

In thinking about the early days and years of what has now become SLA, we see a field that still had its feet firmly grounded in issues of language pedagogy. One way to examine those early years is to look at the journal of *Studies in Second Language Acquisition*, a journal that came into being during the 1970s totally dedicated, as the title indicates, to the field of SLA. In the first issue were comments that reflect the emergence of this 'central, theoretically-oriented core in applied linguistics' (p. iii).[2] It is quite telling that the contents of the first issue reflect what appears to be the ambivalence of the field as it was attempting to identify itself as an area of inquiry in its own right without needing to answer to pedagogical concerns (cf. Hatch's (1979) article telling us to 'Apply with Caution'). Clearly, there were papers such as that of Corder (1978) who was interested in language learning *qua* language learning, or that of Widdowson (1978), who was interested in simplification, or Valdman & Phillips (1978) who also wrote about learner systems, but then there was the paper by Levelt (1978) who tied his comments about learning to language teaching, and the paper by Krzeszowski (1978) on an English Reference Grammar for learners. Even in Volume 3 (1980), there was a special issue titled 'Foreign Language Syllabus and Communicative Language Teaching' (edited by Müller), clearly an area of inquiry that is focused on concerns of pedagogy rather than on concerns of learning. But by 1981, issues of pedagogy were backgrounded with the emer-gence of articles on interlanguage systems, such as the one by Eckman (1981) on phonological difficulty or the one on developmental stages by Meisel, Clahsen & Pienemann (1981), and with the emergence of articles with a focus on learning and how learning theory might affect language teaching. This was seen, for example, in an article titled: 'Language Acquisition Research and the Language Teacher' by B. J. Gadalla (1981).

In sum, on the one hand, we see the field in the late 1960s and 1970s beginning its strong move to deal with issues of non-primary acquisition, while on the other, we see it as having its foot in the camp of pedagogy. And, in fact this is our history. In today's climate, however, the classroom takes on a different perspective and is seen as the locus of learning, with research in the classroom having a strong focus on learning and not just on principles of pedagogy.

In the early years, learning was studied to determine better teaching methods (classroom practices), but with the steady emergence of research in SLA and the development of a body of independent knowledge, the relationship added another dimension – that of using what happens in the classroom as a basis for understanding how learning takes place. This has not eliminated the need for the first emphasis, as I have argued recently (Gass, 1997), inasmuch as pedagogy must be grounded *inter alia* in acquisition.

The initial approach to the study of learner systems came in the 1970s at which time the field was in a particularly strong anti-behaviourist mood. I will not go into detail here (see Ellis, 1994; Gass & Selinker, 1994; Larsen-Freeman & Long, 1991 for elaboration), but suffice it to say that the consequence of this mood, a mood which had its source in psychology and in child language acquisition, was a de-emphasis of the role of the native language and of language input, both of which were, erroneously, associated with behaviourism.

As the field developed, we saw a greater emphasis on learner systems as unique entities, often with studies with a linguistic base in the traditional areas of syntax, phonology, and particularly morphology. In the late 1970s and early 1980s we moved from studies on universals of the typological nature (e.g. Eckman, 1981; Eckman, Moravcsik & Wirth, 1989; Gass, 1979; Gass & Ard, 1984; Rutherford, 1984) to a study of universals based on a theory of principles and parameters (e.g. Clahsen, 1996; Eubank, 1991; Flynn, Martohardjono & O'Neil, 1998; Hoekstra & Schwartz, 1994; White, 1989). Within this framework, the task of SLA research is to determine whether or not learners have access to universal principles of language and to determine what the nature of grammatical knowledge is. But we are still heavily dependent on another source field, that is, linguistics for our theoretical underpinnings. This linguistic thread of research remains with us today and it might be characterised as representing static knowledge in that what one attempts to determine is the type of linguistic knowledge that learners have. Is that knowledge consonant with native speaker knowledge or is it unique to learner systems?

Challenges from Within

There are two main areas of criticism levelled against this line of research. Early studies argued that the access to UG position (e.g. Bley-Vroman, 1989; Schachter, 1988) could not be maintained and arguments were put forth that second language learners did not have access to the same innate mechanism that is responsible for first language acquisition. More recently, we have seen the emergence of what is called general nativism. In general nativist approaches it is argued that one does not have to invoke Universal Grammar (UG) – or any other innate language module – to explain second language acquisition. The main point of general nativist positions is that whatever innate learning mechanisms are available for second language acquisition are also available for other types of learning (e.g. Eckman, 1996; Hamilton, 1996; O'Grady, 1996; Wolfe-Quintero, 1996).

The second area of criticism, and one which I will deal with to a greater extent, relates to special nativist accounts, such as UG, as well as to general nativist accounts. Both special and general nativist positions consider language as an isolated phenomenon. The criticism that is levelled against these approaches is that language is used in context and one cannot understand second language acquisition without a theoretical recognition of this fact. I find this argument not particularly convincing in that it obscures the many ways in which we study second languages – ways that I schematize in Figure 1 (first appearing in Gass (1998)), some of which deal with acquisition[3] and some of which do not.

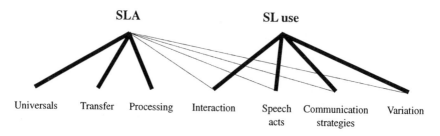

Figure 1 A characterisation of research in SLA second language studies

The thick lines indicate ascertained connections. That is, there is little doubt (or controversy) that the field of SLA encompasses such basic areas as universals, transfer, and processing or that language use entails a study of interaction, speech acts, pragmatics, variation, and so forth. What is less clear and is a matter of current controversy is the relationship between use and acquisition (e.g. What is the relationship between variation and acquisition? Is variation itself a mechanism for learning?). These unconfirmed links are indicated by the thin line. I will return to Figure 1 later in this paper.

In many ways the field of second language acquisition itself appears to be one of great contradictions and in many cases practitioners appear to be content to portray it that way. On the one hand, there are those who claim that there is an innate linguistic system and the debate centres around whether or not second language learners have access to that system and whether or not learners construct their second language systems guided by some sort of innate module. On the other hand, there are those who argue that language acquisition cannot be investigated without considering the context within which language is used. For these individuals, language acquisition is guided by the interactions in which learners are involved and the situational and discoursal context of language use. Within the input/interaction framework, the feedback given in interactions is crucial to learners as they hypothesis-test their way from no knowledge to a reasonably developed second language system. The extent to which interaction and/or some sort of modified input is relevant in determining grammatical knowledge is still under investigation, although there is substantial evidence of its importance. It is in this sense that language in context can be seen as crucial to an understanding of how acquisition takes place.

Stemming from these seemingly opposing views of acquisition is an interest in the ways internal factors (such as those represented by a UG approach to SLA) and external factors (such as those represented by an input/interactionist or variationist approach to SLA) might work together to account for learning. For example, can variationist approaches to the analysis of second language data tell us something about acquisition? To explore the relationship of these approaches is a daunting task, but one which is of interest to me given my research interests in both areas. I have conducted research that focuses almost exclusively on internal factors represented by the work that I have done in (a) language transfer (e.g. Gass, 1979, 1984a), (b) language universals (Gass, 1979, 1983, 1984a,b; Gass & Ard, 1984) , and (c) language processing within the framework of the Competition Model (e.g. Gass, 1986, 1987). But I have also done work that focuses almost exclusively on interactional factors represented by the work that I have done within the input and interaction framework (e.g. Gass & Varonis, 1985a,b, 1986, 1989; Gass, 1997; Varonis & Gass, 1985), much of which was conducted with my colleague, Evangeline Varonis. As mentioned, I have never seen these as contradictory, but only as areas that focus on different parts of the acquisition puzzle, to use an overused metaphor. Importantly, I would argue that one cannot explain acquisition in its entirety through purely external factors, nor can one explain acquisition in its entirety through purely internal factors. Pinker (1994: 277–8) similarly argues that nature provides part of the answer and nurture provides another. Whether or not they are interacting factors, and, if so, in what way, remains to be seen but at the very least they are both necessary although they quite likely address different questions and concerns.

Much of the debate came to a head in the 1990 exchange of papers between Gregg on the on hand and Tarone and Ellis on the other, and the debate continues to this day as was evidenced in a recent colloquium at the AAAL conference (1997). Gregg's position is that a theory of SLA must confine itself to the linguistic competence of L2 learners. My problem here is with the notion of 'confining itself'. Those who work within this framework take as their scope of investigation 'some systematic set of arguments, principles, etc. intended to explain the acquisition of second language competence' (Gregg: 1990: 365). Hence, from the start the scope is, as some might argue, overly limiting, since he, I believe, here means grammatical competence. Tarone and Ellis argue that variability is part of what learners know and hence should be part of a theory of SLA. I would argue that the issue is little more than a definitional one: What are we trying to account for? Those working within a 'grammatical competence' perspective (see, for example, White (1989)) do not deny the importance of studying pragmatic competence or discourse competence. The problem arises when terminological distinctions are blurred, particularly the use of the word competence, a word with both a technical meaning and a lay meaning. By definition a competence theory is not the same as a performance theory; its goal is to characterise mental representations rather than observed behaviour, and it is based on a somewhat different class of evidence (Pylyshyn, 1973: 24 (cited in Gregg, 1989)). The idea is that for grammatical competence there is some sort of formal system; for other types of knowledge, no such formal system exists, making it difficult to argue for a theory of other kinds of competence in the technical sense. This does not make these other areas of inquiry more or less valuable, interesting or worthwhile, or more or less part of what a learner knows; it just makes them different than the types of characterisations that one can have for a theory of grammatical competence. To understand completely the nature of second language acquisition, including the linguistic (I intend this term quite broadly here) knowledge and how that knowledge comes to be, one must take a broad perspective on the scope of inquiry, including all sorts of language-based knowledge, whether we call it competence or not. But the goal by definition is to understand acquisition, that is, the nature of L2 knowledge and how that knowledge comes to be.

My own work in language universals convinces me that second language acquisition is shaped by the nature of language (the extent to which innateness plays a role is still, in my mind, unanswered). On the other hand, my work in input and interaction convinces me that second language acquisition is shaped by the input one receives and by the interactions in which one engages. In other words, second languages are constrained by universals (innate or otherwise) while at the same time second languages are shaped by interactions and/or the sociolinguistic context in which learning takes place. It may be appropriate to think of universals not so much as informing learners of what a possible grammar is, but of restricting their choices (see Schachter, 1983, 1992). It is from this basket of choices that learners must select; input to the learner and the interactions in which they engage help them with that task.

In Gass (1988) (and slightly modified in Gass (1997)), I presented a model designed to capture the fact of multiple roles in acquisition. I argued that universals play one part of the dynamic picture of second language acquisition; our task as second language researchers is to determine the precise nature of the significance of universals and the extent to which they are (or are not) innate. I also argued that input and interaction have a role in understanding how second languages are learned; our task as second language researchers is to determine with precision the nature of that role. But the important point is that both perspectives are necessary.

In a 1994 article in which Eckman picked up on the exchange between Gregg on the one and hand and Tarone and Ellis on the other, Eckman acknowledges that scholarly debate is healthy. However, he also points out that at times debates are not worthwhile and only take up 'time and energy that should be applied to data gathering and analysis' rather than 'advancing and parrying arguments' (p. 3).

I basically agree with Eckman in as much as I do not believe the debate to be a very interesting or worthwhile one, but the reasons for my belief are not the same as those of Eckman. Further, I do not believe that one side or the other needs to be defensive, nor do I believe that one side or the other can or should appropriate all of SLA for themselves while excluding other intellectual avenues. While Eckman argues that the debate, which in this case is the proper domain for a theory of SLA, needs to be decided on empirical grounds, I would argue that the debate has no absolute answer. It has no answer if we mean that one side is part of the winning side and the other is not; both views are winners and need to be essential ingredients. A theory of how second languages are learned must include the nature of abstract linguistic competence as well as sociolinguistic information of the type dealt with in variation studies as well as that dealt with in input/interaction studies as well as an understanding of how language is processed. White (in press) acknowledges the non-inclusive nature of theories when she says: 'It is not the aim of UG-based theories of SLA to account for all aspects of L2 development. These theories concentrate specifically on the nature of IL knowledge' (p. 24).

Much of the distinction centres around certain kinds of knowledge and how learners (children/adults) can possibly attain that knowledge without being explicitly taught it or without being exposed to it in some direct way. Nonetheless, an eventual theory of second language acquisition will need to account *inter alia* for the nature of linguistic knowledge (competence in the theoretical sense) that L2 learners attain, how that knowledge comes to be, how that knowledge is used and how use of knowledge may relate to acquisition (see Liu, 1991; Tarone & Liu, 1995).

It is not necessary that one approach fit into the 'requirements' of another; it is not necessary to claim that one approach *is* SLA and another is not. Sociolinguistic information provides the input into whatever linguistic system has been formulated by the learner. Sociolinguistics can help explain why some input is relevant and other input is not. Understanding what happens in interactions with learners and with language addressed to learners gives us insight into what linguistic information serves as input and how that input is structured and 'primed' for the internal linguistic system (Gass, 1997). This is the job of those who take a sociolinguistic bent on acquisition. What happens in a learner's head once that information is provided is the job of those who have a more linguistic or psycholinguistic bent on acquisition. All of these approaches share the common goal of learning about how knowledge comes about and what that knowledge is.

A Potential Solution to the Problem

In today's literature, much attention is being paid to the concept of attention (Leow, 1997, 1998; Schachter *et al.*, ms.; Schmidt, 1990, 1993a,b,c, 1994a,b, among others). This, to me, plays a central part of the picture and may turn out to be what links the nature and nurture positions. Some of this literature relates in particular to the classroom context and to the debate between focus on form and focus on meaning and, in particular, to the types of tasks (pedagogical or otherwise) that might be beneficial to learning. The other area of emphasis is more directly related to issues of psycholinguistic processing. It is this area that I turn to here.

Given that second language learners are surrounded by L2 data, some mechanism must be available to help them wade through and sort out these data. One way in which the input becomes more manageable is by focusing attention on a limited and hence controlled amount of data at a given point in time. By limiting the data to which one attends, learners can create a set of data that allows them to move from input to output. What this assumes is that language processing is like other kinds of processing: Humans are constantly exposed to and often overwhelmed by various sorts of external stimuli and are able through attentional devices to 'tune in' to some stimuli and to 'tune out' others.

Another concept that is frequently discussed in the literature is awareness. Definitions are somewhat varied, but a common one according to Schachter *et al.* (ms.) is that an individual is able to detect and verbalise the pattern that has been learned (p. 2).

One of the early works devoted to the role of attention in SLA was that of Schmidt (1990; 1993a,b,c; 1994a). Schmidt's main point is that noticing something in the input is crucial to its subsequent role in acquisition. That is, before something can result in intake, it must be noticed. This is not unlike what I have claimed in earlier works (Gass, 1988; 1997) where 'noticing' or what I have called 'apperception' serves as a priming device, or as a prerequisite to intake. Nor is it unlike Slobin's (1985) claim for first language acquisition that children must notice and hold the noticed material in memory as a prerequisite to acquisition. Where my view and Schmidt's part company is that for Schmidt 'intake is that part of the input that the learner notices' (Schmidt, 1990: 139). Thus, for Schmidt once the learner notices something in the input, it automatically becomes intake: 'If noticed, it becomes intake' (Schmidt, 1990: 139).

In considering the concept of noticing, Schmidt argues that all noticing is conscious. This means that a learner in noticing something is conscious of the fact of noticing. In fact, he specifically states that 'subconscious learning' is oxymoronic (Schmidt, 1990: 139).

In sum, noticing in this view, by definition, involves awareness and consciousness. Further, Schmidt (1993b,c) argues that noticing involves a subjective experience and an ability to articulate that experience. While Schmidt (1993b: 25) acknowledges that determining what a learner has or has not noticed is virtually impossible, at least in naturalistic learning situations, he does claim that one can show that something has not been noticed 'by the failure of subjects to report their awareness of a stimulus if asked immediately following its presentation'. Hence, attention is central to any concept of noticing.

There have been a number of recent studies on the role of attention, most attempting to show that attention is a driving force of acquisition. While a review of these studies is beyond the scope of this paper, what I do want to propose is that by carefully understanding attention (and perhaps language processing in general) we will be in a better position to link the ways in which the language available to learners in context is processed, is utilised (or not), and eventually serves as crucial data for the formation of grammars. We will need to explore how attention might affect different parts of language (e.g. lexicon, syntax) – in fact, I am just finishing up an investigation of exactly this point with two of my students. We will need to explore how attention, in whatever form might be appropriate (e.g. explicit rule instruction, error correction), is dependent on individual characteristics such as proficiency levels, another area that I am currently investigating. In this way we will be able to link the external environment with internal capacities.

Challenges From Without

What I have discussed thus far are debates internal to the field today. Where does that leave us as a field? It leaves us with a number of strands that have to be pulled together. It leaves us with the task of determining what the study of SLA in its entirety is. As Long (1998) said in a recent paper entitled 'SLA: Breaking the Siege', the field is under attack. Let me quote from one of the areas of concern to him to give you a flavour of at least one of the attacks. He characterises the attack as one in which it is claimed that 'SLA researchers focus overly narrowly on learners' internal, cognitive processes, ignoring social context', but the attack is different than the Tarone and Ellis contra Gregg exchange. It is different in that it is not part of a squabble amongst participants who have the same understanding of the goals of the field. In other words, there appear to be few shared assumptions. The specific source of Long's consternation is an article in a recent issue of *Modern Language Journal*. Firth & Wagner (1997) critique orthodox SLA research and their paper 'argues for a reconceptualisation of SLA research that would enlarge the onto-logical and empirical parameters of the field' (p. 285). The authors 'claim that methodologies, theories and foci within SLA reflect an imbalance between cognitive and mentalistic orientations, and social and contextual orientations to language, the former orientation being unquestionably in the ascendancy' (p. 285). On the surface, there is nothing wrong with this position. As Long (ms.) states 'Few researchers would deny the *potential* importance of the interactional and socio-linguistic context in which SLA occurs ...' (p. 11). There is no dispute that there is a need to broaden our base and this is what Tarone was arguing, but in reading the article by Firth and Wagner one sees a lack of shared assumptions of what con-stitutes SLA research. Returning to the differentiation I made in Figure 1 between SL Acquisition and SL use, Firth and Wagner demonstrate a confusion between *learners* and *users*; they cut the line between use and acquisition. As they state, the field of SLA has 'led to the prioritising of the individual-as-"non-native speaker"/"learner" over the participant-as-language-"user" in social interaction' (p. 286). But of course we are primarily and foremost concerned with the learner; learners are our subject matter; they are our bread and butter. As Kasper (1997) said in her *MLJ* response to the Firth and Wagner article, after all A in SLA is for acquisition. To me there is an even more general difference as to the scope of inquiry of SLA research. Firth and Wagner state in the article that SLA has a general preoccupation with the *learner*. This makes as much sense to me as would a criticism of chemists' general preoccupation with chemical compounds. After all, I thought that our goal was to study learners in order to find out how learning takes place. But, as Poulisse (1997) correctly notes, '... the acquisition and learning of skills are generally considered to be psychological processes, as are the produc-tion and perception of language. Hence, it is no wonder that many studies of second language acquisition and use take a psycholinguistic approach' (p. 324).

Firth and Wagner go on to talk about the categories of NS and NNS that we use so blithely in our literature. While it is true that we are lax in using those terms, their concern is different. They argue that we should not necessarily use the categories NS and NNS as primary categorisations. They talk about the fact that there are other categories that reflect who these individuals are and that our so-called NSs and NNSs, fit into. They suggest, for example, categories, such as 'father, man, friend, local, guest, opponent, husband, colleague, teacher, team-mate, intimate, acquaintance, stranger, brother, son, expert, novice, native speaker, uninitiated, joke teller, speaker, caller, overhearer ad infinitum' (p. 292) (and perhaps others that designate women rather than men). However, in trying to capture the more complete picture of an individual's persona, they have failed to understand the nature of an empirical paradigm; they have not understood that these categories are not included because they are not deemed to be relevant to the question at hand, which is: How are second languages acquired and what is the nature of learner systems? In other words, no previous research suggests that potential categories, such as father, mother, brother, sister, aunt, uncle are ones that need to be taken into account and no theories are dependent on these concepts. As Firth and Wagner note, there are many categories that individuals can be placed into, some of which they do not mention, for example, hair colour or hand preference. It is a basic assumption of empirical research that categories such as hair colour, that have no theoretical bearing on the question at hand, are not part of a design or do not figure in the analysis, whereas categories such as hand preference, that might be relevant, might be part of a research design or analysis. In other words, relevance has to be established theoretically, in this case insofar as it affects the acquisition of an L2.

I do not want to spend any more time on this criticism of SLA research and the various responses to that criticism since that was done on the pages of the *Modern Language Journal*. What I want to do is think about why what I see as a basic misunderstanding has come about. Why do we have to continually justify our field and explain its goals? No one asks a chemist or an economist what they do. But we do frequently hear naïve views about the field of SLA, views that are freely expressed by those with no expertise to those with expertise. For example, an English professor I know has what we now affectionately call the 'fixed-mouth hypothesis'. According to him, you cannot learn a second language because your mouth gets fixed at a young age. Or, to take another example, at a recent dinner party, someone at the dinner table proceeded to tell everyone that you cannot learn a second language after age 20 – never once turning to me to ask me if there is any evidence for or against this. We all have numerous stories like these. What this suggests to me is that the accumulated specialised knowledge of our field is not recognised as such.

Is the blame for this partly ours? Do we need to articulate better what our field is about? Why does everyone have an opinion? Most SLA researchers have

enough respect for nuclear physics not to utter uneducated opinions or judgements. In Gass (1993) I argued that we should be making greater contributions
to other fields, particularly our source fields. Early research began from a decidedly linguistic perspective, but has now branched off with research influences
from psychology, sociolinguistics, neurolinguistics, and so forth. But information should flow to as well as from the various disciplines. To date, most of the
interaction between SLA and the other disciplines has been unidirectional; that
is, we have drawn from the theoretical insights of other disciplines, but little has
gone from SLA to the source. In other words, developments in other areas have
had implications for theories of SLA, but SLA research has, in general, not had
an impact on the development of theories of other disciplines. To continue to
grow in academia, we need to do more than draw from source disciplines, we
need to be *important* if not *essential* to other disciplines. As we have developed
into a field, we need to ensure our future; we need to guard against isolationism
and move toward integrating our research with the agenda of others. If we enter
into a debate drawing from another field, let's say linguistics, shouldn't we
contribute to the debate by showing how second language data may elucidate
theoretical constructs and issues? (see White, in press).

　　In sum, I have discussed two aspects of SLA. I briefly touched upon the fact
that the field has started from a concern about the classroom and, in some sense,
we're back there albeit from a different perspective. I have also pointed out that
the field has moved away from a decidedly linguistics bent, a static view of
understanding linguistic competence. In so doing, we have become much more
influenced in recent years by a more dynamic view of language learning, one
that includes studies on discourse, on conversation, on pragmatics, on speech
acts, on input, on psycholinguistic processing, on issues of attention and awareness and so forth.

SLA and Language Teaching

　　Thus far, I have been concerned with the general shape of the field of SLA. I
want to return to where the field began and that is its relationship to language
teaching. As I noted above, many of the earlier studies had as their ultimate goal
the betterment of teaching methodologies or pedagogical tools. This general area
of interest has remained in the background throughout the years, but is now
being looked at from a different perspective. Today's emphasis on the classroom
has as an underlying emphasis the basics of acquisition. That is, when we are
considering learning within a classroom context, we are considering theoretical
issues in second language research and how those principles might affect our
teaching. But the relationship is still in debate. A few years ago there was a
discussion on the SLART bulletin board[4] concerning the relationship between

SLA and language teaching. The context of the specific debate was the extent to which an SLA conference should include papers on language pedagogy. Some strongly favoured such inclusion and others argued against such inclusion. Shortly after this discussion, I received a letter from the then president of TESOL asking me to participate in a debate concerning the role of SLA research in a teachers' professional organization. In her letter, the TESOL president said 'Over the last several years, TESOL membership has shifted from an organization of researchers working primarily in institutes of higher education to an organization of educators who teach in a variety of different settings in many different countries. At the same time, other organisations interested in second language research have grown. So, as an organization whose mission is "to develop the professional expertise of its members and other service providers to foster effective communication through English in diverse settings" we need to consider how TESOL's contribution in research is unique but also complementary to the work that goes on in other forums and professional groups.' So within the space of just a few months, two organisations were asking questions of identity: one wondering if pedagogy should be part of it and if so, to what extent and the other wondering if research should be part of it, and if so, to what extent. The question asked by TESOL is: What is the role of research in a teachers' association and the counterpart being asked by SLA conference organizers is: what is the role of pedagogy in a researcher's forum?

The question may be more fruitfully addressed if we do not think of teaching issues versus learning issues as a dichotomy, bur rather as a continuum with pure research issues on one end and purely teaching issues on the other. In the middle there is research in the classroom which can be of at least two sorts: research that is conducted so that we will be better informed about learning and research that is conducted for purposes of teaching – those that address specific effects on learning. The former is clearly part of the SLA mission, the latter perhaps less so.

Reading the Tea Leaves

Of course, one cannot predict with accuracy, but one can think about the trajectory that we are on. We will undoubtedly become more sophisticated as a field as a result of more sophisticated techniques for elicitation. The field of SLA has carved out a niche in its serious attention to issues of elicitation, witness the discussions about acceptability judgements, elicited imitation and sentence matching in the literature. It is likely that we will quickly adopt and adapt techniques used in psycholinguistic processing in gathering neurolinguistic data and so forth. With a wider range of techniques available, I predict that there will be a greater emphasis on what actually is occurring in learners' heads as they process and use language – for example, we will become more interested in which parts of the brain are activated for different functions and how that may or may not differ depending on whether or not one is using a first or a second language. Alongside this emphasis will be a continuation of our role in teacher education and in trying to understand the relationship between the classroom and learning. For example, the study of interaction per se, the study of learners' perception of error correction, an examination of tasks and their contribution to learning and at what stage, will all become major foci. With all of these research areas, we must, however, continue to show that we have a strong contribution to make to understanding the nature of language, the nature of language processing, and how, in general, language is used in a social context. We are an interdisciplinary field with multiple spokes; we must enter into discussions about the nature of the hub that anchors the spokes.

Notes

1. This dating of the field of second language acquisition (SLA) is not unlike Catherine Snow's (1994) placing the beginnings of 'modern child language research' to the 1964 publication of Brown and Bellugi.
2. It is important to note that in today's research climate, many SLA researchers do not associate the field of SLA with applied linguistics, but for many SLA is a branch of linguistics, and consequently a part of cognitive science.
3. I am using acquisition here in a strict sense to refer to what is *learned* of the second language. I am differentiating it from language use and consider both of those to be under the general umbrella of second language studies.
4. SLART is an unmoderated e-mail bulletin board.

References

Bley-Vroman, R. (1989) What is the logical problem of foreign language learning? In S. Gass and J. Schachter (eds) *Linguistic Perspectives on Second Language Acquisition* (pp. 41–68). Cambridge: Cambridge University Press.

Brown, R. and Bellugi, U. (1964) Three processes in the child's acquisition of syntax. *Harvard Educational Review* 34, 133–51.

Clahsen, H. (ed.) (1996) *Generative Perspectives on Language Acquisition.* Amsterdam: John Benjamins.

Corder, S. P. (1978) 'Simple codes' and the source of the second language learner's initial heuristic hypothesis. *Studies in Second Language Acquisition* 1, 1–10.

Corder, S. P. (1967) The significance of learner's errors. *International Review of Applied Linguistics* 5, 161–70.

Eckman, F. (1981) On the naturalness of interlanguage phonological rules. *Language Learning* 31, 195–216.

Eckman, F. (1994) The competence–performance issue in second-language acquisition theory: A debate. In E. Tarone, S. Gass, and A. Cohen (eds) *Research Methodology in Second-Language Acquisition* (pp. 3–15). Hillsdale, NJ: Lawrence Erlbaum Associates.

Eckman, F. (1996) On evaluating arguments for special nativism in second language acquisition theory. *Second Language Research* 12, 398–419.

Eckman, F., Moravcsik, E. and Wirth, J. (1989) Implicational universals and interrogative structures in the interlanguage of ESL learners. *Language Learning* 39 (2), 173–205.

Ellis, R. (1990) A response to Gregg. *Applied Linguistics* 11, 118–31.

Ellis, R. (1994) *The Study of Second Language Acquisition*. Oxford: Oxford University Press.

Eubank, L. (ed.) (1991) *Point Counterpoint: Universal grammar in the second language*. Amsterdam: John Benjamins.

Firth, A. and Wagner, J. (1997) On discourse, communication, and (some) fundamental concepts in SLA research. *Modern Language Journal* 81 (3), 285–300.

Flynn, S., Martohardjono, G. and O'Neil, W. (1998) *The Generative Study of Second Language Acquisition*. Mahwah, NJ: Lawrence Erlbaum Associates.

Fries, C. (1945) *Teaching and Learning English as a Foreign Language*. Ann Arbor: The University of Michigan Press.

Gadalla, B. J. (1981) Language acquisition research and the language teacher. *Studies in Second Language Acquisition* 4, 60–9.

Gass, S. (1979) Language transfer and universal grammatical relations. *Language Learning* 29 (2), 327–44.

Gass, S. (1983) Second language acquisition and language universals. In R. DiPietro, W. Frawley and A. Wedel (eds) *The First Delaware Symposium on Language Studies: Selected papers* (pp. 249–60). Newark: University of Delaware Press.

Gass, S. (1984a) A review of interlanguage syntax: Language transfer and language universals. *Language Learning* 34, 115–32.

Gass, S. (1984b) Empirical evidence for the universal hypothesis in interlanguage studies. In A. Davies, C. Criper and A. Howatt (eds) *Interlanguage* (pp. 3–24). Edinburgh: University of Edinburgh Press.

Gass, S. (1986) An interactionist approach to L2 sentence interpretation. *Studies in Second Language Acquisition* 8 (1), 19–37.

Gass, S. (1987) The resolution of conflicts among competing systems: A bidirectional perspective. *Applied Psycholinguistics* 8, 329–50.

Gass, S. (1988) Integrating research areas: A framework for second language studies. *Applied Linguistics* 9, 198–217.

Gass, S. (1993) Second language acquisition: Past, present and future. *Second Language Research* 9, 99–117.

Gass, S. (1997) *Input, Interaction, and the Second Language Learner*. Mahwah, NJ: Lawrence Erlbaum Associates.

Gass, S. (1998) Apples and oranges: Or, why apples are not oranges and don't need to be. *The Modern Language Journal* 82 (1), 83–90.

Gass, S. and Ard, J. (1984) L2 acquisition and the ontology of language universals. In W. Rutherford (ed.) *Second Language Acquisition and Language Universals* (pp. 33–68). Amsterdam: John Benjamins.

Gass, S. and Selinker, L. (1994) *Second Language Acquisition: An introductory course*. Hillsdale, NJ: Lawrence Erlbaum Associates.

Gass, S. and Varonis, E. (1985a) Variation in native speaker speech modification to non-native speakers. *Studies in Second Language Acquisition* 7, 37–57.

Gass, S. and Varonis, E. (1985b) Task variation and nonnative/nonnative negotiation of meaning. In S. Gass and C. Madden (eds) *Input in Second Language Acquisition* (pp. 149–61). Rowley, MA: Newbury House.

Gass, S. and Varonis, E. (1986) Sex differences in nonnative speaker-nonnative speaker interactions. In R. Day (ed.) *Talking to Learn: Conversation in second language acquisition* (pp. 327–51). Rowley, MA: Newbury House.

Gass, S. and Varonis, E. (1989) Incorporated repairs in NNS discourse. In M. Eisenstein (ed.) *The Dynamic Interlanguage* (pp. 71–86). NY: Plenum Press.

Gregg, K. (1989) Second language acquisition theory: The case for a generative perspective. In S. Gass and J. Schachter (eds) *Linguistic Perspectives on Second Language Acquisition* (pp. 15–40). Cambridge: Cambridge University Press.

Gregg, K. (1990) The variable competence model of second language acquisition, and why it isn't? *Applied Linguistics* 11, 365–83.

Hamilton, R. (1996) Against underdetermined reflexive binding. *Second Language Research* 12, 420–46.

Hatch, E. (1979) Apply with caution. *Studies in Second Language Acquisition* 2, 123–43.

Hoekstra, T. and Schwartz, B. (1994) *Language Acquisition Studies in Generative Grammar.* Amsterdam: John Benjamins.

Kasper, G. (1997) 'A' stands for acquisition. *Modern Language Journal* 81 (3), 307–12.

Krzeszowski, T. (1978) English reference grammar for Polish learners. *Studies in Second Language Acquisition* 1, 85–94.

Lado, R. (1957) *Linguistics Across Cultures.* Ann Arbor: The University of Michigan Press.

Larsen-Freeman, D. and Long, M. H. (1991) *An Introduction to Second Language Acquisition Research.* Harlow, Essex: Longman.

Leow, R. (1997) Attention, awareness and foreign language behaviour. *Language Learning* 47, 467–506.

Leow, R. (1998) The effects of amount and type of exposure on adult learners' L2 development in SLA. *The Modern Language Journal* 82, 49–68.

Levelt, W. (1978) Skill theory and language teaching. *Studies in Second Language Acquisition* 1, 53–70.

Liu, G. (1991) Interaction and second language acquisition: A case study of a Chinese child's acquisition of English as a second language. Unpublished PhD thesis, La Trobe University.

Long, M. (1998) SLA: Breaking the siege. Paper presented at PACSLRF, March, Tokyo.

Meisel, J., Clahsen, H. and Pienemann, M. (1981) On determining developmental stages in natural second language acquisition. *Studies in Second Language Acquisition* 3, 109–35.

Müller, K. (ed.) (1980) The foreign language syllabus and communicative language teaching. *Studies in Second Language Acquisition* 3.

Nemser, W. (1961) *Hungarian Phonetic Experiments.* American Council of Learned Societies. Research and Studies in Uralic and Altaic Languages. Project. 32.

O'Grady, W. (1996) Language acquisition without universal grammar: A general nativist proposal for L2 learning. *Second Language Research* 12, 374–97.

Pinker, S. (1994) *Language Instinct.* NY: William Morrow and Company.

Poulisse, N. (1997) Some words in defense of the psycholinguistic approach. *The Modern Language Journal* 81 (3), 324–238.

Pylyshyn, Z. (1973) The role of competence theories in cognitive psychology. *Journal of Psycholinguistic Research* 2, 21–50.

Rutherford, W. (ed.) (1984) *Second Language Acquisition and Language Universals.* Amsterdam: John Benjamins.

Schachter, J. (1983) A new account of language transfer. In S. Gass and L. Selinker (eds) *Language Transfer in Language Learning* (pp. 98–111). Rowley, MA: Newbury House.

Schachter, J. (1988) Second language acquisition and its relationship to Universal Grammar. *Applied Linguistics* 9, 219–35.

Schachter, J. (1992) A new account of language transfer. In S. Gass and L. Selinker (eds) *Language Transfer in Language Learning* (pp. 32–46). Amsterdam: John Benjamins.

Schachter, J., Rounds, P., Wright, S. and Smith, T. (ms.) Comparing conditions for learning syntactic patterns: Attentional, nonattentional and aware.

Schmidt, R. (1990) The role of consciousness in second language learning. *Applied Linguistics* 11, 129–58.

Schmidt, R. (1993a) Awareness and second language acquisition. *Annual Review of Applied Linguistics* 13, 206–26.

Schmidt, R. (1993b) Consciousness, learning and interlanguage pragmatics. In G. Kasper and S. Blum-Kulka (eds) *Interlanguage Pragmatics* (pp. 21–42). NY: Oxford University Press.

Schmidt, R. (1993c) Consciousness in second language learning: Introduction. Paper presented at AILA 10th World Congress of Applied Linguistics, Amsterdam.

Schmidt, R. (1994a) Implicit learning and the cognitive unconscious: Of artificial grammars and SLA. In N. Ellis (ed.) *Implicit and Explicit Learning of Languages* (pp. 165–209). London: Academic Press.

Schmidt, R. (1994b) Deconstructing consciousness in search of useful definitions for applied linguistics. In J. Hulstijn and R. Schmidt (eds) *Consciousness and Second Language Learning: Conceptual, methodological and practical issues in language learning and teaching* (pp. 11–26). AILA Review – Revue de l'AILA, 11.

Slobin, D. (1985) Crosslinguistic evidence for the language-making capacity. In D. Slobin (ed.) *The Crosslinguistic Study of Language Acquisition* (pp. 1157–256). Hillsdale, NJ: Lawrence Erlbaum Associates.

Snow, C. (1994) Beginning from baby talk: Twenty years of research on input in interaction. In C. Gallaway and B. Richards (eds) *Input and Interaction in Language Acquisition* (pp. 3–12). Cambridge: Cambridge University Press.

Tarone, E. and Liu, G. (1995) Situational context, variation, and second language acquisition theory. In G. Cook and B. Seidlhofer (eds) *Principle and Practice in Second Language Acquisition* (pp. 107–24). Oxford: Oxford University Press.

Tarone, E. (1990) On variation in interlanguage: A response to Gregg. *Applied Linguistics* 11, 392–9.

Valdman, A. and Phillips, J. S. (1978) Pidginization, creolization and the elaboration of learner systems. *Studies in Second Language Acquisition* 1, 21–40.

Varonis, E. and Gass, S. (1985) Non-native/non-native conversations: A model for negotiation of meaning. *Applied Linguistics* 6, 71–90.

White, L. (in press) Special nativism. In C. Doughty and M. Long (eds) *Handbook of Second Language Acquisition Theory and Research.* Oxford: Basil Blackwell.

White, L. (1989) *Universal Grammar and Second Language Acquisition*. Amsterdam: John Benjamins.

Widdowson, H. (1978) The significance of simplification. *Studies in Second Language Acquisition* 1, 11–20.

Wolfe-Quintero, K. (1996) Nativism does not equal universal grammar. *Second Language Research* 12, 335–73.

5 Change and Continuity in Second Language Acquisition Research

FLORENCE MYLES
University of Southampton

Abstract

This paper analyses how two well-established traditions within SLA research illustrate both continuity and change in the discipline. Work undertaken within the Universal Grammar framework, and within the context of the ESF (European Science Foundation) project, are examples of the 'North-American' and 'European' traditions respectively, which have consistently pursued clear lines of inquiry with well-defined research agendas, albeit very different ones.

Recently, their respective research agendas have matured and developed in less incompatible ways. Both approaches have as one of their goals, along their different paths, the description and explanation of early L2 acquisition. This has given rise, in the ESF context, to the notion of *Basic Variety* (BV), and, in the UG context, to the characterisation of the *Initial State*.

Although it would be misleading to equate BV and Initial State, as they remain very different concepts, they nonetheless present some similarities. The BV has been reanalysed recently by its authors using a UG framework. Such dialogue, unthinkable only recently, is a sign of the future, and of the realisation within the maturing field of SLA research that it must be studied as a multi-faceted phenomenon, which benefits from attention from a variety of approaches.

Introduction

When the theme of the BAAL Conference, *Change and Continuity in Applied Linguistics,* was announced my interest was aroused because of my perception of major shifts within second language acquisition research in Europe over the last ten years or so, shifts which have occurred within fairly stable theoretical frameworks. As a regular participant at SLA conferences in different European countries, it has been fascinating to witness the changing nature of the dialogue between researchers from different linguistic schools. For the purpose of this paper, I have chosen to illustrate these changes by following the recent development of two well-established traditions within SLA research, which I call, somewhat simplistically, the 'North-American' tradition on one hand, and the 'European' tradition on the other. Though a gross oversimplification, this is nonetheless a useful dichotomy. By these two traditions, I mean the formalist approach on one hand, substantially influenced by Chomskyan linguistics, and the functionalist approach, more influenced by Saussurian linguistics, on the other. The formalist approach can be illustrated by briefly tracing the development of the Universal Grammar approach to SLA research (see, for example, White, 1989 or Ritchie & Bhatia, 1996 for fuller accounts), and the functionalist approach by looking at the work of the European Science Foundation (ESF) project (see, for example, Perdue, 1993a,b). I will show how their very different research agendas have matured and developed in less conflicting directions recently, and how their attempts at describing and explaining early L2 acquisition have given rise to the creation of two constructs which, although very different in many ways, nonetheless share important aspects. More importantly perhaps, a dialogue has now been established between researchers of the two schools, visible at conferences and in academic journals, a dialogue which would have been unthinkable not so long ago. I will then assess the significance of this dialogue.

Two Different Research Traditions

The ESF project

The European Science Foundation funded project 'Second language acquisition by adult immigrants', is a major research project carried out in the early 80s in Europe. It is a longitudinal study of the early stages of SLA in relatively uneducated immigrants in a number of Western European countries, and it represents an impressive example of international research co-operation between a number of European countries. The project comprised research teams in France (Paris VIII and Aix-en-Provence), The Netherlands (universities in Brabant), Sweden (Göteberg), Germany (Heidelberg) and the UK (Ealing College of Higher Education). The informants were interviewed and recorded over a period of two and a half years in the early 1980s, and the massive databank which was collected then is still being actively used by many researchers, with publications continuing to arise from the project. The languages studied are outlined in Figure 1, and were chosen to enable a comparison of the acquisition of a number of target languages by learners from different, typologically unrelated L1s.

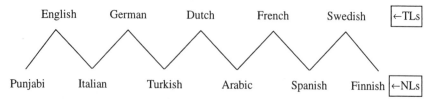

Figure 1 Language pairs in the ESF project

The design of this project has nothing specifically 'European' in itself, and could just as well have been carried out from a 'North-American' perspective, although methodological choices would then have been different. But whereas a Chomskyan perspective would have tried to find out if UG was at work in the interlanguage of the learners by looking specifically at its formal structure (e.g. by eliciting judgements on structures for which native language and target language have different parameter settings), the ESF project asked broader questions, representative of their theoretical allegiance. The aims of the project were defined as follows (Perdue, 1984):

> The project concentrates on linguistic issues: it investigates three general and inter-related questions about second language acquisition by adult immigrants, set out in its Field Manual as follows:
>
> (1) the factors on which acquisition depends;
>
> (2) the general structure of second language acquisition with respect to
>
>> a. the order in which elements of the language are acquired and
>>
>> b. the speed and success of the acquisition process;
>
> (3) the characteristics of communication between native and non-native speakers of a language.

Some of the best-known work arising from the project has been on the expression of temporality and spatial relations, and on utterance structure. The researchers involved in this work have consistently argued that pragmatic universals arising from the organisation of information structure, in terms of topic and focus, are at play. For example, learners were shown to organise linguistic units according to the principle that 'focus comes last, controller comes first', where controller refers to the extent to which one argument is or intends to be in control of another (Perdue, 1995).

Similarly, in the acquisition of spatial relations, learners chose first to express dynamic relations (change of place) rather than the location of objects. ESF researchers then drew explicit parallels with L1 acquisition, and emphasised the fact that the semantico-pragmatic tendencies observed are universal.

Some of the more recent analyses arising from the ESF project will be described in more detail later, but let us conclude this section by stressing the major impact that this project has had on our understanding of the semantic and pragmatic universals which characterise human linguistic behaviour and play an important part in language acquisition, which have typically been dismissed by universalists as peripheral to language, but which deserve our attention too. The ESF work has put L2 semantics and pragmatics well and truly on the SLA map (for a comprehensive report of this work, see Perdue, 1993a,b).

Universal Grammar

The Universal Grammar approach to second language acquisition is probably more widely known, as it has been the source of a huge number of studies. Incidentally, the fact that these studies are normally published in English in the main SLA journals has made them more readily available to a wider research community, and has reinforced the North American domination, together with its lack of awareness of European research. The impact of the UG approach to SLA is due to the tremendous influence of the main current in linguistics in North America, Chomskyan linguistics. The consequences of this geographical dichotomy has been to split the SLA field into two camps (at least), with the UG 'camp' firmly believing they were the only ones truly concerned with the essence of language and its acquisition, and the ESF 'camp' truly convinced that their approach was more comprehensive and therefore more useful.

The Universal Grammar approach to language study has a well-defined research agenda. Its starting premise is that human language is part of our genetic makeup, and that the human mind has a component devoted exclusively to language, which is independent of other mental structures dealing with cognitive abilities generally, although it obviously interacts with them.

The main goal within the UG approach is to understand and characterise the human language faculty, the architecture children are born with which makes the learning of any human language possible. In their effort to characterise this language faculty, UG theorists have put forward a highly sophisticated analysis of the formal properties of language. They have postulated a number of universal principles which are at the core of all human languages, and a series of parameters which limit the variation between languages. For example, all languages are structured hierarchically (phrasal structure – a universal), but the way in which these phrases are ordered varies from language to language (head-first or head-last – a parameter).

Applied to the study of first language acquisition, the aim of such an approach is not only to describe the system a child has to acquire, but also to provide a principled explanation of the fact that children acquire language so quickly and effortlessly, in spite of its highly abstract nature, and at an age when ill-equipped to deal with abstract concepts.

In the context of second language acquisition, the central aim of the UG approach is to investigate the role – if any – played by this language faculty. If, as is claimed, the only difference between languages is in terms of parametric differences, what implications does this have for the acquisition process? Is Universal Grammar also available to adults? What happens when parameter settings are different in the L2? Can we reset parameters? Are principles still available directly or only via the L1? These are the kind of 'top-down' questions such an approach is asking, fundamentally different from the much more global, 'bottom-up' questions underlying the ESF researchers' approach.

In the UG framework, non-structural aspects of language tend to be dismissed as trivial: unless we understand what the essence of language is and how it is represented in the minds of speakers, as well as how it gets to be represented in that way, we are missing the crucial point. The attitude of such researchers was therefore closed to dialogue on anything other than this specific issue: there was no point talking to people interested in other aspects of the learning process or in other aspects of language, as they would not be able to inform us on the nature of formal linguistic knowledge, as defined by UG. The crucial dichotomy introduced by Chomsky between *competence* and *performance* became at the forefront of linguists' minds, with competence being seen by UG researchers as the essence of human language, and with anything concerning language use being dismissed as the domain of performance and therefore outside the domain of linguistic theory proper.

The same was also true in the other tradition: researchers interested in SLA with a broader and less prescriptive agenda found very little of relevance in the very theoretical and technical concerns of UG people. Therefore, you either belonged to one tradition or the other, and opportunities for exchanging views were non-existent.

Beginnings of dialogue

To summarise this very brief historical overview, until very recently (I would say until the last few years at most), we had two well established research traditions: on the one hand, the European functionalist researchers primarily concerned in with the construction of meaning in SLA, and the North-American formalist researchers primarily interested in the construction of formal language properties, and little dialogue between the two.[1]

Many members of the SLA research community in Britain in the mid-80s felt frustrated by this lack of dialogue. If you were an SLA researcher interested in the UG approach, the only platforms for discussing your research would be in America, with small pockets elsewhere, e.g. some British universities, and some universities in The Netherlands. If you were an SLA researcher interested in other approaches, the platform for discussion was a number of general Applied Linguistics venues across Europe, few of them dedicated solely to SLA issues. It was in this context that EUROSLA (the European Second Language Acquisition Association) was set up in the early 90s, in order to create a forum for SLA researchers in Europe. The first few conferences reproduced closely the two 'camps' division, with the UG people keeping to themselves and refusing all dialogue with the 'pragmaticians', and vice versa. Gradually, over the next few years, dialogue started taking place, not always very constructively. In the late 90s, although the differences in approaches are still fundamental, a number of developments have meant that fruitful and constructive dialogue is now taking place, and the last few EUROSLA conferences have seen researchers from both traditions exchanging views. Part of the shift has been the realisation that no one approach can explain all the facts, and that you can believe in a UG-guided component to the acquisition process in order to explain certain morpho-syntactic phenomena, without necessarily believing that UG is the answer to all questions, even at the level of morpho-syntax. With a modular view of language becoming more prominent in theoretical debates (Gregg, 1996; Smith & Tsimpli, 1995), a major research interest in SLA has been how the different modules might develop and interact with one another. Although this outline of the situation might be a somewhat idealised picture of what is actually happening, I believe researchers are now looking at the various dimensions of language in order to answer more specific and focused questions. So, for example, some UG researchers might now recognise that you need to resort to, say, psychological accounts of language parsing in order to understand some aspects of the SLA process, or that pragmatic universals might explain some aspects of language development. Similarly, some functionalist SLA researchers might believe that you need to take account of formal universals in order to explain some SLA facts.

The last few years have been an exciting time for SLA research for those reasons. SLA researchers interested in understanding a range of phenomena typical of the SLA process, and willing to resort to different theoretical approaches in order to do that, do not necessarily feel excluded by impenetrable boundaries between the different 'camps' anymore.

More importantly perhaps, the very different starting points and premises taken by the different schools have all led to similar discoveries, in the finding of universal paths of development, be they syntactic, morphological, or pragmatico-semantic.

Where researchers are now meeting (and disagreeing), is in their attempts to explain these phenomena. But this surely represents the way forward towards building a comprehensive picture of the SLA process, with the development of the morpho-syntactic system, typically the concern of UG researchers, being one of the building blocks, rather than the whole process, and the development of the pragmatico-semantic system, another building block. The emerging dialogue has meant that the complementary nature of the different approaches is being recognised, with for example European functionalists turning to the UG framework in order to explain some of their formal findings.

Recent Developments

The 1997 (13:4) issue of *Second Language Research* (*SLR*) illustrates this dialogue. It is devoted to the 'basic variety', a product of the European approach, in a journal in which the UG approach has traditionally had a very strong presence. In this issue of *SLR*, the 'basic variety' is discussed by linguists from different theoretical perspectives (typologists, ESF researchers, theoretical linguists, UG proponents).

It is necessary, before turning to that discussion, to introduce the basic variety (BV), and to discuss another, UG-based construct, referred to as the 'initial state'.

The *Basic Variety*

What is interesting from the point of view of the present paper is how the very pragmatico-semantic motives behind the analysis of the data in the ESF project have led to some characterisation of learners' early interlanguages in terms of morpho-syntactic properties. One of the major findings of the ESF project is the discovery that all learners, no matter what the source language-target language pair was, could be situated on a three-stage continuum which could be characterised in morpho-syntactic terms. Those three stages (or varieties as they are called in ESF parlance) are:

Pre-basic: Nominal Utterance Organisation (no verbs; NPs pasted together, e.g. *Mary shop*,[2] meaning 'Mary is in the shop/goes to the shop/has a shop etc ...')

Basic: Infinite Utterance Organisation (untensed verbs; no functional morphology, e.g. *Mary go shop*)

Post-basic: Finite Utterance Organisation (verbal morphology appears, e.g. *Mary goes (to the) shop*)

The rate at which learners go through these three stages is highly variable. The pre-basic variety is characterised by the organisation of the discourse around the NP (verbs are missing), with the controller of the action as the starting point. The second stage is labelled the 'basic' variety as it represents a fossilisation level which all learners reach, but not all go beyond. It is organised around an untensed verb, and obeys discourse and semantic constraints based on the actors required by this verb. The basic variety is relatively impervious to morpho-syntactic features of both native and target languages, and includes a limited sub-system of pronouns. During the following stage, the post-basic variety, pronouns, subordination and verbal morphology all make their appearance, and this has major implications for the discourse structure of the learners' utterances. Within the pronominal system, an acquisition order has also been observed: singular pronouns appear before plural, reference to humans before inanimates, and nominative pronouns before oblique.

A great deal of work was also done on the pragmatico-semantic properties of learners' interlanguages, but my purpose here is to show that, in spite of a research agenda paying little attention at the outset to formal properties, the researchers were nonetheless drawn to notice the important role they play.

The *L2 Initial State*

The first serious discussion of the 'L2 Initial State', as a theoretical construct used by UG researchers to label the 'starting point of non-native grammatical knowledge', was in an issue of *Second Language Research* in 1996, where a number of researchers defended different positions about the relationship between Universal Grammar and the initial state of second language learners. Questions addressed in this issue were as follows: Is Universal Grammar working in the same way in L2 adult learners as for children acquiring their L1? If this is the case, are all aspects of UG available from the start, or do some properties mature according to some predetermined schedule, as some researchers believe is the case for young children? Is the L2 initial state the first language of the learner? If so, how does it interact with Universal Grammar?

The three hypotheses outlined are the Minimal Trees hypothesis (Vainikka & Young-Scholten, 1996; Vainikka & Young-Scholten, 1998), the Full access/Full transfer hypothesis (Schwartz & Sprouse, 1996), and the Valueless Features hypothesis (Eubank, 1996). To this would have to be added the position that UG is inoperative in adult L2 learners (Meisel, 1997a,b), and other intermediate positions such as that of Schachter (1996) who claims that UG comes online at different times for different structures, and that for a structure to be acquired with the help of UG, it has to be acquired within a certain window of time. The debate is still very much alive to-date.

The main positions can be summarised as follows:

- The Minimal Trees hypothesis claims that L2 learners transfer from their L1 the lexical categories (N, V, etc. ...) but not the functional categories (such as Tense, Inflection, etc. ...). The result is a learner language which lacks 'grammar', in the sense of inflections, complementisers, etc. ...

- The Full access/Full transfer hypothesis claims that the initial state of L2 acquisition is the final state of L1 acquisition. In other words, all of the L1 grammar is initially transferred into the L2, and development is failure-driven. L2 properties which cannot be assigned a representation by this grammar will force restructuring, and this will be constrained by UG, in the same way as L1 acquisition is constrained by UG.

- Eubank's Valueless features hypothesis claims that the L2 initial state comprises the whole of the L1 grammar, except for the 'strength values' of features under functional heads. Briefly explained, functional categories (such as Infl) have different properties (called features) in different languages. More specifically, some functional heads are said to have 'weak' features or 'strong' features, and this has a direct bearing on morphological realisation in a given language. Eubank claims that, initially, morphology is absent from learner language because learners have not acquired the strength value of features.

- The UG is dead position (Meisel, 1997a) argues that adult L2 learners do not have access to UG, and rely primarily on linear sequencing strategies.

This is a very brief summary of the work on the initial state and on the basic variety, constructs originating from very different research agendas and traditions. By focusing on formal characteristics of early interlanguage systems, these constructs have played a crucial role in enabling dialogue to take place.

At the Crossroads

On the one hand, European researchers, under the influence of Saussurian and Hallydayan linguistics, have put semantics and pragmatics on the SLA agenda, and have consistently refused to look at linguistic structure outside of function and meaning. In a recent article on the BV, Jordens (1997) writes:

> ... the BV ... is a simple language system, in terms of its organizational principles. Form-function correspondences are determined by three types of constraints: *phrasal constraints* which define the patterns in which lexemes may occur, *semantic constraints* which attribute arguments to particular positions (controller first) and *pragmatic constraints* which organize information in connected discourse (focus last). The BV, however,

is more than a simple language system. It is a highly functional means of communication which is similar for many learners for a long period. As such, it is a 'genuine manifestation of the human language faculty' (Klein & Perdue, 1997) which means that the limited set of organizational principles inherent to the BV belongs to the genetical endowment of our species.

(Jordens, 1997: 291–2)

Now, in this definition of the BV, reference to concepts such as 'the human language faculty', and the 'genetical endowment of our species' comes as somewhat of a surprise. This kind of discourse is highly reminiscent of universalists' arguments, and at the centre of their concerns. It is not typical of ESF researchers' concerns. What I believe has happened to provoke this shift is that the very findings of the ESF project, as well as the large body of empirical evidence being gathered in all camps over the last 25 years, including the findings of the ESF project itself, show clearly how systematic learner development is. This has led European researchers, who might not have hypothesised such uniformity, to look towards universals (formal, pragmatic, cognitive) in order to explain some of the features of interlanguages (especially as learners go beyond a very basic level). In 1997, Klein and Perdue even go so far as to reanalyse the BV in terms of Chomsky's Minimalist Programme (Chomsky, 1995), a recent development in UG thinking, arguing that the BV is nothing other than a natural language in which all functional features are weak (explaining the lack of morphology). Now this analysis (which has been criticised and is not unproblematic (Schwartz, 1997)) is reminiscent in a number of ways of the initial state debate mentioned above. One cannot help noticing the similarities with, for example, the Minimal Trees hypothesis (where functional categories are missing initially) or the Valueless features hypothesis (where functional categories are present, but lack strength values). The details of the analysis are not crucial in the context of the present discussion, but the very fact that such an analysis is not only possible, but has been carried out by ESF researchers is very interesting indeed.

Another common point between ESF researchers and UG researchers is that both believe that learner language needs to be investigated as a system in its own right, rather than as a cross between the L1 and the L2. A major difference still remaining, however, is that the ESF people do not believe that systematicity has to follow from strong theoretical presumptions. This has important empirical implications: whereas universalists take their theoretical framework as a starting point and try to test it empirically in their research, the ESF approach is more bottom-up. Both approaches have advantages and disadvantages. ESF researchers, for example, tend to use longitudinal semi-spontaneous data elicitation methods, with small numbers of learners, thereby getting a more sensitive view of development within individual learners, but without being able to tap more deeply embedded characteristics of learner language, nor underlying linguistic representations. The different elicitation methods do not tap the same phenomena, nor do they ask the same research questions. But this does not mean to say that both do not have their place in order to gain a comprehensive picture of the acquisition process.

If it is clear that there has been a shift in the point of view of (some at least) functionalists towards acknowledging a role for universalist formalism, it remains for me to demonstrate that there has also been a shift in the other direction. I believe there has, in a number of ways.

Firstly, the ESF researchers were the first to look at the very early stages of language acquisition, something which UG researchers had not paid much attention to before. They had always been more interested in the development of complex grammatical structures, well beyond the kind of interlanguage used by the ESF subjects. I think the claims made by the ESF team about the pre-basic and the basic varieties forced some UG researchers to question the relationship between UG and early interlanguage. And that led to the very interesting work investigating the initial state.

Secondly, as the universalist (in the Chomskyan sense) approach has developed and been applied to language acquisition issues, the research questions have shifted. The early debate over whether UG (or the LAD, or whatever name is given to the mental framework underlying human languages) is or is not available in SLA has been replaced by more focused and sophisticated questions concerning which aspects of language or language learning it can help us understand (Gregg, 1996; Smith & Tsimpli, 1995), for example:

- which aspects of UG are still available (e.g. principles, parameters, functional features etc. ...) in L2 learning?

- which aspects of learning can UG account for (e.g. which levels of language)?

- does UG compete with other learning devices in L2 learners (e.g. what is the interaction between UG-driven acquisition and 'learnt linguistic knowledge', that is the knowledge which has been learnt by another route such as rote-learning)?

- what is the role of the L1 in the SLA process (e.g. how can the same learner have two conflicting parameter settings within the same mind; what is the effect of L1 settings etc. ...)?

In other words, if UG researchers undoubtedly remain dismissive about work outside their area, the explanatory domain of their approach has narrowed somewhat. UG is not seen any more as a be-all and end-all, explaining everything, but is seen as a highly sophisticated linguistic theory which can shed light on specific aspects of the language system and its acquisition. It is true that UG researchers still see as the primary goal of linguistic theory the description and explanation of the nature of the specific architecture supporting language in the human mind, in all its specificity (i.e. separate from, but interacting with, other cognitive functions), and that it excludes many aspects of language use. But they recognise that we also need to understand how this linguistic system develops, in all its aspects, and how learners learn to access the linguistic system they have constructed, in real time and under the constraints imposed by human processing factors. In other words, because recent developments in linguistic theory and in neurolinguistics have led to a more modular view of the language faculty, Chomskyan linguists are increasingly recognising that it is important to understand not only core linguistic knowledge (shaped by UG), but also how it interacts with other aspects of the language system, including pragmatic and semantic systems, and with other cognitive mechanisms outside the language system. They leave that enterprise to other researchers, but, by and large, do not dismiss it anymore as irrelevant. We have to remember that Chomsky (1986) himself defined the aim of linguistic theory as giving answers to three basic questions about human language:

(1) What constitutes knowledge of language?

(2) How is knowledge of language acquired?

(3) How is knowledge of language put to use?

The presence of (3) in this list is significant; although Chomskyan linguists have generally ignored this question as peripheral, the fact that it figures in the list gives it legitimacy within a Chomskyan view of language. It is also interesting to note that (1) is all inclusive, i.e. encompasses all aspects of human language, even though Chomskyan linguists have traditionally restricted their work almost exclusively to the domain of syntax and morphology. (2) is obviously crucial to our understanding of both (1). and (3), and as a link between them. Towell & Hawkins (1994) have constructed an SLA model which attempts to draw these three questions together.

Conclusion

The SLA research agenda of the two traditions I have briefly explored has remained essentially unchanged, in the sense that UG researchers are still interested primarily in understanding the linguistic representations underlying language competence, and how these representations get constructed in learners, and the functionalists are still primarily interested in how learners construct meaning, by exploring for example the devices they use in order to express semantic concepts such as time and space. That has not changed substantially.

What has changed, however, is that the functionalists have come to realise that pragmatic and semantic constraints, although very useful, are not enough to explain some of the formal linguistic properties exhibited by interlanguages, and that they have to resort to formal constraints in order to characterise learner language more fully. The most striking example of this is of course the recent application of Chomsky's Minimalist Programme by two of the 'key figures' of the ESF project to their own work. This would have been unthinkable not so long ago. This should not be taken to mean, however, that the functionalists have been the only ones to shift ground towards the formalist tradition. They have clearly demonstrated that pragmatic and semantic universals play an important part in the shaping of early interlanguages, if not as much later on. They have also added to the huge body of evidence showing how systematic the construction of L2 systems is, in spite of the fact that their starting premise, unlike universalists, did not push them to look for universals, quite the contrary. This is important, because in spite of the fact that the ESF research design was conceived in order to highlight differences between learners from different language pairs and from different language families, it ended up showing very convincingly how similar the early language systems are in *all* learners, whatever their background. The ESF work has also given prominence to the very early stages of second language acquisition, which had been neglected until then, and which are crucial if we are to understand what learners bring to the task of L2 acquisition.

Moreover, there is now a genuine and constructive dialogue, in spite of (or thanks to) many disagreements. Some ten or 15 years ago, the scene was very different. The theoretical approach you adopted was supposed to explain the whole of the SLA process. Therefore, if you adopted a UG approach, you believed that UG could explain the whole process of SLA, and the emphasis of your research was very much on outlining similarities between L1 and L2 acquisition, and differences would be dismissed as peripheral. The almost exclusive focus of interest was the development of a formal system, with syntax and morphology being prime candidates for study. If, on the other hand, you adopted a functionalist approach, you assumed that differences between L1 and L2 acquisition would be crucial, and that the TL–NL pairs would play a determining role. Both these views are now more subtly qualified, and both traditions have contributed to this more sophisticated understanding.

Notes

1. Again here, forgive the oversimplification; for a more detailed account of the role of a wide range of theoretical approaches in the development of SLA research, see Mitchell & Myles, 1998.
2. My examples.

References

Chomsky, N. (1986) *Knowledge of Language: Its nature, origin and use.* NY: Praeger.

Chomsky, N. (1995) *The Minimalist Program.* Cambridge, MA: MIT Press.

Eubank, L. (1996) Negation in early German–English interlanguage: More valueless features in the L2 initial state. *Second Language Research* 16 (1), 73–106.

Gregg, K. (1996) The logical and developmental problems of second language acquisition. In W. Ritchie and T. Bhatia (eds) *Handbook of Second Language Acquisition* (pp. 49–81). San Diego: Academic Press.

Jordens, P. (1997) Introducing the basic variety. *Second Language Research* 13 (4), 289–300.

Klein, W. and Perdue, C. (1997) The basic variety (or: Couldn't natural languages be much simpler?). *Second Language Research* 13 (4), 301–47.

Meisel, J. (1997a) The acquisition of the syntax of negation in French and German: Contrasting first and second language development. *Second Language Research* 13 (3), 227–63.

Meisel, J. (1997b) The L2 basic variety as an I-language. *Second Language Research* 13 (4), 374–85.

Mitchell, R. and Myles, F. (1998) *Second Language Learning Theories.* London: Arnold.

Perdue, C. (ed.) (1984) *Second Language Acquisition by Adult Immigrants. A field manual.* Rowley: Newbury House.

Perdue, C. (ed.) (1993a) *Adult Language Acquisition: Cross-linguistic perspectives* (Vol. 1, Field methods). Cambridge: Cambridge University Press.

Perdue, C. (ed.) (1993b) *Adult Language Acquisition: Cross-linguistic perspectives* (Vol. 2). Cambridge: Cambridge University Press.

Perdue, C. (1995) *L'Acquisition du Français et de l'Anglais par des Adultes. Former des énoncés.* Paris: CNRS Editions.

Ritchie, W. and Bhatia, T. (eds) (1996) *Handbook of Second Language Acquisition.* San Diego: Academic Press.

Schachter, J. (1996) Maturation and the issue of Universal Grammar in second language acquisition. In W. Ritchie and T. Bhatia (eds) *Handbook of Second Language Acquisition* (pp. 159–93). San Diego: Academic Press.

Schwartz, B. (1997) On the basis of the basic variety ... *Second Language Research* 13 (4), 386–402.

Schwartz, B. and Sprouse, R. (1996) L2 cognitive states and the Full Transfer/Full Access model. *Second Language Research* 16 (1), 40–72.

Smith, N. V. and Tsimpli, I.-M. (1995) *The Mind of a Savant: Language learning and modularity.* Oxford: Blackwell.

Towell, R. and Hawkins, R. (1994) *Approaches to Second Language Acquisition.* Clevedon: Multilingual Matters.

Vainikka, A. and Young-Scholten, M. (1996) Gradual development of L2 phrase structure. *Second Language Research.*

Vainikka, A. and Young-Scholten, M. (1998) The initial state in the L2 acquisition of phrase structure. In S. Flynn, G. Martohardjono and W. O'Neil (eds) *The Generative Study of Second Language Acquisition* (pp. 17–34). NJ: Erlbaum.

White, L. (1989) *Universal Grammar and Second Language Acquisition.* Amsterdam: Benjamins.

6 Rethinking Interactive Models of Reading

MARTIN GILL
Åbo Akademi University, Finland

Abstract

Despite awareness of literacies as forms of sociocultural practice, explanatory accounts of reading typically appeal to cognitive models from which features of context are excluded. A hybrid picture is emerging of diverse literate activities resting on a foundation of universal cognitive processes. This does not reflect a necessary division of academic labour, but the unhappy – ultimately, it will be argued, unworkable – union of opposing theoretical positions, and, as such, is an obstacle to reading research from a sociocultural perspective. This paper examines incoherences in the familiar account, in particular in interactive models and cognitive schemata, which cannot be corrected (although they may be concealed) by empirical investigation; and suggests that it is these, rather than the nature of reading itself, which have encouraged the widespread view that reading remains a 'mystery'. As a potential way out of these difficulties, an integrated model of reading is outlined to which the notion of situated practice is central.

Cognitive Processes, Social Practices

In assessing recent developments in applied linguistics, it will be relevant to take a critical look at the study of L2 reading, where increasingly the standard explanatory paradigm seems out of step with the kinds of phenomena to be explained. The familiar preoccupations of L2 reading research – is L2 reading a language problem or a reading problem?, threshold levels, the nature of skill taxonomies and transfer, the relation of bottom-up and top-down processes, and so on – largely reflect the priorities of language testers and cognitive psychologists, particularly the interest of the latter in what takes place 'behind the eye' during the reading process (cf. Goodman, 1976). At the same time, more recent work in literacy studies has highlighted the importance and possible dimensions of contextual variation in reading, and the inadequacy of generalising about 'the reader' and 'the text' on the basis of short (often contrived, unmotivatéd) specimens of print written in English and read in experimental situations with the object of 'extracting' or 'recovering' meaning, assumed to be the meaning put in by the writer.

The cognitive approach, it is now clear, has lacked any sense of the semiotic status of the written sign, the highly various forms and purposes of writing, and the many contexts in which it is encountered and read, and has ignored its visual aspects – for example, the subtle, socially and materially framed meanings conveyed by differences of script, font, layout, colour, writing surface, use of graphic space, and so on (cf. Harris, 1995). Yet if we hope to understand what readers actually do when they make sense of written texts, what they are capable of doing and need to learn, such matters call for serious attention. It is also clear that differences of reading purpose do not simply represent alternative choices from a neutral inventory, but depend on, and help to constitute, different forms of group affiliation and identity. Moreover, investigation of earlier forms of text and literate practice has shown that the cognitive processes of reading are themselves closely shaped by (in fact, inseparable from) the material facts of text production at different periods and in different settings; hence, the specific skills necessary to read modern printed material, far from being uniform or universal, actually followed from physical and social changes in the nature of the text (cf. Saenger, 1982, 1997).

Since considerations of this kind oblige us to abandon 'the reader' and 'the text' in favour of something more local and less tidy, we might expect them to have a comparable effect on the modelling of the 'reading process' itself. Unfortunately, cognitive reading models offer no means of treating these matters as anything more than relatively trivial surface phenomena, part of the *external* nature of reading, dependent on the *internal* working of largely invariant cognitive processes. Despite the new willingness to bring a greater range of contextual variation to bear on the picture, it remains usual to find models of reading treated as explanatory from which all reference to context is entirely absent, with interest focused instead on the bare internal processes of comprehension, and the extent to which they may transfer between languages. For some, indeed, the pendulum has already swung far enough towards the socially constructed view of reading (cf. Urquhart & Weir, 1998: 8ff).

Evidently something is not working here. Rather than hurry back to build better cognitive models, therefore, it will be worth stopping to examine their nature more carefully. For one thing, the cognitive and social sides of the picture are not straightforwardly complementary; that is, it is simply not feasible to factor in more detail from the context and continue to produce the same kinds of explanatory theories as before. Instead, coming to recognize that reading is a social practice has inescapable consequences for how its cognitive processes should be understood.

Thus the view expressed by Urquhart and Weir that 'we are all interactive theorists now' (op. cit.: 40), and that we now have a fairly sound, uncontroversial understanding of 'the reading process', leaving research free to move forward to sort out its details, is hardly justified. Not that no work has been produced to help us think more clearly about reading and the factors that shape it. But, as I shall argue, the terms in which the cognitive view of reading has been framed, are, as they always were, misconceived. Since we are concerned here with thinking about reading in the wrong way, the need is not for further empirical work to put it right, but for the exposure and correction of the conceptual problems involved. In an applied field, where ideas are regularly taken over from other disciplines, or operationalized for particular purposes, there may be a tendency to ignore such questions, or to leave the sorting out to someone else, and get on with empirical work as usual. This would be a mistake. As Hacker puts it, '[Philosophical confusions] are liable to run unnoticed through an elaborate and sophisticated empirical theory precisely because these conceptual incoherences are present in the very form of the questions the theory addresses' (Hacker, 1991: 122). Since, in this case, the difficulties are likely to vitiate any empirical work that might be done using this theoretical framework, there can (I believe) be no avoiding some attempt to examine and clarify the concepts we work with for ourselves. Any attempt to reconcile cognitive approaches to reading with those which view it as a social practice will inevitably expose a fault line that runs through much work in applied linguistics and is responsible for a good deal of institutional schizophrenia and mutual incomprehension.

The argument that follows draws on Wittgenstein's (1953) critique of mental terms and concepts and the illusions that result from a failure to examine their use in everyday language; in particular, illusions created by the picture of an 'inner process', which he argues have misled our understanding of ordinary human sense-making activities. What makes these illusions so hard to see and so intractable is that they constitute the taken-for-granted background shared by all who engage with the topic, creating both spurious mysteries and equally spurious theories to explain them (cf. Wittgenstein, op. cit. §308; see also Baker & Hacker, 1980: 331ff; Baker, 1998). Wittgenstein claimed that his purpose was to provide therapy for such philosophical ills; certainly, turning back from this to the literature of cognitive reading models may seem like re-entering the mad house, since the ills on display go to the very bottom of the ways in which reading is discussed. What at least I hope to make clear is that to get to where we need to go (that is, across the fault line to an integrated, contextually responsive approach to reading), we should not even try to set out from where we are now.

Conceptual Problems with Interactive Models of Reading

Interactive models generally adopt a 'telementational' view of communication (cf. Harris, 1981) which locates reading in a sequence of operations by which the meaning in the writer's head is dismantled, transmitted and reconstructed in the head of the reader. Reading itself begins with a piece of text and ends with the production of a mental copy of the original message, accomplished by the operation of internal mechanisms and propositional knowledge structures. Many problems arise in relation to this general conception (among other things, it has the effect of turning everyday reading into an astonishing feat, and reading difficulties into cognitive failure); for the purposes of this paper I shall confine my attention to those which threaten the coherence of the reading models themselves.

The mechanical fallacy

One general area of difficulty involves what can be termed the mechanical fallacy. To understand how a car or a computer works we look inside, at the mechanism; to understand how the brain works, we devise sophisticated means to do the same. It is therefore easy to suppose that the right approach to other explanatory questions is to look inside and disclose the mechanism involved. For example, since certain aspects of competent driving – co-ordination of hands, eyes, feet, etc. – clearly occur below the level of conscious attention, it might well seem a natural and necessary part of understanding the nature of driving to look to see what occurs inside the driver's head during the 'driving process'. In fact, however, whatever we learn about any mental phenomena we find there, it will fail to connect with the 'nature of driving', which is something people do with cars, subject to social norms and purposes, hence not 'in the head' at all. This point becomes clearer in relation to a more overtly social institution such as voting (cf. Winch, 1958). If a voting system is introduced into a context where previously there has been no experience of one, how can we establish if people are 'really' voting, as opposed to marking crosses randomly on the voting paper? No-one is likely to argue that looking at what is going on inside their heads during the 'voting process' will help us to determine this, or conclude, from the difficulty of doing so, that voting remains a mystery (although equally no-one need doubt that mental processes are required). In this case, it will obviously be necessary to know what the individuals concerned *think* they are doing, what interpretation they give of their actions, how they were motivated, whether they have any concept of the place of voting in a given 'form of life', the institutional framework in which it acquires meaning, and so on.

The same will apply in the case of reading: knowing about mental processes here is irrelevant to knowing what reading is, or if someone is 'really' reading, reading well, or with comprehension. This may be obscured by the fact that reading is more complex than voting, that it must therefore involve the integration of many different kinds of knowledge and ability, including the unconscious co-ordination of automated skills. It may also seem to be in some sense naturally more interior, since privacy and silence are central features of our paradigm of how it is 'done' – apart from eye movements there may be little to observe in the way of external behaviour (though this, of course, is a cultural and historical fact, not a necessary mental one). Moreover, and more to the point, reading research has for long been the province of cognitive psychologists with a professional interest in internal mechanisms. It would be wrong to press such analogies too far. However, reading has more in common with voting than (say) with car maintenance or computer programming.

The incomprehensible process

The mechanical fallacy rests in part on an ambiguity in the use of the word *process*. Reading is commonly referred to as a process, and, of course, is one, in the sense that it has duration, can be interrupted, resumed, left unfinished, and so on: one can be in the process of reading *Middlemarch*. However, this is not what 'reading processes' are taken to mean in the cognitive literature; here, the notion of process applies to a strictly internal integration of stages hypothesised to occur between the perception of print on the page and the final achievement (or what Samuels and Kamil term the 'click') of comprehension (cf. below), involving (among other things) information about features of letters, word forms and boundaries, lexicon, syntax, semantics, world knowledge and textual conventions. But this is not a process in the previous sense at all. It is automatic, unconscious, and apparently instantaneous. One cannot reasonably be 'in the process of' understanding a word (say, somewhere between recognition of its shape and retrieval of the relevant lexical information). In this case, as Wittgenstein notes (1974: 155), the temptation is to suppose that we are in the presence of some special or *incomprehensible* kind of process. And, as he implies, this is naturally the most engaging case of all.

And, sure enough, it seems to be generally agreed that, when it comes to reading, 'we are up against a major mystery' (Eskey, 1973: 72; cf. Spiro, 1980: 266; Clarke, 1988: 114; Barnett, 1989: 38). However familiar, it still in some sense eludes us. According to a reviewer in *The Times Higher Education Supplement*:

> We can probe the chemical composition of stars in far-off galaxies and analyse the neural chemistry of our brains. But in the realm of the mind and

consciousness our understanding is primitive. As yet no one can give much account of what is taking place in your head as you read this sentence.

(Robinson, 1995: 18)

Reading, it is implied, is inaccessible to explanation; more precisely: until we understand these internal, mental processes, we will have no real grasp of what *reading itself* actually is. Not only does the search for inner mechanisms tend to make them mysterious, it also confers on them greater credibility, as constituting the true (hidden) essence of the phenomenon of interest. The dominance of the cognitive paradigm has made such assumptions seem largely unproblematic – part of the neutral background in which we work. Yet, paradoxically, for the cognitive theorist it is not the existence of these internal processes that is in any doubt, or even, ultimately, 'mysterious' at all: what *is* mysterious is the performance of the skilled reader, the fact that we all normally do it with such effortless ease.

It is important here to keep in mind Wittgenstein's familiar dictum that 'an "inner process" stands in need of outward criteria' (Wittgenstein, 1953: §580). Private comprehension is something about which nothing whatever can be said unless it becomes outwardly manifest. We can only know if readers have understood a text by seeing what they say or do, and readers learn what to say or do through social exchange with expert members of their own community. Without evidence of this kind, the final 'click' of the mechanism will be entirely empty.

Agency

The following is a fairly representative statement of the cognitive modellers' idea of the processes involved in reading comprehension:

> Reading comprehension is considered to be a complex behaviour which involves conscious and unconscious use of various strategies, including problem-solving strategies, to build a model of the meaning which the writer is assumed to have intended. The model is constructed using schematic knowledge structures and the various cue systems which the writer has given (e.g. words, syntax, macrostructures, social information) to generate hypotheses which are tested using various logical and pragmatic strategies. Most of this model must be inferred, since text can never be fully explicit, and, in general, very little of it is explicit because even the appropriate intensional and extensional meanings of words must be inferred from their context.   (Johnston, 1983: 17; cf. Carrell, 1991: 161)

As the careful avoidance of any human subject in this example shows, however, there is no clear indication of exactly who or what actually does the reading and comprehending. This may not always be obvious since it is part of the mechanical fallacy that an explanation in terms of mechanisms is in fact a *final* explanation – i.e. in giving it, we have reached the end of the explanatory process, beyond which the problem becomes purely metaphysical: this is just how things are. In other words, it may seem reasonable to assume that the reading processes are automatic and so, in effect, agentless: they carry *themselves* out. It is one of the pernicious consequences of the dominance of mechanical explanation that arguments of this type are seldom questioned.

Yet, as the philosopher Charles Taylor argues, a machine can only be said to 'act' in relation to human purposes; that is, machine activity is entirely parasitic on human activity; whereas the latter has significance in its own right, the former does not (Taylor, 1985: 193–4; for Taylor, it is this property of 'significance' and self-understanding, rather than the issue of 'consciousness', that marks the crucial difference between people and machines). Hence, explaining human understanding in terms of a built-in 'comprehension machine' explains nothing at all; comprehension, understanding, and reading can only be predicated of whole human agents, not some internal part – as shown by the oddity of saying (for example): 'my brain understands the text, but I don't' (cf. Kenny, 1991). The fact that we don't say this reflects a conceptual rather than an empirical fact. It makes clear, in fact, that reading models seek to combine elements across an unbridgeable category distinction.

None of this (to repeat) should be taken to mean that there are no mental phenomena connected with reading, or that they may not be legitimate objects of study. But it does suggest that they are not part of 'what reading is', as it relates to readers as normal human agents in the complex and densely textured everyday world. To borrow Harris' terms, the confusion here is that of mistaking the *biomechanical conditions* of reading for its *macrosocial meanings* (Harris, 1995). One of the reasons why we should treat 'interactive' views of reading with caution is that they tend to rest on (and ignore) precisely this confusion.

Schemata

Reading research has shown particular interest in high-level knowledge structures; indeed, Urquhart and Weir are critical of applied linguists for their over-emphasis on this aspect of reading at the expense of such matters as word recognition. The idea is that, in the last phase of the reading process, incoming ('bottom-up') information from the page is compared with a pre-existing mental catalogue of schemata containing ('top-down') knowledge about the world, in particular its regularities, normal states, typical events, etc. This is the primary sense in which models of this type claim to be 'interactive' (although my use of the passive here again avoids attribution of agency – i.e. who or what does the comparing).

It is also worth noting how misleading the ubiquitous 'bottom-up'/'top-down' metaphor is, since these terms are applied indiscriminately to both a distinction between phenomena 'inside the head' and 'outside the head' (e.g. Samuels & Kamil, 1984), and to a distinction between smaller units of information derived directly from the text and larger units supplied partly or wholly by the reader (both entirely 'inside the head'). In the latter case there can be no 'bottom-up' representation of individual words that does not already presuppose a 'top-down' interpretation; equivocation between the two senses helps to conceal the incoherence of trying to model reading from raw print to final understanding as a single process.

But even if the input to the process is apparently clear – i.e. the words and other symbols on the page, the raw data on which the reader's visual and cognitive machinery go to work – what exactly is the output? The standard answer seems to be 'comprehension', although there are differences over what this means precisely. In general, the end point of the process is conceived of as the construction (or possession) of an appropriate mental representation, corresponding to the 'meaning' of the text, and for which the existence in the reader of 'schematic knowledge structures' is a crucial precondition, as in cognitive accounts of understanding more generally (Garrod, 1986: 226; Johnson-Laird, 1983: 156). Thus Carrell and Eisterhold describe comprehension as the achievement of consistency between textual information and a stored schema (Carrell & Eisterhold, 1988: 79). According to Samuels and Kamil: 'We experience the click of comprehension when there is a match between textual information coming in from outside the head with the concepts stored inside the head' (Samuels & Kamil, 1984: 206). Conversely, failure to understand may be attributed to the absence of the relevant mental schema (Rumelhart, 1980: 48).

But how do we know that ours *is* a relevant schema? (cf. Brown & Yule, 1983: 240f), or that we are applying it 'correctly'? (it would, of course, be circular to reply 'because we experience the 'click of comprehension', or 'because we all understand the text in the same way'). Once again, the inevitable question is: who exactly inspects the schema in order to judge the closeness or appropriateness of the match? In fact, possession of a mental representation cannot be the criterion for our having understood a text, because knowing that it is appropriate already *presupposes* this understanding. In other words, deciding whether or not schemata are appropriate in a given context can only be a matter of normative judgement (therefore, public), not a private cognitive reflex; hence schemata can have no *explanatory* function at all in relation to comprehension (cf. Putnam, 1988: 30). And, if this is so, interactive reading models are in grave difficulty.

Automating comprehension

This is, in effect, a further version of the mechanical fallacy. Whatever their differences, these models share a confidence in the ability of cognitive modelling to automate the reading process up to *and including* 'comprehension' itself (Samuels and Kamil refer to modelling 'the entire process from the time the eye meets the page until the reader experiences the 'click' of comprehension'; 1984: 185). The only way this can be done is by importing a neutral, reader-independent pattern or model – i.e. one that explains itself – and assuming it to be built into the cognitive system, where it can be taken to work automatically, in advance of any conscious interpretation by the reader. Thus, according to Perfetti, 'in well-written texts ... relevant schemata are triggered (activated) by text contents' (Perfetti, 1986: 23) (the choice of verb once again signalling absence of agency): cues in the text simply *cause* the correct schemata to function and comprehension to proceed.

In the cognitive account, this schematic mental representation is therefore a condition and criterion of comprehension. Yet even if this might be a plausible model for a machine, it has no bearing at all on the human case. In the human case, there can be no escaping the necessary relation of comprehension to a person who comprehends, who recognises the representation to be what it is; as noted, the only criterion for comprehension is the ability to make some kind of publicly assessable response, not the unconscious operation of internal algorithms. The inevitable conclusion is that internal accounts of this kind leave reading comprehension exactly where it was.

Gaps in communication

Internal schemata not only provide a criterion for individual comprehension, but also ensure effective communication by compensating for lapses and defects in performance. In the case of reading, they supply details omitted from the written text, allowing its 'gaps' to be properly 'filled' (Samuels & Eisenberg, 1981: 62; cf. Urquhart and Weir: schemata belong to the theory 'that text is never complete'; 1998: 63). By evoking a schema, it is argued, writers (and speakers) are able to omit details that 'must', in this Platonic sense, 'really' be there.

The assumption that mutual understanding requires identity between representations in the sender's and receiver's minds, and that normal communicative performance is therefore at best an 'imperfect 'or 'approximate' copy of (true) underlying competence, belongs firmly to the 'telementational' view of communication (cf. above). In fact, however, we do not judge the adequacy of any representation by its correspondence to some fully specified ('literal') model, whatever that might mean. While it is true that readers can usually supply further details if required to (for example, by a comprehension test or a psychological experiment), there is no need to imagine the latent presence of a schema to account for this ability, any more than it is necessary to suppose some ideally complete internal representation of the human figure to 'underlie' our ability to understand a matchstick drawing; in fact, it would be completely misleading to do so (especially since there can be nothing *in* the mental representation itself to tell us how to understand it). Understanding, it is worth repeating, involves justification; and the question of adequacy is decided in relation to the function and the context in which a representation occurs (the matchstick drawing would make an inadequate portrait, but could form part of an effective diagram of an accident; cf. Wittgenstein, 1953: §74, 204f). How much is needed in a given context is not fixed, but specified by conventions and purposes that are ultimately decided by the community of those who produce/use the representations concerned. And this again is a social and historical fact which is ignored by the cognitive approach. Moreover, as literacy studies have taught us, to hold up such representations as the timeless universal criteria of understanding (or remembering) introduces a bias towards western concepts, and, in reality, reveals the extent to which they too are products of specific cultural circumstances.

Schemata, therefore, are not features of mental organisation that causally mediate understanding. Instead, to understand how schemata are explanatory we must look to the nature of publicly constituted practices. Understanding involves recognising that a particular text is interpretable within a given, socially established schematic framework. If this has psychological reality (which it undoubtedly may), it would appear to be by backward projection from genres or ways of seeing established through social exchange.

In this connection it is relevant to note that while Bartlett's (1932) study is routinely cited as among the earliest to focus on the constructive role of schematic organisation in memory, it tends to be ignored that his theory placed the schema firmly in a social context (cf. Shotter, 1990). In Bartlett's view, it was vital that 'the 'schema' determined reactions of one organism are repeatedly checked, as well as constantly facilitated, by those of others' (op. cit.: 206) in social interaction. He interpreted his experimental evidence as showing that 'both the manner and the matter of recall are often predominantly determined by social influences' (op. cit.: 244), and devoted the latter part of the book to an extended discussion of the ways in which memory is socially constructed.

Summary

In sum, what interactive models of reading are concerned with is 'machine reading', i.e. the specification of a programme designed to process printed text in a roughly human-like way, taking into account an analysis of its relevant dimensions. And there is no doubt that thinking about these dimensions has proved helpful in getting us away from the idea that reading simply involves decoding. But machine reading will differ from human reading exactly as machines differ from humans: that is, above all, it will be devoid of any intrinsic significance or autonomous capacity to make sense (hence, therefore, it won't actually *be* reading). While it may be possible to build a computer programme to emulate the various biomechanical stages involved in fixating, matching printed words with words already stored in a list, even, perhaps, classifying a situation described in a text as belonging to a given pre-programmed pattern labelled, e.g. 'having a meal in a restaurant' (although the computer itself will not have done the labelling or 'know about restaurants'), it will not be possible to add all these (or integrate them) and claim that the computer has 'understood' or 'has comprehension of' the text. Nor will it be legitimate to imply that, because this is how we might design a machine to process text, this is how human beings (or 'the human brain') do it. And if we insist that the human brain is, in fact, an information processing device of exactly this kind, then we simply build into it these machine properties – above all, lack of significance – and still leave the question of how *people* understand texts exactly where it was, with the puzzle simply pushed further back into the system. On these grounds alone, therefore, it must be concluded that the cognitive notion of comprehension ultimately fails.

An Integrated Alternative

A solution to the difficulties outlined here clearly cannot be to propose another model in the same cognitive/interactive framework. However, it is possible at least to suggest the starting point for an alternative. An integrated approach to reading would start from the assumption that what comes first is not mental processing but meaning. A competent reader engages with a text in the expectation that it makes sense – i.e. is coherent and has a meaning; not a private one, but public and intersubjective, and always open to revision. These properties are established by the community of readers, and are inseparable from the association of texts with ends regarded by them as valuable, and embodied in characteristic material forms.

Understanding is therefore to be explained, not by reference to internal processes, but to the culture, where particular genres and accepted ways of talking about them are familiar because its members have learnt their use (cf. Wittgenstein, 1967: 29, 33). In particular, readers learn, through interaction with others in various contexts, to participate in recognised forms of discourse and styles of reasoning, and the meanings they make available, and to operate with them in ways acknowledged by the community as being purposeful and making sense. Though sometimes restrictive, as in a case such as Heath's Roadville

(Heath, 1983), and unevenly distributed through the community as a whole, sense-making activities of this kind are nonetheless socially constructed not mentally programmed. Learning is therefore not simply a matter of extending autonomous mental structures, and need not have a single end or be confined to childhood, but, given suitable conditions, will involve gaining increased command of the expressive potential of the various means available in a given setting.

An account of this type will imply a dynamic relationship between activity and cognition ('for acting in the world is the skilled practitioner's way of knowing it'; Ingold, 1990: 8). That is, cognitive functions are not prespecified in detail, but develop in relation to the use of culturally elaborated 'tools', among other things literate practices, making it artificial to separate what takes place 'in the head' from what takes place 'on paper' (cf. Wittgenstein, 1974: 99; Wertsch, 1991). By abandoning the narrowly information-orientated view, it also becomes possible to include in the picture the other learned capacities we possess – for example, the vast array of physical schemata that guide our actions and shape both the physical and institutional environment in which these actions occur, techniques learnt through imitation and experience, establishing the continuities on which the coherence of the everyday world depends (including, for example, the accommodation of muscles to holding a book, adopting a certain reading posture, etc.), for which there need be no internal mental correlates.

Past attempts to impose idealised versions of 'our' reading behaviour on those with different practices, expecting to reproduce in these new settings the cultural and intellectual value they have for us, now appear naive. However, preoccupation with cognitive reading processes and skills is likely to make a comparable mistake, by implying that their application or transfer to a second language setting is internal and instrumental, unconnected with the local meaning of the activities in which they are involved. By contrast, the approach proposed here is, necessarily, sensitive to context. Emphasis on reading practices helps to direct attention away from the hermetic relation between reader and text, and the nature of cognitive structures, to the ways in which reading acquires meaning for readers, and the kinds of activity and interaction it promotes. It suggests that the key consideration will not be the nature of mental processing but the coherence of the activity engaged in. If competent readers approach reading as coherent in the sense described, an ability to do this in a second language will depend on the extent to which the new activity is seen as fitting a familiar pattern, hence on experience of the uses and values associated with varieties of literate practices. Where settings differ greatly, little of what is recognised in one community may transfer unchanged to another. Problems of assimilation are likely to be accentuated where particular genres, or the institutional setting (e.g. schooling) in which they are articulated, are viewed as intrusive or irrelevant. On the other hand, in the most fruitful cases, a given, non-indigenous genre or practice will be assimilated to locally appropriate ends.

Considerations of the kind briefly sketched here would seem to be more relevant to second language reading viewed as a situated, purposeful activity (as opposed to decoding acontextual instances of written language), than a search for evidence of whether, or how well, putative reading mechanisms may work in a given case. And, as with voting discussed earlier, the best way to establish what is going on will be to find out what readers think they are doing, whether it makes sense to them, and what sense it makes.

Conclusion

When probed, cognitive models of reading reveal a tangle of overlapping misconceptions which leave them, however they may be designed in detail, fundamentally unworkable. The alternative conception of reading presented here stands opposed to the mental processes and propositional knowledge systems of the cognitive approach. Its ultimate justification rests on Taylor's distinction between the kinds of explanation appropriate to the working of a machine, on the one hand, and to human behaviour on the other: namely, that machines do not perform actions except with reference to human purposes. The 'cognitive machine' is not a special case in this respect. If we are to avoid continued unhelpful conflict between the observed phenomena and available explanatory paradigms in L2 reading research, therefore, the development of an alternative approach, perhaps along the lines proposed, should be a priority.

References

Baker, G. (1998) The private language argument. *Language and Communication* 18, 325–56.
Baker, G. and Hacker, P. (1980) *Wittgenstein: Meaning and Understanding: Essays on the philosophical investigations* (Vol. 1). Oxford: Blackwell.
Bartlett, F. (1932) *Remembering: A study in experimental and social psychology.* Cambridge: Cambridge University Press.
Barnett, M. (1989) *More than Meets the Eye. Foreign Language Reading: Theory and practice.* Englewood Cliffs, NJ: Centre for Applied Linguistics and Prentice Hall.
Brown, G. and Yule, G. (1983) *Discourse Analysis.* Cambridge: Cambridge University Press.
Carrell, P. (1991) Second language reading: Reading ability or reading proficiency? *Applied Linguistics* 12, 159–79.
Carrell, P., Devine, J. and Eskey, D. (eds) (1988) *Interactive Approaches to Second Languages Reading.* Cambridge: Cambridge University Press.
Carrell, P. and Eisterhold, J. (1988) Schema theory and ESL reading pedagogy. In P. Carrell *et al.* (eds).
Clarke, M. (1988) The short circuit hypothesis of ESL reading – or when language competence interferes with reading performance. In P. Carrell *et al.* (eds).

Eskcy, D. (1973) A model programme for teaching advanced reading to students of English as a foreign language. In R. Mackay, B. Barkman and R. Jordan (eds) (1979) *Reading in a Foreign Language: Hypotheses, organisation and practice*. Rowley, MA: Newbury House.

Garrod, S. (1986) Language comprehension in context: A psychological perspective. *Applied Linguistics* 7, 226–38.

Goodman, K. (1976) Behind the eye: What happens in reading. In H. Singer and R. Ruddell (eds) *Theoretical Models and Processes of Reading* (2nd edn). Newark, Del.: International Reading Association.

Hacker, P. (1991) Seeing, representing, describing: An examination of David Marr's computational theory of vision. In J. Hyman (ed.).

Harris, R. (1981) *The Language Myth*. London: Duckworth.

Harris, R. (1995) *Signs of Writing*. London: Routledge.

Heath, S. (1983) *Ways with Words: Language, life, and work in communities and class-rooms*. Cambridge: Cambridge University Press.

Hyman, J. (ed.) (1991) *Investigating Psychology: Sciences of the mind after Wittgenstein*. London: Routledge.

Ingold, T. (1990) Society, nature and the concept of technology. *Archaeological Review from Cambridge 9*, 5–17.

Johnson-Laird, P. (1983) *Mental Models*. Cambridge: Cambridge University Press.

Johnston, P. (1983) *Reading Comprehension Assessment: A cognitive basis*. Newark, Del.: International Reading Association.

Kenny, A. (1991) The homunculus fallacy. In J. Hyman (ed.).

Perfetti, C. (1986) Cognitive and linguistic components of reading ability. In B. Foorman and A. Siegel (eds) *Acquisition of Reading Skills: Cultural constraints and cognitive universals*. Hillsdale, NJ: Lawrence Erlbaum Associates.

Putnam, H. (1988) *Representation and Reality*. Cambridge, MA: The MIT Press.

Robinson, A. (1995) Old scripts, new insights. *Times Higher Education Supplement* 13th October 1995, 18.

Rumelhart, D. (1980) Schemata: The building blocks of cognition. In R. Spiro *et al.* (eds).

Saenger, P. (1982) Silent reading: Its impact on late medieval script and society. *Viator* 13, 367–414.

Saenger, P. (1997) *Space Between Words: The origins of silent reading*. Cambridge: Cambridge University Press.

Samuels, S. and Eisenberg, P. (1981) A framework for understanding reading processes. In F. Pirozzolo and M. Wittrock (eds) *Neuropsychological and Cognitive Processes in Reading*. NY: Academic Press.

Samuels, S. and Kamil, M. (1984) Models of the reading process. In P. Pearson (ed.) *Handbook of Reading Research*. NY: Longman.

Shotter, J. (1990) The social construction of remembering and forgetting. In D. Middleton and D. Edwards (eds) *Collective Remembering*. London: Sage Publications.

Spiro, R. (1980) Constructive processes in prose comprehension and recall. In R. Spiro *et al.* (eds).

Spiro, R., Bruce, B. and Brewer, W. (eds) (1980) *Theoretical Issues in Reading Comprehension*. Hillsdale, NJ: Lawrence Erlbaum Associates.

Taylor, C. (1985) *Human Agency and Language: Philosophical papers* (Vol. I). Cambridge: Cambridge University Press.

Urquhart, A. and Weir, C. (1998) *Reading in a Second Language: Process, product and practice*. Harlow: Addison Wesley Longman.

Wertsch, J. (1991) *Voices of the Mind: A sociocultural approach to mediated action.* London: Harvester Wheatsheaf.

Wittgenstein, L. (1953) *Philosophical Investigations* (G. Anscombe (trans)). Oxford: Blackwell.

Wittgenstein, L. (1967) *Zettel.* G. Anscombe (trans); Anscombe G. and von Wright, G. (eds). Oxford: Blackwell.

Wittgenstein, L. (1974) *Philosophical Grammar.* Kenny, A. (trans). Oxford: Blackwell.

Winch, P. (1958) *The Idea of a Social Science and its Relation to Philosophy.* London: Routledge and Kegan Paul.

7 Continuity and Change in Views of Society in Applied Linguistics

BEN RAMPTON
King's College London

Abstract

This paper starts out by looking at a general shift in the humanities and social sciences, where it is the interface between modernity and post-/late-modernity rather than the encounter between tradition and modernity that is now becoming the dominant problematic. It outlines some of the signs of this shift in sociolinguistics, and then argues that this makes applied linguistics more intellectually mainstream than it has perhaps been in the past. Even so, there may be some enduring blind spots.

Introduction

Starting from the assumption that applied linguistics is a 'pluri-centred' field and that Hymes' 'socially constituted' linguistics is as much a part of applied linguistics as anything else (see Hymes, 1977, Rampton, 1997), the first two-thirds of this paper focus on sociolinguistics, arguing that at least in its anglo-phone versions, sociolinguistics over the last 40 years or so has been profoundly affected by two rather different historical and epistemic problematics. The first of these can be identified as the encounter between tradition and modernity, while the second lies at the interface of modernity and late/post-modernity. I shall outline a number of themes that can be seen as emblematic of these two different junctures, and then in the last third of the paper, I shall turn to the applied linguistics of second and foreign language teaching. The applied linguistics of language teaching, it seems to me, is rather better positioned at the modernity/postmodernity interface than it was in the tradition–modernity problem space, and, within language study, one could even suggest that language-teaching linguistics is in the vanguard. Even so, I would be reluctant to draw an entirely rosy picture, and so, in the final part of the paper, I shall point to what I think is an area of continuing weakness in applied linguistics in Britain.

Sociolinguistics at the Interface of Tradition and Modernity

The interface between 'tradition' and 'modernity' has been enormously formative for the social sciences. According to Giddens:

> sociology has its origins in the coming of modernity – in the dissolution of the traditional world and the consolidation of the modern ... With the arrival of industrialism, the transfer of millions of people from rural communities to cities, the progressive development of mass democracy, and other quite fundamental institutional changes, the new world was savagely wrenched away from the old... Sociology was born of the attempt to track [this] ..., but until well into the twentieth century was itself rather too strongly stamped by the context of its own origins.   (1990: 15–16)

I cannot comment on how fair this is to sociology, but it certainly makes sense if one looks at anglophone sociolinguistics from the 1960s.

Starting with the seminal conference at Yeshiva in 1966, one of the central missions of sociolinguistics was to make modern institutions, especially schools, more hospitable to socially and ethnically diverse populations – populations which, in one way or another were generally thought to be non-modern. In the process, debates about the relationship between children and schools threw up a huge array of dichotomies, and these ranged across:

- *modes of expression*, which were supposed to be either vernacular or standard, oral or literate, concrete or abstract, implicit or explicit, narrative or argumentative, metaphorical or rational, contextualised or decontextualised, particularistic or universalistic, etc.

- *types of social organisation*, where it was home vs. school, close networks vs. open networks, homogeneous vs. heterogeneous, solidarity- vs. status-based, mechanical vs. organic, etc.

- *social categories*: host–migrant, white–black, majority–minority, male–female, middle-class/working-class.

Sociolinguists often devoted very considerable energy to contesting these polarities and the long collocational chains that they tended to form – chains which would counterpose particularistic vernacular oral narrative in traditional close working class networks to literate, universalistic argument within the status-oriented modern middle class. But whether they were for or against, whether or not they were trying to uncouple associations like these or to reverse the idea that it was a question of better vs. worse, dichotomous thinking of this kind had a very deep hold in the 1960s, 1970s and 1980s, serving as a central battleground in the work of scholars such as Labov, Hymes, Bernstein, Wells, Heath and Cummins. Indeed, there is a sense in which the arguments look like modernity's struggle to define itself through a process of contrast and comparison, and quite a few of the terms recurring in the sociolinguistic debate – 'decontextualisation' and 'universalistic' for example – resonate with the philosophical underpinnings of liberal modernity.[1] (For fuller discussion, see Rampton, 1999.)

Admittedly, much of the specificity of the work of particular scholars is lost when they are grouped together within a particular historical and epistemic juncture in this manner, and so I would like to go one step further and suggest that, on the whole, there was a very strong current of romanticism in sociolinguistics. Looking back at this period, Bernstein talks about the dominance of a model of competence which saw everyone as 'inherently competent, ... [as] active and creative in the construction of valid worlds', 'announced ... the universal democracy of acquisition', 'celebrated ... everyday oral language' and was suspicious of 'official socialisers' (Bernstein, 1996: chaps 3 & 7).[2] In line with this, a great deal of work in sociolinguistics declared itself opposed to the narrow prejudices of policymakers and popular opinion, and argued instead that subordinate and marginal groups had an authenticity and integrity of their own. In fact, though, it was very hard to challenge modernity's cornerstone values, or to do more than rehabilitate modernity's others along modernist lines. The main strategy in this advocacy was to try to show that the behaviour of these non-standard groups was systematic and coherent – it was justifiable, in other words, in terms of the rational values of system and coherence that modernity rated most highly – much higher, for example, than sanctity or splendour.

Indeed at this point we enter a rather general critique of linguistics itself – a critique that perhaps gets its most succinct and powerful expression in Pratt's 1987 paper 'Linguistic Utopias'. Pratt connects a commitment to system-in-grammar and coherence-in-discourse to the notion that language competence is shaped through a process of socialisation to consensual norms, and she calls this cluster of ideas 'the linguistics of community'. Yes, right from the start, sociolinguists took issue with Chomsky's idealisation about the homogeneous speech community, and language diversity and variation were obviously an article of faith. But even so, the belief was that this diversity was describably structured, and whenever they met it, the sociolinguist's strongest instinct was to root out what they supposed was an orderliness and uniformity beneath the surface, an orderliness laid down in the early years of community belonging. One can see this in the variationist's quest for the vernacular; in research on code-mixing and code-switching, where the emphasis was on systematic patterns established within relatively stable bilingual in-groups; and in work on cross-cultural conflict and misunderstanding, where the problem was attributed to the gap between integrated cultural and linguistic systems. As Pratt says, 'when social division and hierarchy [*were*] studied, the linguist's choice [was] often to imagine separate speech communities with their own boundaries, sovereignty, and authenticity, ... giv[ing] rise to linguistics that seeks to capture identity, but not the relationality of social differentiation' (1987: 56, 59, 61).

What would the alternative be? To address this, it is worth now turning to the new historical and epistemic problematic that is coming to replace the tradition/ modernity juncture.

Sociolinguistics at the Modernity/Postmodernity Interface

In a 1992 paper entitled 'A sociological theory of postmodernity', Zygmunt Bauman summarises a number of major differences between classical sociology and the late-modern perspectives that are becoming increasingly influential. A number of these differences are by now fairly familiar, but for the sake of what I would like to say later it is worth flagging up one or two.

Whereas modernist sociology saw 'society' and other collective entities as unified and integrated totalities, there is a feeling now that that idea was rather uncomfortably based on an idealisation of the nation state, and that, instead, 'the reality to be modelled is ... much more fluid, heterogeneous and under-patterned than anything sociologists have tried to grasp intellectually in the past' (Bauman, 1992: 65). In terms of human behaviour and development, classical ideas about our actions gaining significance from their function in the social system give way to the view that what we do plays a major role in shaping the habitats we live in, and far from being socialised into the norms of a social group whose monitoring subsequently keeps us morally in line, there is much more of a sense that we 'assemble' ourselves from a plethora of changing options, deciding what is right and wrong for ourselves. Methodologically, social science gives up its dreams of being a legislator, a 'healer of prejudices' and an 'umpire of truth', and instead, the best it can do is operate as a translator and interpreter.

These ideas are now fairly well-rehearsed, but their relevance to sociolinguistics is made very clear in an incisive paper by Nik Coupland, in which he looks back over 10–15 years of sociolinguistic work on language and ageing, providing an account of perspectival shift that corresponds very closely to the points that Bauman makes. For example, what Coupland originally conceptualised as an objective description of discrete age-groups, he now sees as an analysis of how people construct their own and other people's age identities in interaction, and when he and his colleagues needed to account for particular interactional data, it was the strategic complexity and creativity of speakers that was most striking, rather than how they played out or reflected supposedly stable beliefs about ageing or attitudes to old age.   (Coupland, 1997: 33)

If I turn to my own work, there have been some broadly comparable shifts in the view of ethnicity. It is no longer enough to see ethnicity as either cultural inheritance or as the strategic/political accentuation of inheritance – it is also necessary to reckon with the ways in which ethnic forms, products and symbols are marketised and disseminated as desirable commodities, life-style options and aesthetic objects (see Rampton, forthcoming a). All in all, whether it is age- or ethnicity-based, belonging to a group now seems a great deal less clear, less permanent and less omni-relevant than it did 15 years ago. We are now much more conscious that community membership doesn't just happen to a person, but that much of it is created in the here-and-now. And, as it becomes harder to think of communities as separate sociocultural blocs, it becomes necessary to reconceptualise the politics that dominated debates about language and culture for much of this century. This is what Table 1 attempts to chart, and in the last column on the right, there is a potted resume of some of the key characteristics of the perspective that Bauman and Coupland discuss.

Table 1 Four orientations to cultural diversity

Interpretation of linguistic diversity:	*I* *Diversity as deficit*	*II* *Diversity as difference*	*III* *Not diversity, domination*	*IV* *Deficit, difference and domination as discourse*
View of culture:	Culture as elite canon/standard.	Cultures as sets of values, beliefs & behaviours.	Culture as reflection of socio-economic relations.	Culture as the processes and resources involved in situated, dialogical sense-making.
Approach to language:	Prescriptivism: norms and standards to be followed.	Descriptivism: system & authenticity of non-standard forms.	Determinism: language either subordinate to, or a distraction from, structures of political & economic domination.	Social constructionism: reality extensively constructed through institutional discourse and discursive interaction.

View of research:	Neutral, objective, informative.	Neutral, objective, advocate. scientific imperialism.	Part of apparatus of hegemony; scientific giving voice to subjugated knowledge.	Either regime of truth/discipline, or empowering,
Descriptive concerns/ focus:	The canon. The Other lacks culture & knowledge.	The Other's autonomy & integrity.	Self & Other in larger system. local sites.	Global & national discourses, diaspora & multi-
Philosophical & political emphasis:	Superiority of 'Us'. 'Them' at fault.	Relativism. Cultures incommensurable: 'we' can't say 'them' at fault. groups.	Power. Capitalist oppression. Resistance through the unity of oppressed	Power, difference & contingency. 'Them' resists, or sees things differently.
Assumption about the world:	Universals & grand narratives: development/ modernisation/ global markets.	Grand narratives maybe, but celebration of the subplots.	Universals and grand narratives: imperialism/ dependency.	Universals and grand narratives disclaimed.
Intervention strategy:	Assimilation	Multiculturalism anti-imperialism	Anti-racism/	Anti-essentialism
Typical politics:	Conservatism	Liberal pluralism	Marxism	Post-modernism

There are two points to make about this table. First, if one takes, for example, the ideas along the right hand side, they are obviously rather broad and general. They could be loosely linked to names like Berger & Luckman, Giddens, Hall, Bourdieu, Foucault, etc., but I would not claim a spotless pedigree for them and that is really the point. What they signify is not so much a substantive theory, consisting of claims open to empirical refutation, as what Brumfit (1997) calls a new *Zeitgeist*, and what others might describe as a new ontology, a new set of non-refutable, metaphysical presuppositions about the fundamental qualities and forces at work in the phenomena and processes being studied (see Cohen, 1987: 275–80). I shall return to this towards the end of the paper, but in the meantime, I hope that the chart makes some kind of intuitive sense. If one works with urban populations in Britain, then the four columns should be recognisable as assimila-tion, multiculturalism, anti-racism and anti-absolutism/anti-essentialism, and if one is more concerned with English abroad, then maybe Quirk can be placed in the first column, Kachru in the second, Phillipson the third and Pennycook the fourth.

The second point to clarify about the chart is that, in spite of the left to right movement, it would be a mistake to interpret it as the final triumph of post-modernism. To different degrees in different quarters, all four of these perspectives are alive and well, and in fact it is because of *unresolved* conflicts of perspective that I spoke of the *junctures* of tradition-and-modernity and modernity-and-post-modernity. It is sometimes imagined that any even half-favourable mention of post- or late-modernity means the abandonment of all commitment to scientific method, but that is a grossly unwarranted inference: the sociolinguistics that I shall refer to puts a great deal of emphasis on being logical, empirical, careful, sceptical and systematic, and more generally I would certainly say that such qualities are important for the discovery, analysis and reporting of phenomena beyond our ordinary imagining. The difference is, though, that people are now probably much more sensitive to the limitations of their methods, and they are also more aware of the historical specificity of the traditions they are working in. Although that may not sound very much, it is enough to produce quite a major shift in the agenda of sociolinguistics, and I would like to sketch a little of this out in the next section, looking at how several basic sociolinguistic ideas are being recast – specifically 'speech community', 'linguistic self-consciousness', 'regularity' and 'variation'.

Some Late Modern Sociolinguistic Themes

'Speech community' has never been a very settled term, but for quite a long time scholars considered it to be an empirically identifiable 'real' thing – a body of people who interacted regularly, who had attitudes and/or pragmatic rules in common, and who would be the largest unit that, in any given study, one could generalise about empirically. In the last decade or so, this has broken down, and instead the notion of 'community' has gone two ways in sociolinguistics.

In one direction, 'speech community' has been funnelled down into research on 'communities of practice', where there is close-up analysis of face-to-face interaction in a number of rather well-established settings and social relation-ships like workshops, classrooms and professional groups of one kind or another (see Eckert & McGonnell-Ginet, 1992; Lave & Wenger, 1991; Goodwin, 1994). There is a rejection here of the correlational tendency in sociolinguistics, which treats speakers as if they were 'assembled out of independent modules: [e.g.] part European American, part female, part middle-aged, part feminist, part intellectual' (Eckert & McGonnell-Ginet, 1992: 471; Goffman, 1964), and instead there is a commitment to ethnography and to micro and often multi-modal description of the lived texture of situated experience. This synchronises well with post-modern uncertainty about grand theoretical totalisations, and if social totality has been 'dissipated into a series of randomly emerging, shifting and evanescent islands of order' (Bauman, 1992: 189), then research on communities of practice seems particularly well-pitched.

In the other direction, 'community' explodes outwards when it is analysed as a semiotic representation in ideological discourses that construct and naturalise very large groupings (e.g. Anderson, 1983; Gal & Irvine, 1995; Gal & Woolard, 1995; Joseph & Taylor, 1990). Particularly in the work on language ideologies, there is a great deal of interest in how a spread of people gets constituted as a 'community' in the first place, how 'linguistic units come to be linked with social units', languages with peoples (Gal & Irvine, 1995: 970). A substantial part of this work is historical, and its angle on modernist illusions differs from the one that one finds in the research on communities of practice. In communities-of-practice research, presuppositions about systemic totality are treated as a source of contamination to be avoided in any empirical account, but in the work on language ideologies, totalising ideas are actually treated as focal objects of analysis themselves, and there are accounts of the social, political and discursive processes involved in the institutionalisation of entities like nation-states and autonomous languages.

At this point of course, linguistic self-consciousness becomes an issue, and research on language ideology and the 'imagining' of community pays a great deal of attention to the political role that philology and linguistics have played building and maintaining nation-states. In fact, though, it isn't only academics whose beliefs about language both influence and are shaped by politics and social practice. Linguistic reflexivity (or 'metapragmatic awareness') is increasingly seen as a crucial feature in all language use, and one of the effects of this is to unseat tacit, *unselfconscious* language use from the throne it has occupied in sociolinguistics for the last 30 years (Lucy, 1993; Cameron, 1995). Instead, *artful performance*, where there is 'heightened awareness of both the act of expression and the performer' (Bauman, 1986: 3; Bauman & Briggs, 1990), moves from the margins to the centre of sociolinguistics, and in Bakhtin's terms, 'direct unmediated discourse, directed exclusively toward its referential object, as an expression of the speaker's ultimate semantic authority', loses its supremacy, making way instead for 'doublevoicing', where there is an uneasiness in speech produced by its penetration by other people's talk (1984).

Overall, this shift of interest from style to stylisation and reflexive intertextuality makes the premium that sociolinguistics has always put on the unconscious and the repetitive seem rather 'Fordist'.[3] Elsewhere, Bauman (1992a: 192) suggests that in late modernity, '[s]ignificance and numbers have parted ways'. 'Statistically insignificant phenomena may prove to be decisive,' he suggests and, if he is correct, then regularity, consistency and system lose their primacy and our focus needs to extend to the unusual and *spectacular*. To do that, of course, we need a conceptualisation of language in psychological and social process that is rather different from, for example, Labov's, but in fact there are resources quite close at hand, first of all in the linguistics of practice rather than in the linguistics of system, and secondly in the shift from 'variation' to 'transposition' as a way of envisaging linguistic movement across settings, time and space.

There is obviously a very considerable pedigree to the linguistics of practice (see Hanks, 1996; Verschueren, 1999), but for present purposes the key point lies in the priority given to situated action in the relationship between language and language-use. Instead of seeing language-use simply as system output, *language* as a set of social conventions or mental structures is reduced to being just one among a number of semiotic resources available for local text production and interpretation. And instead of the system itself being viewed as the main carrier of meaning, meaning is analysed as a process of here-and-now inferencing, ranging across all kinds of percept, sign and knowledge. By definition, spectacular texts rupture expectations of regularity and co-occurrence but, since we are always plugging holes with whatever we can gather from the contingent links between different semiotic modes and levels anyway, that's obviously not fatal.

Once one treats language as playing only a subsidiary part in meaning, and once one says that local and historical context play a constitutive rather than ancillary role in communication, then it is also difficult to see *variation* as an adequate frame for analysing communicative processes across social space and time. Labovian sociolinguists take the identity of language system for granted, and they see it as their task to describe the parts and properties of the system that adjust to different situations. But if you're interested in situated meaning and you see people as getting to this through immersion in all the contingent particularities of a given context, then the first thing you have to do if you want to understand communication across time and space is to try to work out how people construct semiotic objects that will hold together long enough to carry over from one context to the next, going on after that to look at what people make of it the other end. The key words here are *en*textualisation, *trans*position and *re*contextualisation', and again, these are concepts that one can usefully use to study the spectacular. If a spectacular practice or event is actually significant, then obviously it can't be just done once and forgotten, and there has to be some record or memory of it which gets circulated over time and space. With transposition rather than variation as a conceptual framework, one looks beyond the producer's communicative competence and their flexible-but-durable underlying disposition to (a) the multiple people and processes involved in the design or selection of textual 'projectiles' which have some hope of travelling across settings, (b) the alteration and revaluation of texts in 'transportation', and (c) their embedding in new contexts. This is in fact a topic that is now becoming increasingly significant in linguistic anthropology (Bauman & Briggs, 1990; see also Silverstein & Urban (eds), 1996).

Overall, I would say that apart from the reproductive groupings that tend to be studied in the research on communities of practice, there is a shift of interest in sociolinguistics from 'production-within' to 'projection-across', from the 'use-value' to the 'exchange-value' of a language practice. Indeed, it is not hard to see this as part of the much larger movement in the social sciences, where instead of trying to define the core features of any social group or institution, the focus has turned to the flows of people, knowledge, texts and objects across social and geographical space, to the production and policing of boundaries of inclusion and exclusion, and to experiences of indeterminacy and ambivalence. Pratt sees the 'linguistics of community' being replaced by a 'linguistics of contact' which, among other things that there is not space to go into, is likely to shift the ground from 'negotiation' and 'competence' as foundational concerns to getting-attention-in-the-first-place – see Gee (1998) on 'recognition work' – to *non*-competence and to the management of 'ignorance'.[4]

At this point, however, I would like to switch my focus, and ask what significance these shifts could have for the kind of work that has traditionally been called applied linguistics? What implications do all these shifts of interest in sociology and sociolinguistics have for the identity of, for example, the applied linguistics of foreign language teaching?

Applied Linguistics in Late Modernity

It is probably worth admitting straightaway that if one follows the romantic model of competence that Bernstein attributes to sociolinguistics and many other social sciences in the 1960s, 1970s and 1980s – if one is committed to 'the universal democracy of acquisition' where everyone is inherently competent and official socialisers are suspect – then the applied linguistics of language teaching doesn't look terribly appealing. Admittedly, there is some alignment with this competence model in ideas about the integrity, autonomy and authenticity of language learner language in interlanguage theory, and communicative language teaching also looks in the same direction. Even so, my guess is that much of the tension in the 1960s, 1970s and 1980s between ELT/EFL on the one hand and English mother-tongue teaching on the other can be explained in terms of major differences in the extent to which they could commit themselves professionally to the competence model that Bernstein describes. It is also likely that the competence model has been one of the main factors that has made modern foreign language education seem so uninspiring to sociolinguists. Certainly, if one looks through *Language in Society* or any number of introductory sociolinguistics textbooks, it is hard to find even a passing reference to instructed foreign languages, and if you're principally committed to rehabilitating rich but repressed community knowledges, it's not difficult to see why. In Britain anyway, there is hardly anywhere where German and French are locally rooted community languages, and if you cut out the teacher, then there's no foreign language at all (see Rampton, 1999b for fuller discussion).

What happens, though, when the humanities and social sciences turn to new topics and there is a growth of interest in cultural flows, in boundaries and margins rather than centres, and in uncertainty and ambivalence? What happens if the climate of the times changes, competence models lose their intuitive appeal, and instead, discussion turns to the political economy of language, to the uneven production, circulation and distribution of symbolic and cultural resources, to ideology, exclusion, legitimation and resistance? What happens if anti-essentialism moves in, and we start to wonder whether feelings of group belonging aren't themselves socially constructed in the here-and-now? The answer, of course, is that the applied linguistics of other-language teaching-&-learning starts to look a bit different. It is hard to think of any other area of language study which is as centrally concerned with fluidity, marginality and transition, with what people can't do with language and with how they get by with what they can, and whatever your flavour – whether it's interstate agents or postcolonial flaneurs, whether it's Quirk, Kachru, Phillipson or Pennycook – there is longstanding involvement with globalisation and the management of transnational communication. Indeed, once one becomes wary of metaphors about roots, one starts to wonder why it is that we routinely assume that minority kids *shouldn't* invest in German as a foreign language – maybe it's actually a very welcome escape from weary language ideologies that are habitually pigeon-holing their voices within dominant discourses about ESL and community languages.

In fact, that is not the only way in which new directions in sociolinguistics turn out to be a traditional staple for language-teaching applied linguistics. Far from being the distinctive product of late modern experience, reflexivity and self-consciousness about language have been constitutive features of foreign language education since time immemorial, and coming very often out of language teaching itself (unlike their colleagues in modernist sociolinguistics), applied linguists have never been properly socialised into doctrines about language research being ethically neutral and 'linguistics being descriptive, not prescriptive' (c.f. Cameron, 1994: 21).

I am not suggesting that the applied linguistics of language teaching has been a coherent academic programme, guided by the ideas of radical linguistic thinkers like Le Page and Tabouret-Keller or Harris. Obviously, the concerns and engagements of language-teaching applied linguistics are very large, diffuse and amorphous and, in my view anyway, there is still really quite a lot that could do with conceptual refitting. But just as clearly, though, there is much more involved here than a family of hillbillies waking up to find that they're sitting on an oil-field.

If one rereads, for example, Criper & Widdowson's 1975 paper on 'Sociolinguistics and language teaching' in the *Edinburgh Course in Applied Linguistics,* one sees a much sharper understanding of idealisation as a situated strategy, and of the limits of sociolinguistic generalisation, than anything to be found in introductory sociolinguistics textbooks. This is a line that Widdowson worked out more explicitly in his papers on models and fictions (1984), and a little later on it is matched by Brumfit's (1984) argument that, as well as 'knowledge that' and 'knowledge how', there is 'knowledge of what it is to ...' – '"knowledge of what it is to be a language teacher" has a legitimate claim to be considered in methodological discussion'. Applied linguistics worked out its rejection of naive descriptivism quite a long time ago, at a time when naive descriptivism still dominated orthodox sociolinguistics, and it was not simply abandoning it for some kind of crude back-to-basics prescriptivism.

My guess is that one half of this epistemological reflexivity came from talking to sceptical teachers working on real world language problems, and that the other came from applied linguistics' precarious position in the academy and its need both to differentiate and justify itself to linguists. But whatever the sources, from the mid-1970s on, scholars such as Widdowson, Brumfit and Strevens were reflecting on positional knowledge, interdisciplinarity and the 'real world' in ways that anticipate a good deal of what is being said today. And indeed, in my view, it was neither an accident nor a revolution that made BAAL Annual Meetings such an important arena for some of the most celebrated recent developments in British sociolinguistics. In terms of international profile, both critical discourse analysis and the new literacy studies stand out in British sociolinguistics; my impression is that from the late 1980s onwards, much of the debate around this work went on at BAAL annual meetings (much more, for example, than at the Sociolinguistics Symposia); and my contention is that, in spite of any regrets he now might express, the critical reflexivity of someone like Widdowson did a great deal to open the ground for it.

Overall, then, I would suggest that the applied linguistics of language teaching stands to gain a good deal from the epistemic shifts I described earlier, and that after years of trying to fight for respectability and inclusion in the academic mainstream, there are a number of ways in which it is really rather well-positioned at the juncture between modernity and postmodernity.

Having said that, however, I am not entirely satisfied that my arguments have achieved the right balance between praise and burial and so, in the last part of my paper, I feel I ought to try and identify some ways in which there may still be some work to be done to enhance our understanding of language, discourse and social processes. So this is what I shall attempt in the last section.

The Neglected Situation

In 1964, Goffman wrote a paper called 'The Neglected Situation': at the time, a great deal of new ground was being broken, both in the description of language and in the documentation of social factors that affected it, but scant attention was being paid to the distinctive properties of the arenas where language and social factors came together. Since that time, we have been given a very impressive battery of descriptive tools, by Goffman and a range of other schools and paradigms: the ethnography of communication, conversation analysis, inter-actional sociolinguistics, critical discourse analysis, etc.

But in Britain anyway, though there are certainly some very notable excep-tions, there is not an enormous amount to compare with the traditions associated with scholars like Erickson, Gumperz, McDermott, Ochs or the Goodwins. Just how good are British linguists, I wonder, at looking at situated practice, and, outside conversation analysis, just how far does protracted immersion in the detailed particularities of situated interaction figure as a routine practice in British applied linguistics?[5] Exactly how willing are British applied linguists to sign up to the relatively inaccessible technicalities of a theoretical framework while accepting that these technicalities will have only a *sensitising* role, relevant and interesting only to the extent that they illuminate a bit more of the interaction that's being examined? And when things don't work, how happy are we to spend time learning a new apparatus that we think will tell us more about what we're looking at (rather than devoting ourselves to correction of the original theory)? How seriously do we take the recognition that hasty com-parison blinds one to the complex cultural and semiotic ecology that gives a phenomenon its meaning? How patient are we in the move from one case to the next, and when some kind of theoretical structure starts to emerge, how far do we judge it by the justice it does to our holistic sense of the data, rather than, say, the neatness of its fit with other theories? How long are we willing to wait to feed into the things that everyone else is talking about, and when we do, how freely do we admit to the number of interpretative steps we've taken in coming to such a connection?

Edge & Richards (1998) provide a very coherent formulation of questions like these, and researchers are obviously going to differ in their answers. But my own view is that if we really do think that situated interaction is a key site for the production of social reality, if we're really serious that culture and social relations are both reproduced and created anew in interactional activity, that actors draw on unevenly distributed resources in locally and historically specific circumstances, and that these circumstances are themselves enabling and con- straining to different degrees, then we can't take short-cuts or trust any ready- made theory to tell us what's going on. Instead, we need the kind of painstaking, bottom-up methodology that I really only became fully conscious of when I taught on a methods course with Celia Roberts and read Erickson's marvellous 1985 paper on 'Qualitative methods in research on teaching'. To encapsulate why this matters, I would like to refer very briefly to McDermott's paper on inarticulateness (1988).

McDermott has done a great deal of far-reaching classroom micro-ethno- graphy that is both open and technically very sharp, and rather than treating inarticulateness as a matter of individual ability, he thinks in terms of 'well orchestrated moment[s] in which inarticulateness is invited, encouraged, duly noted and remembered, no matter how much lamented' (1988: 38). At such moments, there are likely only to be 'mutterances ... grunts, groans, quips, exple- tives and a wide range of nonsense in the service of apparently unformulated ends. Fluency is missing' (ibid: 42). But at other times, there is 'breakthrough, words flow, new things are said, and the world is temporarily altered' (ibid). Inarticulateness and breakthrough make up two ends of a continuum, but the difference between them can sometimes be a very fine one, and McDermott is particularly interested in exploring the way in which inarticulateness might represent not a disability, but 'an invitation to listen in a new way' (1988: 40).

In my view, there is a dual truth here for the applied linguist, both as speaker and listener. There is no doubt that applied linguists are often under a lot of pressure to come up with a fast line for the punters, and you can probably only do that by thinking with principles and theories ready-to-hand. The risk, though, is that everything you produce falls at the midpoint of McDermott's continuum – 'mundane talk', where 'a person can fill up time with words, but only in service of a status quo'. Worse than that, there is a risk that you lose the capacity to 'listen in a new way'. Personally, I don't think that Critical Discourse Analysis is *outstandingly* good at giving itself to the interactional data, but some of the main criticisms that applied linguists have directed at it make me worry that we're losing sight of the kind of interpretative project that McDermott is calling for. Both Widdowson (1995: 513) and Stubbs (1997) take CDA to task for not being a substantive theory, whereas I would welcome it as a different ontology, as a set of assumptions that may not be refutable in themselves, but that allow us to formulate new kinds of claim close to the data where issues of testability and falsification really do come into play.

So all in all, I would say that there is still quite a bit of work to be done developing micro-ethnography in British applied linguistics. I agree that micro-analysis sometimes feels like lotus-eating, and I know from personal experience that, when you're talking about something, the ethnographic habit of saying 'well yes but it's more complex than that' can be really annoying, especially when your critic can't really tell you what you're missing. On the other hand, there is a massive agenda for discursive, social and applied linguistic analysis in Ortega Y Gasset's observation that

> [t]wo apparently contradictory laws are involved in all uttering. One says 'Every utterance is deficient' – it says less than it wishes to say. The other law, the opposite declares, 'Every utterance is exuberant' – it conveys more than it plans and includes not a few things we would wish left silent.
>
> (Ortega Y Gasset, cited in Becker, 1995: 5)

If you seriously want to tune to that, is it really enough being fluent, accurate, smart and supportive? Or is some kind of reverence for the complexity and plenitude of situated interaction the most basic requirement, however irritating or inhibiting that might sound?

Notes

1. The liberal tradition is complex and contested, but among other things, it can be characterised in terms of
   (a) a strong sense of reason as impartiality, with the reasoner standing 'apart from his own emotions, desires and interests ... abstracting ... away from the concrete situation' (Frazer & Lacey, 1993: 48);
   (b) a belief that public and private realms shold be clearly separated, with state activity limited to the public sphere and human diversity and difference regarded as private (ibid: 47);
   (c) an a-historical and 'disembodied' view of the individual, seen as having a 'moral primacy ... against the claims of any social collectivity' (Gray, 1986: x) and grounded in the 'presocial or transcendent features of human beings' (Frazer & Lacey, 1993: 45);
   (d) an insistence that the legitimacy of the state be based on consent and on a public and universal conception of law committed to rationality (ibid: 49–50).
   (e) a conviction that social reality is knowable, and that social policy and technology might be used to ameliorate poverty, unhappiness and other ills (ibid: 50).
   Within sociolinguistics, these values have been at issue in the debates about concrete vs. abstract, etc. modes of expression, in disputes about the extent to which school and other instututions should recognise different home cultures, in the argument with Chomsky, in the hypostatization of system and coherence, and lastly, in the commitment to social intervention. (For fuller discussions of liberal modernity relevant to sociolinguistics, see Scollon & Scollon, 1995: Chap. 6; Collins, 1998; Heller, 1999).
2. This can be seen, for example, in the title of Labov's classic paper, 'The Logic of Nonstandard English', or alternatively, in Bernstein's failure to make very much of the metaphorical capacities which he attributed to restricted code.
3. Gee *et al.* characterise Fordism as follows: '[w]orkers, hired from the head down had only to follow directions and mechanically carry out a rather meaningless piece of a process they did not need to understand as a whole, and certainly did not control' (1996: 26).

4. The salience of non-shared knowledge makes the tranditional priority given to 'competence' look over-optimistic, and instead, ignorance looks likely to become a substantive issue for theory and description. In our complex cultural environment, says Hannerz, it is more important to 'know ... one's own ignorance, [to] know ... that others know something else, [to] know ..., whom to believe, [to] develop ... a notion of the potentially knowable' (Hannerz, 1992: 45).

5. I would very much welcome correction to this, but it seems to me that there are three kinds of Applied Linguistics that really flourish in Britain. First of all there is generalist research, an applied philosophy of language use that sees itself as having a sensitising role, helping professionals to identify principles in practice, running with technical concepts as long as they have heuristic value for a relatively uninitiated readership. Second, there is data-oriented empirical work that is willing to work with the analytic concepts developed by the generalists, but that in my own view anyway, moves rather quickly to the description of teachers teaching and learners learning, maybe without fully recognising just how problematic and contested the identities of 'teacher', 'student' and 'learning' can be in everyday classroom life. Lastly, there is empirical work that is aligned with specific models of language and communication to which it owes its principal loyalty, and that uses data to test and develop elements in this overall theory. I leave it to the reader to supply illustrative examples!

References

Anderson, B. (1983) *Imagined Communities: Reflections on the origin and spread of Nationalism.* London: Verso.

Bakhtin, M. (1984) *Problems in Dostoevsky's Poetics.* Minneapolis: University of Minnesota Press.

Bauman, Z. (1992a) *Intimations of Post-modernity.* London: Routledge.

Bernstein, B. (1996) Sociolinguistics: A personal view. In *Pedagogy, Symbolic Control and Identity* (pp. 147–56). London: Taylor & Francis.

Brumfit, C. (1984) *Communicative Methodology in Language Teaching.* Cambridge: Cambridge University Press.

Brumfit, C. (1997) Theoretical practice: Applied linguistics as pure and practical science. *AILA Review.*

Cameron, D. (1994) Putting our theory into practice. In D. Graddol and J. Swann (eds) *Evaluating Language* (pp. 15–23). Clevedon: BAAL/Multilingual Matters.

Cameron, D. (1995) *Verbal Hygiene.* London: Routledge.

Clifford, J. (1992) Traveling cultures. In L. Grossberg, C. Nelson and P. Treichler (eds) *Cultural Studies* (pp. 96–116). London: Routledge.

Cohen, I. (1987) Structuration theory. In A. Giddens and J. Turner (eds) *Social Theory Today* (pp. 273–308). Oxford: Polity.

Collins, J. (1998) *Understanding Tolowa Histories: Western hegemonies and native American responses.* London: Routledge.

Coupland, N. (1997) Language, ageing and ageism: A project for applied linguistics? *International Journal of Applied Linguistics* 7 (1), 26–48.

Criper, C. and Widdowson, H. (1975) Sociolinguistics and language teaching. In J. Allen and S. Pit Corder (eds) *Papers in Applied Linguistics: Edinburgh course in Applied Linguistics* (Vol. 2) (pp. 155–217). Oxford: Oxford University Press.

Eckert, P. and McConnell-Ginet, S. (1992) Think practically and look locally: Language and gender as community-based practice. *Annual Review of Anthropology* 21, 461–90.

Edge, J. and Richards, K. (1998) May I see your warrant, please? Justifying outcomes in qualitative research. *Applied Linguistics* 19 (3), 334–56.

Erickson, F. (1985) Qualitative methods in research on teaching. In M. Wittrock (ed.) *Handbook of Research on Teaching* (3rd edn) (pp. 119–61). New York: Macmillan.

Fairclough, N. (1992) *Discourse and Social Change.* Oxford: Polity.

Frazer, E. and Lacey, N. (1993) *The Politics of Community.* Hemel Hempstead: Harvester Wheatsheaf.

Gal, S. (1989) Language and political economy. *Annual Review of Anthropology* 18, 345–67.

Gal, S. and Irvine, J. (1995) The boundaries of languages and disciplines: How ideologies construct difference. *Social Research* 62 (4), 967–1001.

Gal, S. and Woolard, K. (1995) Constructing languages and publics: Authority and representation. *Pragmatics* 5 (2), 129–38.

Gee, J., Hull, G. and Lankshear, C. (1996) T*he New Work Order: Behind the language of the New Capitalism.* Westview Press.

Gee, J. (1999) *An Introduction to Discourse Analysis.* London: Routledge.

Giddens, A. (1990) *Social Theory and Modern Sociology.* Oxford: Polity.

Goffman, E. (1964) The neglected situation. *American Anthropologist* 66 (6), 133–6.

Goodwin, M. H. (1990) *He Said She Said Bloomington.* Indiana University Press.

Goodwin, C. (1994) Professional vision. *American Anthropologist* 96 (3), 606–33.

Gumperz, J. (1982) *Discourse Strategies.* Cambridge: Cambridge University Press.

Hannerz, U. (1992) *Cultural Complexity: Studies in the social organization of meaning.* NY: Columbia University Press.

Harris, R. (1981) *The Language Myth.* London: Duckworth.

Heller, M. (1999) *Linguistic Minorities and Modernity.* London: Longman.

Joseph, J. and Taylor, T. (eds) (1990) *Ideologies of Language.* London: Routledge.

Kachru, B. (ed.) (1982) *The Other Tongue.* Oxford: Pergamon.

Lave J. and Wenger, E. (1991) *Situated Learning: Legitimate peripheral participation.* Cambridge: Cambridge University Press.

LePage, R. and Tabouret-Keller, A. (1985) *Acts of Identity.* Cambridge: Cambridge University Press.

McDermott, R. (1988), Inarticulateness. In D. Tannen (ed.) *Linguistics in Context: Connecting observation and understanding* (pp. 37–68). NJ: Ablex.

Pennycook, A. (1994) *The Cultural Politics of English as an International Language.* London: Longman.

Phillipson, R. (1992) *Linguistic Imperialism.* Oxford: Oxford University Press.

Pratt, M. L. (1987) Linguistic Utopias. In N. Fabb *et al.* (eds) *The Linguistics of Writing* (pp. 48–66). Manchester: Manchester University Press.

Quirk, R. (1990) Language varieties and standard language. *English Today* 21, 3–10.

Rampton, B. (1997) Retuning in applied linguistics. *International Journal of Applied Linguistics* 7 (1), 3–26.

Rampton, B. (1999) Deutsch in Inner London and the animation of an instructed foreign language. *Journal of Sociolinguistics* 3 (4).

Rampton, B. (forthcoming a) Crosstalk, language crossing and cross-disciplinarity in sociolinguistics. In N. Coupland, C. Candlin and S. Sarangi (eds) *Sociolinguistics and Social Theory.* London: Longman.

Rampton, B. (forthcoming b) Speech community. In J. Verschueren, J-O Ostman, J. Blommaert and C. Bulcaen (eds) *Handbook of Pragmatics.* Amsterdam: John Benjamins.

Scollon, R. and Scollon, S. (1995) *Intercultural Communication.* Oxford: Blackwell.

Stubbs, M. (1997) Whorf's children: Critical comments on Critical Discourse Analysis. In A. Ryan and A. Wray (eds) *Evolving Models of Language*. Clevedon: BAAL/ Multilingual Matters.

Verschueren, J. (1999) *Understanding Pragmatics*. London: Edward Arnold.

Widdowson, H. (1984) 'Applied linguistics: The pursuit of relevance' and 'Models and fictions'. *Explorations in Applied Linguistics* 2 (pp. 7–20 & 21–7). Oxford: Oxford University Press.

Widdowson, H. (1995) Review of Fairclough 1992. *Applied Linguistics* 16 (4), 510–6.

8 Talking Disability: The quiet revolution in language change

MARIAN CORKER
University of Central Lancashire

Abstract

This paper concerns continuity and change in 'disability' discourse. It first outlines the different forms of disability discourse that have emerged over the last three decades and focuses, in particular, on those discourses that frame disability as a significant dimension of social inequality and social exclusion. The paper then goes on to show how these different discourses are played out in the situated social interaction of deaf children with their peers, both disabled and not disabled, and with adults, using data gathered in ethnographic fieldwork and informal interviews from the *Lives of Disabled Children* project. Data analysis uses an interactional sociolinguistics approach that concentrates particularly on conversational strategies and repertoires that act to reinforce and resist disabling practice.

Continuity and Change in Disability Discourse

Disability, like most dimensions of experience, is polysemic – that is ambiguous and unstable in meaning – as well as a mixture of 'truth' and 'fiction' that depends on who says what, to whom, when and where. Discourses relating to disability might therefore be viewed in terms of the 'different languages used in representing different social practices from particular points of view' (Fairclough, 1995: 56). The last 30 years or so has seen a movement from a discourse that constructs disability as functional impairment, tragedy, deviance, incompetence or dependence, to a range of discourses that are framed by an understanding of disability as a dimension of social inequality and oppression (Corker & French, 1999). These discourses are engaged in a struggle in and over language, yet disability is probably the last remaining dimension of social inequality to receive the critical attention of an applied linguistics that is caught between those who argue that 'language reflects society' and those who believe that 'language marks identity'.

'Old' disability discourse emphasises the division of individual disabled people into a large number of objectified medically and scientifically determined impairment categories, each of which are described in terms of their relationship to the arbitrary category 'normal', which itself remains unexamined. Because 'society' assumes a role of 'care' and 'benevolence', old disability discourse is therefore not *of* disabled people so much as *about* (particular and largely negative perceptions of) disability. Such discourses are typified by the individual or medical model of disability, and will henceforth be referred to as *impairment discourses.* Their history is well documented in the literature on social exclusion, the social construction of dependency and the institutionalisation of disabled people (see, for example, Barnes, 1990, 1991), and what linguistic analysis there is of 'disability' is very much concentrated in this area. Examples might include error analysis of speech and language impairment, miscommunication and problematic talk (Coleman & dePaulo, 1991) and communication disorder (Kovarsky, Duchan & Maxwell, 1999).

'New' disability discourses (Corker, 1999a) – or social models of disability – are *of* disabled people. That is, they have developed from within collective organisations of disabled people – or new social movements. Social models of disability are founded on a conceptual distinction between disability and impairment, in much the same way that some feminists attempt to distinguish gender from sex. Starting from this foundation, there are two main ways in which disability itself is then conceptualised that reflect some of the tensions surrounding a number of core sociological dichotomies such as structure/agency and society/ individual. First, in a materialist analysis that draws heavily on neo-Marxist perspectives, it may be seen as a form of oppression that is *socially created* by structures, processes and policies which institutionalise inequality in Western society (Oliver, 1990). Such analysis, in its focus on social structure, tends to take the view that 'language reflects society' and, since society is oppressive, 'disabled identities' are produced as by-products of oppressive practice (Barnes, 1996). This is why the term 'disabled people' is preferred because it marks disabled people as an oppressed group, but when used in isolation it also presents disabled people as lacking in agency. To contest this, disabled people have collectively organised to produce two main, though not always distinct forms of *collective identity* that are built on some concept of 'disability pride' (Morris, 1991; Linton, 1998). First, disabled people can be viewed as *a new social movement* – a 'political identity' that mobilises a politics of resistance. Second, disabled people self-define as *a social minority* or *'community of practice'* (Wenger, 1998) engaged in the production of a counter-culture that has a developing lexicon of 'disability language'. This includes the defiant reclamation of terms such as 'crip', 'freak', 'gimp' – narratives of resistance, opposition, transgression and competition that rehearse 'conventional formulae in non-conventional ways' (Butler, 1997: 147).

The discourses enacted by the collective identity in its various forms will be referred to as *disability discourses*. However, charting continuity and change in disability discourse has been problematised in two main ways – hybridity and hegemony. When discourse relating to disability is studied historically and dynamically and in terms of shifting configurations of discourse types, it is also possible to see the emergence of a number of *hybrid discourses* characterised by the contingent use of terms such as 'people with disabilities' (Corker, 1999b). This term may, for example be employed

- in 'people first' language, such as that promoted by the organisation of people with learning difficulties, *People First*, in order to project 'positive' images;

- as a marker of distance from and/or denial of the political and social ideology of the disability movement, in particular from the movement's notion of institutionalised oppression;

- as a means of dichotomising concepts of personhood and disability, often privileging (particular understandings of) the former through self-denial of impairment and the impact it has on the life of the person.

These different meanings engage in a struggle in and over language and shifts between them both constitute and are constituted by wider processes of social change. Different meanings clearly imply different power relations that have differing abilities to shape and transform the discourse practices of society and its institutions relating to disability (Corker, 2000). I have suggested elsewhere that 'people with' language in its second and third configurations is an example of the more subtle discursive dimensions of modern elite impairment discourse that dominates the media, medical, legal, political, bureaucratic or scholarly text and talk (Corker, 1998; 1999b). For example, though the second and third usages may seem similar, they are actually very different discursive formations in that the second represents a denial of disablement by powerholders that presupposes a definition of disablement that excludes them as part of the problem. This is causally related to the third usage – the individual's denial of (their own) impairment which may be part of 'internalised oppression' and/or the strategy of 'passing' in order to appear 'normal'. It is also true that the term 'disabilities' is highly metaphoric and metonymic. 'Disabilities' can refer both to the particularistic barriers that are faced by disabled people and to the individual model of disability. In other words, at times it means disability in the social model sense and at other times it means impairment in the social model sense. The most significant aspect of these varied meanings is that they can signify a commitment both to the disabled people's movement and to the social practices that oppress disabled people. As such, the term 'people with disabilities' is itself a dual performative, or what Homi Bhabha (1983: 22) might describe as the 'double articulation' of affirmation and prejudice.

However, these different meanings also co-exist in a climate of hegemony where *impairment* discourses are 'naturalised' – 'employed as if they were common-sense, apolitical statements' (van Dijk, 1993). Impairment discourses (and impairment-dominant hybrid discourses) dominate the mass media and government policy. They therefore act as 'linguistic conventions that structure the meanings assigned to disability and the patterns of response to disability that emanate from or are attendant upon those meanings' (Linton, 1998). Inequalities in social power and access imply that disability discourses do not always achieve the ritualised status that enables them to exert manifest influence on the main domains of social reproduction or elitist discourse. Indeed, there is often overt censorship of *disability discourses*. Such a climate also tends to reinforce a division between minority and majority languages through practices such as 'verbal hygiene' (Cameron, 1995) and language planning that places an emphasis on 'linguistic purism' (Thomas, 1991), and these practices can extend to the language relationships within oppressed communities.

It is here that the growing interest of linguists in Sign language as a 'proper' language problematises the study of disability discourse. Sign language users ('Deaf' people) self-define as a linguistic minority rather than in terms of the impairment category 'hearing-impaired'. In Britain, this group comprises 40–70,000 adult Deaf people – or about 3–4% of 'severely' hearing-impaired people – depending on the statistical source used. The Deaf community generally rejects the term 'disability' as a self-referent, though disability is defined in terms of 'impairment discourse', and regards deaf people who use spoken language as 'really' disabled. However, it is important to emphasise that access to Sign language itself is politically and geographically constructed with the result that it is very unevenly distributed in terms of use (see, for example, Lucas, 1995). Moreover there is an important sense in which 'Deaf culture' is a product of elitist discourse, where 'linguistic units become linked with social units' (Gal & Irvine, 1995: 970), rather than of the lived experience of deaf people as a community of practice (Corker, 1996, 1998, 2000).

Deaf Children Talk 'Disability'

Priestley (1998: 89, his emphasis) notes that 'it is not sufficient to identify disabling social values unless it can also be shown *how* they become disabling'. One way of doing this is at the level of ideology because discourse, as Gee (1990: 144) suggests, is closely linked to the distribution of social power and to social hierarchy, control over particular discourses can lead to the acquisition of social goods (money, power and status) in a society. Nevertheless, their influence is perhaps best observed at the local, micro-level, in *everyday* 'text' and 'talk'. Indeed, as Hymes (1996: 98–9) suggests, 'saying ... might be the aspect of life most within the power of persons in a community to change'. It is to everyday social practice that this paper now turns. The following three sub-sections present data gathered in ethnographic fieldwork and informal interviews from a two-year ESRC funded project, *Lives of Disabled Children* (Award number L129251047), which are analysed using interactional sociolinguistics (see Hoyle & Adger, 1998). This analysis concentrates particularly on conversational strategies that reinforce and resist disabling practice in order to show the difference between different kinds of disability discourse in social practice. Further, in order to explore the issues raised above, analysis deliberately focuses on *deaf* children's interaction with their peers, both disabled and not disabled, and with adults, and how this highlights disability as situated performance. It will address whether deaf children's talk may be of relevance to van Dijk's (1996: ix–x) arguments about 'preferential access to and control over public discourse and its consequences for the manufacture of consensus', given that for this group disabling barriers include barriers to language, information and communication.

Impairment discourse

The first example (transcript A) is taken from a mainstream Social Education class where non-disabled children and adults formed the large majority. My colleague John Davis (JD), is providing access to the group's communication for me (I am deaf) by typing into a small computer. Sometimes, this typing includes 'silent' reflexive observations which are built into the process of recording data and which represent a condensation of the research process, with commentary and analysis between researchers happening simultaneously with the activity being investigated (these comments are italicised). The teacher begins by instructing the class that they are to divide into groups and each group is to represent a particular charitable 'cause' which must decide why they deserve to get a large source of funding. She begins to name the 'causes'.

Transcript A: Contemporaneous typed notes of spoken exchange

1. **JD:**   *(to MC) The teacher just used the word 'handicapped'*
2. **Robbie:**   (joking, derisively) Bill behind us – **he's** handicapped ...

3. **Teacher:** Each group has x million ti organise and choose what ti spend it on. One of the choices is ti spend money on facilities for the handicapped.' (general laughter)

4. *JD:* *(to MC) The groups are arguing about which 'cause' they should take on*

5. **Jim**: We're Drugs, but they aren't behind us – they're Oxfam.'

6. **Robbie:** We're Oxfam .. 'You should be with us.'

7. **Teacher:** Robbie's group is 'Facilities for ti handicapped' (class laughs).

8. *JD:* *(to MC) This is completely lacking in disability awareness. Teacher has no idea, nor do the kids and there is nothing here to break the stereotypes. Robbie's group have now changed their 'cause' to Deprived Inner City – he had a lot to do with that .. wonder why?*

9. **Amy:** (almost drowned out) We're 'Facilities for ti Handicapped'.

10. **Teacher:** (to Robbie's group) 'Oh you've changed – di yi think you can argue be'er for that?'

11. *JD:* *(to MC) The group furthest away of four girls are singing 'Money Money Money – it's a rich man's world' and the teacher doesn't intervene*

    ***   (disruption continues)

12. **Teacher:** Why d' we need to feed the poor in the Third World?

13. *JD:* *(to MC) No real answer so she moves on to Oxfam, but she's lost control – no one's answering so she's stopped speaking and waiting for control but they are not giving her it ....*

14. **Teacher:** 2nd year we cannot continue if you are being silly. ... Tell me why Oxfam should get the money?

15. **Jim:** It helps to get money and that's all we thought about ... people in Sudan are starving since the way ...

16. **Teacher:** How would they normally feed themselves?

17. **Robbie:** With difficulty!

18. **Teacher:** (losing her temper) Are we gonny get to handicapped nit? (uproar increases) ... Could every one just be polite. This is social education – you're expected ti be able to speak ti other people ... Right Colin – that's your final warning – oot you go.' (class quietens)

19. **Amy:** We think handicapped (noise increases) should get more attention 'cos we get attention, so should them ... so need more money for facilities....

20. **Teacher:** You're not presenting this terribly well ...

21. **Amy:** (no response)

22 . **Teacher:** So ... the two that came out most were one for deprived area and drug addicts (big cheers from this group) ... One of the reasons that you said more on drugs and the inner city is because they're closer to home ... Sudan's too far away.

This transcript shows the use of a number of sociolinguistic distancing and silencing strategies that perform impairment discourse. The tone, in some ways, is set by the teacher's distancing strategies through her lack of 'knowledge of the history and culture of the Other' (Todorov, 1982: 185). This is evident in her choice of the term 'the handicapped' (turn 1) to describe disabled people, a description that is no longer regarded as politically correct, and the way in which the activity associates it with 'charity' discourse – 'facilities *for* the handicapped'. She continues to reinforce a particular stereotype of disability with her approach to the whole activity. However, the young people in this example demonstrate not only that they share a stereotyped knowledge of disability, which they do not attempt to disguise, but also that there is strong collective pressure to reinforce this knowledge through disruptive social action (2, 3, 7, 9,18 and 19). Every time the word 'handicapped' is used, the general level of noise in the class increases to the point where the girls who eventually 'represent' this group are silenced. They are forced to surrender to the class consensus that this is a 'no-go' topic (21).

But there are other forms of meaning here also. First, there are two deaf children in the group who are 'silent witnesses' to these events. What is the meaning of this silence and does it influence the performance of the communicative event? Second, Robbie (who has dyslexia and 'emotional-behavioural difficulties'), at the start of the dialogue (2), also distances disability by transferring the label 'handicapped' along with its connotations to Bill, who is not (visibly) disabled but is being particularly disruptive. Robbie's language in association with the term 'handicapped' (2) might be contrasted with the different intensity of language he uses later on in the dialogue in relation to feeding the starving in Sudan (17). Both examples are humorous – and in this context it is worth noting Rosaldo's (1990) observation that humour and satire are effective tools of minority discourse – but he uses more derision in turn 2. When 'his' group is subsequently publicly referred to as 'facilities for the handicapped' by the teacher (7), the group change their 'cause', apparently following Robbie's leadership. This brings to mind Bhabha's notion of the stereotype as 'a complex, ambivalent and contradictory mode of representation, as anxious as it is assertive' (1994: 70).

Hybrid discourse

In transcript A, deaf children were in a minority. However, in the next transcript (Transcript B), which is extracted from a focus group in a residential school, structured very loosely around the topic of disability and school, the group, including the researcher, are deaf.

Transcript B: Translation of video-taped focus group conducted in sign language

49.	MC:	What I want to ask you is a different question. You talk about problems, you say disabled people have problems OK. Isn't that the same as what Glen Hoddle said about disabled people being punished for past?
50.	Chris:	Glen Hoddle had said he thought people were disabled now because they had been bad in previous lives
51.	MC:	Yes .....
52.	Alan:	(laughs) I don't know who G.H. is or anything about them (to Chris) Who is G.H.?
53.	Lee:	(to MC) I don't think Glen Hoddle (signs G.H.) realised what he was saying, he must have been in a dream world.
54.	Chris:	(to Alan) It's the England Football Manager (signs 'M', not MANAGER)!
55.	Alan:	(to Chris, laughs) What their Mother? (to MC) I don't know who you're talking about sorry. Who is it?
56.	Maria:	(annoyed) I'm not interested in Glen Hoddle!
57.	MC:	You're not interested in Glen Hoddle?
58.	Maria:	(Shakes head).
59.	Alan:	Because......
60.	Ruth:	Because he's a boring person.
61.	MC:	But I thought you said you were .... interested in deaf people ...
62	Alan:	I think it is difficult sometimes for me to communicate .....
63.	Ruth:	Well I wish I was hearing, I do ... I wish I was hearing.
64.	Alan:	.......I can.... I don't simple things, you know do everything. I can't be a policeman and work in a police station or be a fireman. I can't because I'm disabled. If I was in danger in those situations I couldn't hear people shouting to save me before, I don't know, I got crushed to death or something.
65.	Ruth:	I agree.
66.	MC:	OK, so if your mother was pregnant and she knew the baby was deaf and the doctor said that it can be aborted, what should she do?
67.	Maria:	*I* would have it aborted, I don't let it be born deaf. If it was *mine* I would, I'd want it to be hearing. Deaf people can't have the jobs we want, all we have is anything to do with Sign Language.
68.	Alan:	It is always difficult for deaf people to find work because we can't do everything. Really there should be more things for deaf people and not concentrate on who has hearing and who don't ...
69.	Ruth:	But what about hearing aids?

70 . **Alan:**   I wish that in the future there will be some operation that would make deaf people hearing, I really do....

71. **Maria:**   Things will only improve a long way in the future .... and *it's not fair!*

This exchange begins with a reference to Glenn Hoddle, who was the manager of the England national football team until he rose to notoriety because of his use of 'impairment discourse'. Because this school had a very dominant 'football culture', and the issue was frequently discussed by the children, it is here used as a 'lead' into the topic of disability. The resulting interaction is a complex mixture of disabling self-talk that uses 'I' language (62), disabling stereotyping of deaf people that uses 'we' language (64 and 67–8) and very subtle disabling practice (52 and 55) which would only be visible to an insider. Both Lee (who is Chinese) and, to a lesser extent, Chris (who is from a Deaf family) tended to abbreviate terms that might be difficult to fingerspell 'accurately' to the first letter of the word (e.g. Glenn Hoddle becomes G.H. and 'Manager' becomes 'M', which is also the sign MOTHER). Alan, who had initiated a conversation the day before on the subject of Glenn Hoddle and knew what the issues were, is teasing Lee and Chris about their 'primitive' signing, whilst distancing himself from them using the guise that he does not understand them. This is one example of the 'double performative' described earlier. Alan's behaviour irritates Maria and Ruth (56–60), who signal this irritation by marginalising the topic as 'boring'. Alan then reclaims the centre ground by drawing attention to himself through disabling self-talk, which is legitimated in the responses of both Ruth and Maria, and in a different way, through the silence of Lee, Chris and also Angie, who does not figure in this exchange at all. Thus the group arrive at some consensus that 'they' are disabled, without actually mentioning the word disability, but they frame their experience of disability with *impairment* discourse.

Transcript B is extracted from a much longer transcript that is full of examples of different hybrid discourses. At times the children's talk gives more weight to impairment discourse and at other times there is more emphasis on disability discourse, for example in references to the 'unfairness' of disabling practice. However, it is also clear that they do not understand disabling practice as *constituting* disability because talk about disability is framed predominantly by the lexicon of impairment discourse – 'we can't do' something rather than 'we're not allowed' to do something. (see Corker, 2001, forthcoming for examples of the latter). Indeed, in situations where I attempted to introduce disability as a social phenomenon, there did seem to be some resistance to it. For example, in an interview with Linda, in the same school, the following exchange took place:

Transcript C: Translation of video-taped interview conducted in sign language

77. **MC:**   So what do you think about disabled people?
78. **Linda:** About disabled people...... I like them. It must be horrible to be disabled but there is nothing wrong in it. I certainly wouldn't think or say what Glenn Hoddle said, I would do that. It's horrible and the teasing, it's not nice.
79. **MC:**   Do you think you're disabled?
80. **Linda:** No
81. **MC:**   No?
82. **Linda:** Someone did say to me that deaf is disabled, is that true or not?
83. **MC:**   I'm asking you, what do you think?
84. **Linda:** No.
85. **MC:**   You don't think so?
86. **Linda:** No, what about you?
87. **MC:**   Disabled has many meanings and maybe when I use the word disabled, I mean something different from you. So I would say yes, I think I am disabled.
88. **Linda:** (laughs) Why, you don't look disabled. You can walk naturally. Disabled people have funny walks, you know like KG here. They have a funny walk and they are disabled and you are deaf and are not disabled. Other people have said that you are deaf so that means that you are disabled but I think I am deaf but I'm not disabled. If you have a funny walk then you are and I am not. If I was disabled that would really upset me I think I would always wish that I could walk properly. So not being able to walk or see is disability – not me.

This is a different kind of hybrid discourse where there is a recognition of and aversion to disabling practice in relation to *other* disabled people, who are referred to as 'them' (78), coupled with a rejection of the label 'disabled' when applied to the deaf self (80, 88), deaf people (84 and 86) *and to me* as a deaf person (88). In the latter example, it is interesting that 'disability' is associated with how someone 'looks', with a lack of 'natural' performance and with 'tragedy' ("If I was disabled that would really upset me I think I would always wish I could walk properly"). But impairment discourse is retained and reinforced to the point where, when I suggest I *am* disabled, Linda contests this perception.

Disability discourse

Overt reference to disability that was framed by disability discourse was almost non-existent in the talk of deaf children we worked with, irrespective of context and location. On one level, the incidence of disabling self-talk could reflect the power of hegemonic impairment discourse, but on another it may reflect the access these young people have to particular discourses and communicative events. There were, however, a number of clear examples of the use of discourse as a social resource in the *resistance* of disabling practice. That is, some of the deaf young people recognised disabling practice and took steps, usually collectively, to change the situation by reinforcing their own world view. In the final transcript (D), which involved 'silent' Angie from the focus group with a different, younger group of deaf students, a classroom assistant's drawing of the boundaries between deaf and hearing sparked the following exchange:

Transcript D: Contemporaneous translation from sign language

1.	**Carol:**	Get me a protractor ...
2.	**CA:**	Why don't you get off your lazy backside and get it yourself?
3.	**Angie:**	(shouts) You swear, you swear ...
4.	**CA:**	Stop shouting at me, I'm not deaf
5.		Angie and Carol simmer and Angie turns her back on the CA. She is doing addition and asks MC to check her work from time to time – she won't ask CA. MC notices that Mike is using a calculator to do his work. Carol sees MC looking over at him
6.	**Carol:**	Oh look ... Mike use a calculator. Not allowed
7.	**CA:**	You're not allowed to use that Mike
8.	**Mike:**	I am I am. [the teacher] say so
9.	**Angie:**	(mutters in sign) They never let girls use them (to MC) You think she (nods towards teacher) a good teacher?
10.	**MC:**	I don't know. I've only met her twice.
11.	**Angie:**	Well look at her now and tell me
12.	**MC:**	That won't help
13.	**Angie:**	She tell you I hit her or something ...
14.	**MC:**	(noticing teacher is watching) Angie thinks I can tell if you're a good teacher by just looking at you.
15.		Carol laughs scornfully
16.	**Angie:**	Want a calculator because Mike have – (to teacher) get me a calculator
17.	**Teacher:**	They're in the bottom drawer
18.	**Angie:**	Get me one
19.	**Teacher:**	It would be nice if you said please ..
20.	**Angie:**	(grudgingly) Pullleaase ..
21.		Teacher gets up to get the calculator
22.	**Angie:**	(to MC, back to CA) She got a big quivering bottom!
23.		Carol has a problem with her hearing aid – she thinks tube is

blocked. We all try to unblock it but I suspect that this is a diverting tactic because everyone now wants their hearing aids unblocked. They have a puffer device which Angie tries to puff directly into her ear.

24. **MC:**   Don't do that. It dangerous ...

25. **Angie:** That not true ...

26.   Angie then uses the puffer to mime other kinds of puffer devices , e.g. a scent puffer and the CA takes it away from her, cross her arms so that the puffer rests close to her breast.

27. **Angie:** Are you blowing up your breasts now?

28. **MC:**   (laughs)

Angie objects to the CA swearing (3) and the CA, who has been caught out responds by reinforcing her power as a hearing person (4). Angie and Carol allow this boundary to remain intact and then reinforce it by enlisting my help with their work instead of the classroom assistant's whilst monitoring my reactions. Mike is drawn into the dialogue when the direction of my eye gaze is tracked by Carol (5) and she uses Mike to bait the classroom assistant to tell him off (7). This reinforces a 'good adult' (me)/'bad adult' (CA) distinction. Angie colludes with Carol's intervention by using a similar strategy to bait the teacher whom she first suggests is sexist (9) and then suggests might try to influence my impression of Angie in a negative way (13). She also tries to seek reassurance that I am 'on her side' by asking me what I think of the teacher (9). When I am non-committal (10–12) and then involve the teacher (14), this enables Angie and Carol to aggravate the teacher further both directly (turns 15–21) and more subtly (22) with the use of humour. I am included in the joke about 'quivering bottoms' but the CA is not because Angie turns her back on the CA, thus deliberately excluding her. The next stage in the disruption (23–27) involves both drawing attention to their deafness through the use of *impairment* discourse, specifically by adopting the role of deaf people as hearing aid users, and an amusing 'play upon signs' that uses the iconicity of Sign language. This is a different way of emphasising deaf that contests impairment discourse. The classroom assistant is again forced into the disciplinary role (26) which Angie then deflates with humour (27).

Concluding Remarks

All of these examples perform disability in a number of contested ways even if disability itself is not named. When it is named, it performs impairment discourse and so provokes strong resistance in the form of denial. One way of looking at this is that it happens because impairment discourse is highly salient and ritualised, and is *therefore most accessible to those who lead institutiona-*

lised or marginalised lives. As Judith Butler (1997) suggests, the 'force' of ritual is that it is repeated in time and hence maintains a sphere of operation that is not restricted to the moment of the utterance itself. Thus, impairment discourse 'wounds', even when it is not owned by the self. Social transformation would require similar ritualisation of alternative knowledges that match this power to 'wound' with the power to affirm, but ritualisation requires collective organisation and access to knowledge which may be impeded by disabling practice. If this were the case, I would argue that we would expect to see more restrictions on the roles that are adopted and used in social interaction, both by deaf children and by those around them, than we do in the above datasets. However, what we actually see is evidence of the creativity of deaf children's *localised* resistance to inequality. Certainly, it is true that the only difference between the young people in transcript A and transcript D is that the latter use Sign language. In both examples, control of and change in the communicative event is performed collectively to reinforce particular versions of disability and to distance others, and in both, the children's strategies are labelled by adults as 'naughty' and therefore requiring 'discipline'. There are however differences in the way that discipline is enforced.

In transcript A, the teacher reinforces the majority consensus that 'disability' is a no-go topic through her collusion with the 'silence' of the deaf children. The only overt challenge lay in the reflexive commentary by the researchers, but this too was forced to remain silent as we were expected to 'observe' only. In transcript D, the classroom assistant's assertion of her 'hearing' status and the way in which she chooses as a result to dissociate herself from what she saw as 'deaf behaviour' is regarded in a negative light by Angie and Carol. (In a different kind of way, Linda has difficulty with my use of the label 'disabled' as a self-referent, but only because she sees the label to mean impairment, which she then projects back by way of challenge.) In transcript D, Carol and Angie assume control of the communicative event, both in terms of moving the topic away from the ascribed topic of the lesson and in terms of disrupting the formal learning that can take place, by legitimating each others' communicative strategies and roles. In this context, it is important to recognise that signing is highly visible and much of what occurs is therefore visible to the whole class, excepting those whose Sign language is not very proficient, as was the case with the teacher, or whose view is temporarily interrupted. When they *choose* to do so, Angie and Carol are able to exclude or marginalise 'undesirable' members of the group (the classroom assistant and the teacher) through their body practice. This has a very similar local effect to increasing the volume of noise in order to exclude the topic 'handicap' in the Social Education class (transcript A). Indeed it is precisely because of this similarity that transcript D is given as an example of the performance of *disability* discourse because, in transcript C, the balance of inequality is tipped in favour of the children.

128   CHANGE AND CONTINUITY IN APPLIED LINGUISTICS

What is interesting, however, is that attempts to change the direction of the communicative event through the imposition of adult authority can only be *temporarily* effected as, once particular strategies are exposed, either by the children themselves or by adults, they are re-used by others in the group in order to maintain the group's consensus. This kind of exchange is frequently interpreted in the field of Deaf Studies as indicating that Deaf people are *not* disabled and deafness should therefore be conceptually distinguished from disability. However, I would suggest that there is an alternative interpretation – one that embraces the displacement of alternative forms of disability discourse because they are at odds with how deaf children 'see' disability and because seeing is knowing in deaf experience. This is where transcript C is of critical importance.

In conclusion, I want to propose that though communication impairment – or what McDermott (1988) might describe as 'inarticulateness' – has often been regarded in terms of individual ability, these children's experiences should be seen as part of a move towards the representation of inarticulateness as 'not a disability, but an invitation to listen in a new way' (1988: 40). However, all of these exchanges, except perhaps the first, show the urgency of deaf children's agency in situations they perceive to be discriminatory. When agency involves the creative use of hybridity or allows children to gain control of the communicative event, this can be a tremendously empowering experience for them. Thus if they are to be viewed as competent social actors rather than passive 'victims', and if some notion of critical language awareness' is to be developed, it also seems important to consider 'articulate inequality'. To paraphrase Hymes (1996: 65), 'saying' ultimately cannot change the structural inequities that make it rational for centres and margins of power alike to combine in social destruction, nor change interests that find it reasonable to allow institutionalised inequality. But it can have demonstrable local effects and, because 'discourse is everywhere', the scrutiny of our own and that of others – the task of applied linguistics – 'is a lens that may sometimes focus light enough to illuminate and even start a fire.'

References

Barnes, C. (1990) *'Cabbage Syndrome': The social construction of dependence*. London: Falmer.
Barnes, C. (1991) *Disabled People in Britain and Discrimination: A case for anti-discrimination legislation*. London: Hurst & Co.
Barnes, C. (1996) Theories of disability and the origins of the oppression of disabled people in western society. In L. Barton (ed.) *Disability & Society: Emerging issues and insights*. London: Longman.
Bhabha, H. K. (1983) The other question: The stereotype and colonial discourse. *Screen* 24 (4), 18–36.
Bhabha, H. K. (1994) *The Location of Culture*. New York: Routledge.
Butler, J. (1997) *Excitable Speech*. New York: Routledge.

Cameron, D. (1995) *Verbal Hygiene.* London: Routledge.

Coleman, L. M. and dePaulo, B. M. (1991) Uncovering the human spirit: Moving beyond disability and 'missed' communications. In. N. Coupland, H. Giles and J. M. Wiemann (eds) *'Miscommunication' and Problematic Talk.* Thousand Oaks, CA: Sage.

Corker, M. (1996) *Deaf Transitions.* London: Jessica Kingsley.

Corker, M. (1998) *Deaf and Disabled or Deafness Disabled?* Buckingham: Open University Press.

Corker, M. (1999a) 'New' disability discourse, the principle of optimisation and social change. In M. Corker and S. French (eds) *Disability Discourse.* Buckingham: Open University Press.

Corker, M. (1999b) 'See the person (not the disability)': Deconstructing the politics of visibility and the performance of 'positive' images. *Disability Studies Quarterly* 19 (3), 191–205.

Corker, M. (2000) Disability politics, language planning and social policy. *Disability and Society* 15 (3), 445–61.

Corker, M. (2001, forthcoming) 'They don't know what they don't know' – the social constitution of deaf childhoods in everyday interaction. In A. James, P. Christensen, A. Prout and S. McNamee (eds) *Sites of Learning.* London: Falmer.

Corker, M. and French, S. (eds) (1999) *Disability Discourse.* Buckingham: Open University Press

Fairclough, N. (1995) *Discourse and Social Change.* Cambridge: Polity.

Gal, S. and Irvine, J. (1995) The boundaries of language and disciplines: How ideologies construct difference. *Social Research* 62 (4), 967–1001.

Gee, J. P. (1990) *Social Linguistics and Literacies.* New York: Falmer Press.

Hoyle, S. M. and Adger, C. T. (eds) (1998) *Kids Talk: Strategic language use in later childhood.* New York: Oxford University Press.

Hymes, D. (1996) *Ethnography, Linguistics, Narrative Inequality: Toward an understanding of voice.* London: Taylor & Francis.

Kovarsky, D., Duchan, J. and Maxwell, M. (1999) *Constructing (In)Competence: Disabling Evaluations in Clinical and Social Interaction.* Mahwah, NJ: Lawrence Erlbaum.

Linton, S. (1998) *Claiming Disability: Knowledge and Identity.* NY: New York University Press.

Lucas, C. (ed.) (1995) *Sociolinguistics in Deaf Communities.* Washington: Gallaudet University Press.

McDermott, R. (1988) Inarticulateness. In D. Tannen (ed.) *Linguistics in Context: Connecting observation and understanding.* NJ: Ablex.

Oliver, M. (1990) *The Politics of Disablement.* Basingstoke: Macmillan.

Priestley, M. (1998) Constructions and creations: Idealism, materialism and disability theory. *Disability and Society* 13 (1), 75–94.

Riggins, S. H. (ed.) (1997) *The Language and Politics of Exclusion.* Thousand Oaks, CA: Sage.

Rosaldo, R. (1990) Politics, patriarchy and laughter. In A. JanMohammed and D. Lloyd (eds) *The Nature and Context of Minority Discourse.* NY: Oxford University Press.

Shakespeare, T. (1999) What is a disabled person? In M. Jones and L. A. B. Marks (eds) *Disability, Divers-ability and Legal Change.* The Hague, Martinus Nijhoff.

Thomas, G. (1991) *Linguistic Purism.* London: Longman.

Todorov, T. (1982) *The Conquest of America.* New York: Harper.

Van Dijk, T. A. (1993) *Elite Discourse and Racism.* Newbury Park, CA: Sage.

Van Dijk, T. A. (1996) Discourse, power and access. In C. R. Caldas-Coulthard and
    M. Coulthard (eds) *Texts and Practices: Readings in Critical Discourse Analysis* (pp.
    84–104). London: Routledge.
Wenger, E. (1998) *Communities of Practice: Language, meaning and identity.* Cam-
    bridge: Cambridge University Press.

9 Critical Discourse Method of Field: Tracking the ideological shift in Australian governments 1983–1986

BERNARD McKENNA
Queensland University of Technology

Abstract

This paper presents an efficacious methodology for analysing ideological shifts over time. It draws on over 100 documents, mostly parliamentary debate, from the period of Australian Labor Party governments from 1983 to 1996 to track the shift in labourist discourse during the 13 years of Labor rule.

This methodology reconfigures Fairclough's (1989, 1992) critical discourse method. An attractive feature of Fairclough's method is that it avoids the Foucauldian trap of dissolving structural foci of power by overemphasising the capillaries. That is, Fairclough understands that social relations at the capillary level make sense only in terms of the overarching relations to the means of production and their reinforcing hegemony.

The paper is in three parts:

(1) An outline of my theory of discourse

(2) Applying Fairclough's critical discourse methodology

(3) Evaluating The Critical Discourse Method.

Theoretical Basis

This methodology uses critical post-structuralism and language theory. It assumes that discourse is bounded by three determining elements: spatio-

131

temporal location, macrostructure, and the microstructure inhabited by people (subjects) engaged in daily practice. It assumes that discourse provides a range of possible object, subject, and ethical configurations. That is, various macro-structural aspects provide possible discursive formations from which emerge, at an intermediate level, discourses that, in turn, at the micro-structural level provide texts and utterances instantiating 'objective reality', subject positions, and ethical dispositions.

This analysis does not consider the micro-level of spatio-temporal location – the physical site in which humans go about their business, or their socio-cultural environment – as this is more properly undertaken in ethnography, conversation analysis, and document analysis. Rather, it considers the macrostructure, the overarching rationalities that provide coherence to discursive formations by rationality, faith, authority, or tradition. Such rationalities construct humans socially and construct reality 'objectively'. This is not inconsistent with the way that Foucault (1972) identifies types of discursive formations as occurrences where one can discern a regularity of themes, order, correlations, positionings, and functionings between a number of statements (p. 38). In brief, human beings apprehend material reality by objectifying the world through discourse, and by comporting themselves in subjectivities that allow them to operate upon that material reality in practical and ethical ways.

My definition of *discourse* is largely consistent with Foucault and Fairclough. Discourse is an 'unconscious structure of conscious thought as the *a priori* organ-ising principle' of what people think and say, and so constrains the expression of thought to operate within certain limits (Bannet, 1989: 164). These limits are the epistemic and ethical bases of the discursive formation, which are then manifested in the range of possible statements in a given discourse (Foucault, 1972: 191). According to Fairclough (1995), discourse is a way 'of signifying areas of experi-ence from a particular perspective' (p. 134). This paper limits itself to analysing the construction of an 'objective reality' of material conditions in Australia from 1983 to 1996. Discursive formations maintain unity, not by epistemologically freezing the object, but by regulating the space in which the 'various objects emerge and are continuously transformed' (Foucault, 1972: 32). The 'space' within which a discursive formation operates is regulated by the relationship between 'institutions, economic and social processes, behavioural patterns, systems of norms, techniques, types of classification, and modes of characterisation' (p. 45).

Discourses vary at different rates according primarily to the relations of power within the macrostructure through dialogical and dialectical encounter. All texts derive from discourses, and operate socially in one of three ways or a combination of these: exclusion and monologism ('the forces of stasis and fixity'), dialogism, and dialectic ('movement, change and diversification'). The steps from monologism to dialectic form a continuum from low to high agency of discourse participants: as Bakhtin says, the communicative sphere is 'the terrain of a ceaseless battle between ... the centripetal tendency towards integration and the centrifugal forces towards usurpation and new formations' (Gardiner, 1992: 34).

An industrial relations dialectic began in the 1980s in Australia when right-wing forces criticised the macro-structural arrangements of power. Cravenly, the Hawke Labor Government incorporated much of the discourse to maintain relevance to the new discursive thrust (Luke, Nakata, Singh & Smith, 1993; Stewart, 1990; Stilwell, 1986). Labor policy was 'marked progressively by the development and implementation of a technocratic rationality' (Luke *et al.*, 1993: 140) and ignoring the distributional implications. This discursive capitula-tion led to a new macro-structural rationale (the 'overarching rationality'), changed the modalities of the workplace, and reconstructed the institutional framework (awards replaced by enterprise bargaining) that had remained intact since the inception of the Conciliation and Arbitration Commission in 1904.

Although as Gramsci argues, hegemonic domination is primarily economic, it is not a totalising hegemony. Hegemony is best understood in terms of the options to coerce (or be coerced), or to seek consent (or give consent). Gramsci and Foucault agree that 'the operations of power and their success depend on consent from below' (Holub, 1992: 29). Gramsci's notion of consent implies the need to 'transform' oneself, 'for in "consenting" ... social reality becomes something *other* than what it would have been, had the act of consent not occurred' (Hoffman, 1984: 124–5). Bourdieu (1991) similarly asserts that all symbolic domination presupposes that those who submit, engage in a form of complicity 'which is neither passive submission to external constraint nor a free adherence to values' (pp. 50–1).

To summarise, I adopt Gramsci's notion of a hegemonic formation as 'a social and political space' unified through the imposed logic and political relations on the inhabitants of that space. In the economic sphere, a stage is reached where the corporate interests of one group 'transcend the corporate limits of the purely economic class, and can and must become the interests of other subordinate groups too' (Gramsci, 1971: 181–2). As a consequence, the prevailing ideology propagates itself by creating a relative discursive unity in society's macro-structural configuration, and within the subjects themselves. At this stage, ideology becomes hegemonic.

Fairclough's Critical Discourse Methodology

Operationalising these theoretical concepts to analyse Australian industrial relations proved less difficult than one might imagine given the combination of neo-Marxist and Foucauldian theories of the social, with Bakhtinian and Hallidayan theories of language. Such an approach combines the supra-sentential notions of ideology, hegemony, and power with the intersentential specificity of textual analysis. Fairclough's method is particularly useful because it yields such a rich lode of information at the textual level, and at the discursive level. More importantly for this research is that it provides through the Foucauldian notion of fields a means of identifying the diachronic shifts in ideology.

Fields

Fairclough (1992: 45–7) develops the concept of field from Foucault (1972) to look at the interdiscursive relationship of texts. Three forms of discursive coexistence (*presence, concomitance,* and *memory*) configure an 'enunciative field'.

The first level of my analysis of individual texts uses field theory to link one text with another to track the diachronic shifts in the 'objective' world from text to text. Texts belonging to a field of **presence** are those 'formulated elsewhere and taken up in discourse, acknowledged to be truthful, involving exact description, well-founded reasoning, or necessary presupposition' (Fairclough 1992: 46). The field of presence also involves those discursive elements deliberately excluded for being incorrect.

Concomitant texts, are those that interdiscursively 'concern quite different domains of objects, and belong to quite different domains of objects, and belong to quite different types of discourse, but … serve as analogical confirmation, or … as a general principle and as premises accepted by a reasoning, or … serve as models that can be transferred to other contents' (Foucault, 1972: 58). I modify this to mean emergent discourses or, as Fairclough says, 'statements from different discursive formations' (1992: 46). Although not elaborated much by Fairclough, the concept of emergent discourses is crucial in a diachronic discourse model. Because texts do not simply emerge, it is important to identify the discursive domains from which they come: that is, discursive fields concomitant with the traces of the emergent discourse. Thus it is necessary to identify antecedent discourses, a concept consistent with the proposition that 'the utterance is related not only to preceding, but also subsequent links in the chain of speech communication' (Bakhtin, 1994: 87).

Finally, the field of **memory** includes those discourses that simply fade out. It does not include explicitly rejected discourses (listed in the field of presence). Instead, these texts are a little like the fading out of clothing fashions or hairstyles. For this reason, identifying texts from the field of memory requires careful tracking if their disappearance is to be recorded.

Textual analysis

The textual analysis uses two complementary analyses: linguistic analysis and interdiscursive analysis (Fairclough, 1995: 188). The analysis begins with descriptive textual analysis and then interprets this from a macrosociological (interdiscursive) perspective.

Because systemic functional linguistics (SFL) treats the grammar of the text as the 'realisation of a discourse' it is used here to analyse text. The task of grammar is to encode the various meanings deriving from these various functions of discourse into articulated structures (Halliday, 1979: 22). Because SFL assumes mutually predictive (solidary) relations between the text and the social context in which the text occurs, it does not consider texts as decontextualised entities for grammatical analysis; rather, SFL assumes that texts realise social practices (Halliday, 1979). Because ideology is embedded in everyday discursive practices, a textual analytical method founded on the link between language and social practice is clearly appropriate.

Thus, the analysis works on the assumption that there are traces of the social in the text. By analysing text, the social is made evident. The text and discourse analysis is therefore organised around this fundamental understanding. Figure 1 outlines the analytical method.

Level 1: Textual Analysis
Word Level
  Lexical Choices (includes lexical strings)
  Nominalizations (part of grammatical metaphor)
  (Literary) Metaphor
Grammar Level
  Process Type
  Modality
  Theme and Subject
  Cohesion
  Coherence

Link: Context

Level 2: Discourse Analysis
  Intertextuality
  Interdiscursivity
  Fields (Presence, Concomitance, and Memory)
  Subject and Ethos

Figure 1 Overview of the textual analysis

Starting the analysis

Before starting the linguistic analysis I identified labourist discourse to establish an original field of presence. I did this by analysing many documents from the trade union and parliamentary wings of the Australian labour movement from 1879 to 1975. After tracking the diachronic shifts in the ideological position of labourism, I established the extant discursive features of labourism in 1975 (when Labor was last in power). These are set out in Figure 2.

Field of Presence

Security for workers should be provided through appropriate wages and conditions, the social policies of a Labor government, and the vigilance of the trade unions in the workplace.

Societies are best understood and managed from a communitarian, not individual or enterprise perspective.

Economic policy should assume that governments intervene in an economy to provide the citizen with a buffer against economic fluctuations.

Field of Concomitance

Although committed to distributing the national wealth and income more equally, a Labor government assists wealth creation by liberating the talents and skills of the citizenry.

Economic nationalism should be promoted so that the citizen has an economic stake in the nation.

The sense of nationhood is not jingoistic, but one that acknowledges the region in which we live, our regional identity.

Field of Memory

Nationalisation of the means of production no longer appropriate, although government enterprises should co-exist with private enterprise.

Figure 2 Field analysis of Labourism at 1975

Corpus for analysis

This abridged analysis looks only at the period from February 1983, one month before the Hawke Labor Government was elected, to the calling of an early election in late 1984.[1] The documents include the *Accord*, an agreement between the ACTU and the then Labor Opposition, and a *Communiqué* issued from the first economic summit that occurred within a month of Hawke's election. The rest of the documents, 43 in all, are taken from the House of

Representatives *Parliamentary Hansards.* These documents were selected in a meticulous analysis of *Hansards* on the basis that they related to industrial relations.

Critical discourse analysis: ALP Government 1983–4

The first *Accord* not only helped Labor win the 1983 election, but also provided a public perception of industrial harmony between the government and the union movement's peak council (ACTU). During Labor's rule there were seven 'Accords'. This analysis begins by analysing the original Accord document, as this provides the discursive foundation of the Labor Government. In office, the Labor government quickly assembled an extra-parliamentary 'summit' at the end of which participants signed a *Communiqué,* that in a dialectical sense set labourism on the defensive against capitalist orthodoxy. Despite this, the analysis of the third document, the Governor-General's speech, suggests that the Labor government was re-establishing its labourist heritage.

These documents reveal emerging dialectical discourses of labourism and neo-liberalism.[2] However, the analysis of the *Hansards* debates reveals the emergence of a wider interdiscursivity and newer, emerging discourse of consensual technocracy within the Government's discourse (concomitant discourse). This paper now presents the findings of these three documents and the Hansards debates, 1983–4, providing a field summary at the end of each.

Document 1: Accord between Australian Labor Party and the ACTU, February 1983

One month prior to the federal election, the Accord describes the prevailing economic conditions (crisis), and identifies the course of action that a Labor government should adopt.

Crisis

This document identifies a crisis of troubling new economic phenomena: *simultaneously high ... unemployment and inflation* for which there are no specific remedies. They eschew *conventional economic policy* because it will not *maintain a situation even remotely resembling full employment.* The metaphor, *unemployment trap,* connotes a lack of control. They dialectically distinguish themselves from neo-classical ideology, claiming that the conservatives' wages freeze is *manifestly unfair* because it exacerbates the inequity of that distribution.

The Accord lacks confidence: *no new policy approach, however radical and innovative, will be capable of meeting in the short term, the parties' prime objective of full employment.* The ALP and the ACTU have *the shared understanding that change must occur if growth is to ensue.* Central to the new policy is a *mutually agreed policy on prices and income,* distinguishable by considering the *longer term advantages* compared with the *short sighted expediency* of the conservatives. Consistent with traditional labourist discourse, policy will be directed to *alleviating unemployment and redistributing income and wealth.*

Trade-off

The central Accord metaphor of a 'trade-off' denotes a reciprocal relation between capital and labour. The Labor Government will establish a *pricing authority* in return for the *maintenance of real wages.* Through a *centralised system of wage fixation,* workers would be compensated for rising prices and share the benefits of increased productivity.

In government, Labor would adopt clearly labourist policies: full employment, communitarianism, corporatism, and protectionism.

Full Employment

The Accord's objective of full employment is *of paramount concern* because widespread unemployment is *abhorrent.* The Accord assumes that *wage justice for low wage earners* will overcome poverty, as well as *reducing tax on low income earners,* [and] *raising social security benefits.* Workers and non-workers would be cohesively linked by *the social wage.*

Communitarianism

The document acknowledges the *importance of the shared commitment to facing those difficulties through humane policies based on consensus.* The prices-and-income policy would effect *an equitable distribution of real disposable income* with *the goal of maintaining and gradually improving the living standards of all Australians.* Industrial relations would be characterised by *co-operation, not confrontation.*

Corporatism

Trade unions would significantly influence policy decisions in industrial development, technological change, immigration, education, and health. The Labor government would be [*i*]*nterventionist* using a *planning mechanism* requiring the *co-ordination of the ministries covering economic planning, industry and trade.* The new Labor Government would use *detailed economic planning* rather than market forces. This corporatist discourse is clearly antithetical to liberal free market discourse, which is identified and despatched to a field of negative presence. Market-based economic management is *ad hocery*; and recent history has revealed the *hopelessness of* [market-based] *policies.*

Discursively, the Accord unequivocally upholds the following labourist fields of presence:

- Security for the worker provided through appropriate wages and conditions.
- Communitarian societies, not individualistic or enterprising.
- Economic policy assumes that governments intervene to buffer the citizen against economic fluctuations.

A concomitant discourse of protectionism emerges. It merges with economic nationalism in dealing with transnational corporations. International free trade must be subordinate to national interests: *changes to protection in the future will be determined within the planning mechanisms in which unions and business will play key roles.* The *unfettered actions* of transnational corporations (TNCs) *will be regulated.* These are unequivocal, unmodalised statements.

Figure 3 summarises the field analysis of Labourist discourse in the Accord document.

Presence
Full employment is paramount for workers.
Communitarian concern with eliminating poverty.
Government intervention in economy to regulate prices and incomes.

Concomitance
No distinction made between employed and unemployed in terms of right to decent standard of living.
Corporatist approach allows union involvement in decision making.
Globalised economy recognised

Memory
Labour's dialectical relationship with capital replaced by co-operation.

Figure 3 Field analysis: Accord 1983

Document 2: National Economic Summit Communiqué

On winning office, Hawke called a National Economic Summit (NES), which was attended by business, trade union, and NGOs representatives. The Summit provided the first dialectical encounter, blunting the preceding strongly labourist discourse. A dialectic emerges from the separate expressions of concern by employers and the trade union movement. Labour's capitulation to employer interests before parliament had even sat is evident in the lexical analysis. Discursively, it is also evident in the emergent discourse of international competitiveness and by the incorporation of the profit principle in labour's own discourse.

Employer Concerns

In expressing concern about the *overall unit costs of production and their importance in preserving the competitiveness of business*, employers disguised the dialectical relationship between profits and wages. Business argues that *increased profitability is now essential if new investment is to be generated at an effective level.* By not claiming profit as a reward for entrepreneurial risk taking, profit is discursively represented as socially useful, indeed 'essential', a clever ploy by capital to meet the discursive framework within which it needs to operate. The nominal group, *unit costs of production*, recasts the wages-profit nexus in a new technocratic discourse. Business is concerned

> with overall unit costs of production and their importance in preserving the competitiveness of business and therefore its ability to survive, expand and create jobs.

Because wages generally constitute the greatest component of production costs, the nominal group *unit costs of production*, a feature of technocratic discourse, blunts the obvious struggle between capital and labour. This technocratic term is then obliquely related to the market mechanism through the notion of competition. Business survival is related to the social activity of creating jobs, not to the business's desire for more profit. Thus any discursive features of neo-classical economics are recast into socially-oriented discourse.

The employers also disable a fundamental 'trade-off' Accord element of the unions when the Labor Government agrees that the proposed prices authority would not be a *bureaucratic body which artificially tinkers with prices.* The use of *artificially* literally naturalises market forces as a means of determining price, rather than the 'artificial' one agreed in the Accord.

Union Concerns

By contrast, the unions' concerns are tame. Although emphasising *the role ... of real wages ... in job creation*, the trade unions modify their claims for real wage maintenance as *an objective over time,* and agree to offset even this with government social wage expenditures. Furthermore, they concede that the *prices surveillance should not ... deny an adequate return on investment.*

Shared Discourse (Dialogism)

The NES Communiqué contains much shared discourse: a crisis exists; the need for co-operation and restraint; acknowledging each other's legitimate claims; that the disadvantaged need protection; the desire for improved confidence and high growth rates. However, although the unions agree to a *centralised approach to wage fixation*, where stronger unions agree to the *suppression of sectional claims*, capital and management agree only that those on non-wage incomes be *encouraged to agree to have their fees determined on a voluntary basis.* Thus workers' incomes are externally fixed, management incomes may be voluntarily determined.

The tripartite approach to technology is strangely passive. The grammar of the Communiqué statement that *the adoption of new technology may be the only means of remaining competitive* is agentless, modalised, and nominalised. The limited agency suggests that the economy is being driven by technological developments beyond the participants' control. Such limited agency is evident in the later emerging technocratic discourse.

The lexico-grammar clearly shows that the onus of economic recovery would fall on labour. This is evident in the closing Objectives that state that the government will *devise machinery for achieving the necessary restraint, including methods of wage fixation, influencing non-wage incomes, and price surveillance.* Reformulated the sentence states that restraining machinery will be devised to **fix** wages (*wage fixation*); **influence** non-wage incomes, and **survey** prices (*price surveillance*). Clearly the impact of this machinery is more restraining of wages (being fixed) and far less restraining on non-wage incomes and prices.

In summary then, the NES Communiqué emphasises the potency of information (technocratic discourse), and blurs the capital-labour dialectic by using the nominal group, *unit costs of production.* Because of its absence, the commitment to full employment is now in the field of memory. Further debilitating labourist discourse is the acceptance of a fundamental element of capitalist discourse (field of presence status): the Profit–Investment–Jobs nexus. This nexus is inherent in the claim that:

> *to achieve the growth in GDP and employment ..., increased profitability is now essential if new investment is to generated at an effective level.*

When unpacked, this statement reads that profits are necessary for investment that, in turn, is necessary to create jobs. Each of the two logical links is, at the very least, debatable.[3]

The Accord's strident labourist response to international capital is considerably muted in the Communiqué. Whereas the Accord asserts that transnational corporations will be regulated by the state, the Communiqué states simply that *every corporation ... should behave in accordance with the interests of the nation.* This modulated statement places no demands on corporations such as there are to fix workers' wages.

With this weakened labourism, the Labor government then began its parliamentary life.

Document 3: The Governor-General's Speech

Although the government gives *the highest priority to ... restoring sustained growth,* the speech displays few traits of labourist discourse. *Full employment* is not mentioned and conservative economic discourse is drawn on to explain that the *severe budgetary constraints it has inherited* will limit its commitment to job creation. This discursive withdrawal is evident also in references to government intervention and manufacturing industry policy.

Government Intervention

The greatest slippage from labourist discourse is evident in the government's stated intention to intervene in the economy. In discursive terms, what the new government does is to combine the consensus discourse of the NES, with a concomitant technocratic discourse, evident in the statements about economic knowledge. This fusion allows the government to represent itself as the hand-maiden of a consensus decision reached as a result of the substantial information now at its disposal. By emphasising information, the government reveals a technocratic, rather than ideological, approach to economic issues: *an essential ingredient to the success of the Conference was the dissemination of information to an extent not previously attempted in Australia.* In future, *this process of information-sharing* will be *essential to the making of sound economic decisions.*

The new government distances itself from policy formulation and limits the ideological exchange or dialectic. Policy is executed not because of labourist ideology, but because it has been formulated by the technocratically competent. The primary technocracy, the Economic Planning Advisory Council (EPAC), is created *to advise on economic developments and provide a forum for community consultation on national economic and social strategies.*

Manufacturing Sector Policy

The Accord labourist discourse is also compromised in manufacturing policy: *a strong, competitive manufacturing industry* will *be of crucial importance to* [the] *Government's efforts towards national recovery and reconstruction.* The adjective *competitive* interdiscursively links this with neo-classical economics. The absence of references to planning and to integrating with wider social and economic objectives further links this policy with neo-classical discourse.

Thus on its first day of parliament sitting, the new Labor government has been discursively constrained by a hegemonic orthodoxy, although this constraint is blurred somewhat by the concomitant discourses of technocracy and neo-classicism. The field analysis of Labor discourse at this stage (early 1983) is provided in Figure 4.

Presence
Create a More Equal and just society
Eliminate massive unemployment
Price Control
Consultative forum on economic and social strategies (corporatism)

Concomitance
Sustained growth
Budgetary constraints (fiscal prudence)
Dissemination of information

Concomitance
Sustained growth
Budgetary constraints (fiscal prudence)
Dissemination of information
Competitive industry
Incentives to research and development

Memory
Globalism

Figure 4 Field analysis – April 1983

Document 4: House of Representatives Debate 1983–4

Despite the discursive triumph of capitalist orthodoxy, conservative (LNP) members of parliament vigorously attacks the NES and the Communiqué. Their dialectic is not just anti-union – predictable for conservative political parties – but is one that allows a significant re-emergence in their own discourse of neo-classical economics within a neo-liberal universe. They do this by simultane-ously drawing on the discourse of small business – big business had become cosy with the PM – and by portraying the government as lacking *the courage to stand firm against ... trade unions* [who] *are really telling the government what to do.* The small enterprise owner is the new underclass in a corporate state dominated by *bully boy* unions. One Liberal backbencher argues that:

> *trade unions, socialism and small business are not compatible, because entrepreneurship, diligence, profit and the creation of wealth which small business means and is all about, are threats to the union movement.*

A discordant and a cohesive collocation is presented here. The discordant one claims that trade unions and small business are incompatible. The cohesive collocation links *entrepreneurship, diligence, profit, and the creation of wealth* with small business. Clearly these latter collocations have deep roots in the antecedent discourses of neo-classical economics. The Labor Party responds to these ideological attacks mostly by contrasting the new consensual order with the conflictual old order; and attempting to establish this new order as a universalising orthodoxy: *We need to get together, not shout at each other.* The Labor government is suggesting that class-based politics is irrelevant.

Although the Hawke Government maintains some of its labourist discourse, the analysis reveals that its discourse is largely colonised by neo-liberal discourse. It also reveals two emerging discourses (concomitance): *Consensual Technocracy*; and *Flexibility Discourse.*

Labor Adopts Neo-Classical Discourse

While maintaining some vestiges of labourist discourse, the Labor Government simultaneously incorporates the fundamental neo-classical claim that increased private sector profit is necessary to create more jobs. This *Profit– Investment–Jobs* nexus is seen in backbencher Mr Bilney's statement:

> *It is quite clear to honourable members on this side of the House that there will not be a genuine, sustained, lasting, recovery unless jobs are created in the private sector. ... The Government is well aware that ... profits need to be such that investment can take place and jobs can be created.*

Using *It is* and *there will be* eradicates modality, thus presenting an existential state of being for an anticipated future. The first existential process (verb) is emphasised by the adjective *clear.* The subject-complement, a noun-clause (with an embedded conditional clause), *that there will not be ... the private sector,* is therefore presented as an unequivocal universal statement of fact. After creating this 'objective' state of being, Bilney then builds a syllogistic argument from this 'objective' premise in the first sentence. Thus the contorted syllogism runs:

- Only the private sector creates jobs.
- The private sector needs profits.
- If profits, then investment
- If investment, then jobs.

Bilney's universal claims and reasoning are strongly supported by other Labor members, and Mr Howard, then Deputy Leader of the Opposition, who claims that *an increase in the profit share from ... [is] essential if new employment opportunities [are] to be created.*

Consensual Technocracy

The essence of consensual technocracy is that an idealised classlessness is made possible by operationalising *independent, objective* data into *plans,* which are the blueprints from which managers make neutral decisions. Introducing the EPAC Bill, Treasurer Keating states the *Government will have available to it ... independent advice ... which will be invaluable to the process of economic policy formulation.* Elsewhere, the nominal group *broad indicative planning* is used to separate this sort of planning from socialism. EPAC's apparent objectivity, based on *knowledge*, is to be mediated through a *representative* body external to parliament. According to Keating, *knowledge sharing ... plays an integral part in establishing a common perception.* The nominal group *common perception* means that participants apprehend a shared objective reality, which is possible only if ideology is negated because we draw upon common contextual resources. In this way, public policy is sanitised by appearing to be not ideological, and is dialogical, not dialectical, because of *consensus.* However, this technocracy, the Economic Planning Advisory Council, lacks agency as its analysis will allow *the nation to try to assess the longer term trends and to seek to influence them in a desirable direction.* From the outset, the Labor Government's combined technocratic and neo-classical discourses make it indistinguishable from the conservatives.

Flexibility Discourse

A subtly emerging concomitant discourse is *flexibility* in industrial relations matters. Inflexible industrial relations processes collocate negatively with the freedom that business needs. Thus, it is necessary to *remove some of the inflexibilities in the present systems.* This nominal lexical feature of flexibility increasingly dominates the economic discourse of government and opposition. The conservative deputy leader claims that the *redeeming feature* in the US economy *has been a remarkable downward flexibility of US wages.* Applied to the labour force, *flexibility* implies downward movement, or diminution. Applied to capital, it implies the neo-classical assumption that capital is free to maximise production or profits or markets. For example, the Opposition Leader congratulates the government when it deregulated the financial markets and floated the exchange rate because they *increase the flexibility of the economy.* This freedom of enterprise is represented as an *environment* that governments are supposed to provide. Restraining business, the Opposition represents as *being strapped ... with more and more bureaucratic red tape,* or as *controls and regulations which* [are] *squeezing industry.* These metaphors provide a contrasting corollary of flexibility.

Labor's Capitulation

In blending neo-classical economic with technocratic discourse the Labor government forced the labourism of the Accord into the field of memory. The conservatives were strategically successful in identifying wage fixation as virtually the only definite agreed action in the *NES Communiqué.* The *nexus between unemployment and wage rises* was presented as a virtual iron law. Centralised wage fixing thus became the focus of the government's economic policy because it would *ensure that the living standards of wage and salary earners and the non-income earning sectors of the population are maintained over time with movements in national productivity.* In this way the government's communitarian commitment was overwhelmed by economic management discourse to the extent that wage restraint became the defining point of Labor's management credentials. Roles reversed when the Labor Treasurer, Keating, castigated the Liberal opposition for having *no idea how to restrain wages in a recovery,* and by proclaiming the Profit–Investment–Jobs nexus as axiomatic:

> *if we hold wages down long enough we will get a bigger restoration of the profit share, higher investment and growth.*

In other words, by 29 November 1983 when Keating made this statement, labourist discourse is completely supplanted by capitalist discourse: game, set, and match. The Minister for Employment and Industrial Relations, Mr Willis, incorporated both technocratic and neo-classical economics boasting that the

> *level of real labour unit costs will be back to the level of a decade ago. ... Such an outcome is conducive to ... a continued improvement in our level of economic competitiveness.*

History now reveals that capital was strategically successful. Wages increased by one-third of the increase in prices, and the wages share fell considerably to allow profits a greater share of the national product.

The Labor Government continually referred to fulfilling its part of the Communiqué *trade-off* by restraining wages, effectively shifting attention away from management responsibilities. On one of the few occasions when the focus was broadened beyond labour costs, a minister, Mr Duffy, identified other elements that could improve economic performance such as new investment, upgrading facilities, tighter management, and improved work practices. Duffy also draws on 19th-century socialist discourse, now part of the memory field, to assert that the labour movement has a *duty to investigate deeply the remote sources of our actual condition.* In other words, Duffy's statement provides one of the few instances where labour actually (indirectly) challenges the neo-classical episteme.

Labor could claim to be the party of fiscal responsibility contrasting with the ineptitude of the previous conservative government, which Keating claimed *went beyond the limits of fiscal responsibility.* PM Hawke asserted that the conservative government *was totally incapable of taking the hard decisions that were necessary for the economic management of this country.* Fiscal policy is a discursive domain, although often dominated by technocratic discourse, in which labourist concerns about the redistribution of wealth and income are fought out. The conservatives dialectically positioned themselves as anti-socialist, anti-taxation and government expenditure. For example, the Opposition Leader stated this ideological distinction:

> *the choice will be between a socialist government which spends more,* [and] *adds to the debt of this nation ... and the Opposition, which is dedicated to*

achieving growth and development through the private sector and to freeing up that private sector through proper economic management of the public sector.

Far from challenging these assumptions, the Labor government claimed greater competence in reducing the size of government. Explaining the government's 1984 budget, a minister asserted that the budget *strikes an appropriate balance between the need to reduce the deficit and the need to ensure a continuance of economic activity until private investment picks up.* Terms like *appropriate balance* and the *need to reduce the deficit* clearly identify this as neo-classical orthodoxy because appropriateness and needs are meaningful only within this shared episteme.

The Labor Government depoliticised this neo-classical discourse by technocratising it. For example, Hawke stated that he would ask EPAC *how a government may be able to establish the fairest possible revenue base in this country,* as though 'fairness' is just another variable to factor into an econometric equation, and not the very grounds of ideological difference. Absent from Labor's debate is any textual evidence of traditional labourist demands for equality and fairness.

The clash of ideologies: What clash?

Contrasting with Labor's weak labourism throughout the first two years of Labor Government are the conservatives' unchallenged neo-classical assumptions:

- *free enterprise is the best way of achieving economic growth which will result in jobs.*
- *only through the private enterprise sector and through individual initiative* [will] *Australia get itself out of this mess.*
- *The market-place will work and it must be allowed to work.*

Rather than challenge this hegemonic discourse, Labor incorporated it, concomitantly, into its own. As an hegemonic discourse and material practice, neo-liberal capitalism defines the necessary conditions – characterised lexically as *climate* or *environment* – for its existence. The government

- *should be ... encouraging a climate for the growth of business* (conservative backbencher).
- *must create an environment in which ... business has the capacity and incentive to invest and grow* (Opposition Leader).

Significantly, there is no equivalent *climate* for the worker. Instead, the Minister for Employment and Industrial Relations stated, 14 months into Labor's office, that the lowest real labour unit costs in a decade is *very conducive to the creation of an environment which is highly conducive to an increase in private investment.* By this stage, the interdiscursive mix of technocracy and neo-classicism is complete.

Labor's Discourse Fields After One Term (1983–4)

The following summarises the discursive situation at the end of 1984 when the Hawke Government called a snap election.

Field of Presence

Not one of the three labourist fields of presence (i.e. maintaining previous discourses in an intertextual chain) contained in the original Accord remained intact by the end of 1984. The only surviving item in the field of presence is the modified one that unions have a vital role to play in representing the working classes. Only one minister draws on the memory field to ask about the structural sources of the current condition.

Field of Concomitance

The concomitant discourses (i.e. new discursive links) used in the early years of the Hawke Government were conflicting and inconsistent. They included:

Labourist-inclined discourses:

- corporatism involving state, capital, and labour;
- consensus discourse, de-ideologising the labour-capital dialectic.

However, technocratic discourse incorporates a hegemonic economic orthodoxy based on neo-classical principles.

Neo-classical inclined discourses

Labor's discourse is interdiscursively infused with the nominals of the market-place and flexibility. It also adopts the conservative doxa[4] of Profit-Investment-Jobs and the need for 'business confidence'.

Field of Memory

Two important features of labourist discourse slip from the Hawke Government's discourse: regulation of transnational corporations; protectionism is ambivalent.

Evaluating the Critical Discourse Method

Resting upon a critical theory of discourse, this method uses two analytical approaches: (inter)discourse analysis and lexico-grammatical text analysis. These approaches identified diachronic discursive shifts into fields of presence, concomitance, and memory. The fields of presence and concomitance provided the overarching rationalities that become hegemonic as the Labor Government and unions consented to the objective and ethical constraints of the blended discourses. This hegemonic rationality is linguistically instantiated in the texts of the parliamentary debate records (*Hansards*) and official documents. An important finding from the emerging, or concomitant, discourses is technocratic discourse (described elsewhere in relatively exact lexico-grammatical terms: see McKenna & Graham, 1999).

This dual analytical method proved efficacious because it helped to identify contemporary and emergent discourses. These discursive features revealed the rapid capitulation of labourist discourse to neo-liberal politics and neo-classical economics. This capitulation is confirmed by the consigning to the field of memory those discursive features that had defined labourism: worker security; income and wealth redistribution; government intervention; and communitarianism.

Notes

1. My doctoral thesis covered the entire period of government to March 1966.
2. Neo-liberalism in this paper refers broadly to the ideology based on individualism and political libery. Neo-classical economics refers to principles of free trade and private enterprise. The decisions of *homo economicus* acting out of self-interest to maximise their utility thereby maximises social utility and efficiency of production.
3. e.g. the division of profit into re-investment and dividends is at the discretion of the firm and may not lead to job creation at all. Investment is quite often directed to replacing and deskilling labour, a problem that is compounded in Australia which is a capital importer (cf. Argy, 1998).
4. Doxa constitute the 'common sense' of everyday practice in which people draw upon 'self-evident' maxims (Bourdieu & Eagleton, 1992).

References

Argy, F. (1998) *Australia at the Crossroads: Radical free market or a progressive liberalism?* St Leonards: Allen and Unwin.
Bakhtin, M. M. (1994) From M. M. Bakhtin, Speech genres and other late essays (translated by M. Holquist and C. Emerson). In P. Morris (ed.) *The Bakhtin Reader: Selected writings of Bakhtin, Medvedev, Voloshinov* (pp. 81–7). London: Edward Arnold.
Bannet, E. T. (1989) *Structuralism and the Logic of Dissent: Barthes, Derrida, Foucault, Lacan.* Urbana & Chicago: University of Illinois Press.
Bourdieu, P. (1991) *Language and Symbolic Power* (edited by J. B. Thompson; translated by G. Raymond and M. Adamson). Cambridge UK: Polity Press.
Bourdieu, P. and Eagleton, T. (1992) Doxa and common life: In conversation. *New Left Review* 191, 111–21.
Fairclough N. (1989) *Language and Power.* Essex: Longman.
Fairclough N. (1992) *Discourse and Social Change.* Cambridge: Polity Press.
Fairclough, N. (1995) *Critical Discourse Analysis: The critical study of language.* London & New York: Longman.
Foucault, M. (1972) *The Archaeology of Knowledge.* London: Tavistock.

Gardiner, M. (1992) *The Dialogics of Critique: M. M. Bakhtin and the theory of ideology.* London & New York: Routledge.

Gramsci, A. (1971) *Selections from the Prison Notebooks* (edited by Q. Hoare; translated by G. Nowell Smith). London: Lawrence and Wishart.

Halliday, M. A. K. (1979) *Language as Social Semiotic: The social interpretation of language and meaning.* London: Edward Arnold.

Halliday, M. A. K. and Martin, J. R. (1993) *Writing Science: Literacy and discursive power.* London: Falmer Press.

Hoffman, J. (1984) *The Gramscian Challenge: Coercion and consent in Marxist political theory.* NY: Basil Blackwell.

Holub, R. (1992) *Antonio Gramsci: Beyond Marxism and postmodernism.* London & New York: Routledge.

Luke, A., Nakata, M., Singh, M. S. and Smith, R. (1993) Policy and the politics of representation: Torres Strait Islanders and Aborigines at the margins. Paper from James Cook University of North Queensland.

McKenna, B. J. and Graham, P. (1999) Technocratic discourse: A primer. Manuscript submitted for publication.

Stewart, R. (1990) Industrial policy. In C. Jennett and R. Stewart (eds) *Hawke and Australian public policy: Consensus and restructuring* (pp. 105–36). South Melbourne: Macmillan.

Stilwell, F. (1986) *The Accord and Beyond: The political economy of the Labor Government.* Sydney & London: Pluto Press.

10 'Risk is the Mobilising Dynamic of a Society Bent on Change'[1]: How metaphors help to stabilise the developing discourse of the learning society, and how they don't

ALISON PIPER, *University of Southampton* and
CHARMIAN KENNER, *Institute of Education, University of London*

Abstract

Discourses of culture, politics and social life are 'characterised by debate around a relatively small set of key words which frequently occur' and which 'gain stability when they fit into a schema' (Stubbs, 1996: 159, 162). This paper aims, in both a theoretical and methodological sense, to develop this notion of keyword-based stability, and to do so with particular reference to metaphor. In using the developing discourse of 'the learning society' as an example, it examines metaphors associated with two words – change and learning – at a point where government policies for learning articulate with contemporary social theories of change in late modernity. The data of the study consist of an 850,000-word corpus of recent British and EU literature on lifelong learning. Using concordances to manipulate this data, the study demonstrates how the analysis of large scale repetitional patterns of collocation makes it possible to reveal metaphors which represent covert but conflicting agendas within the official discourse of the learning society – metaphors of change as motion and learning as a journey. In analysing their implications for discourse stability, the paper concludes by examining the notion that 'metaphor constructs, motivates and constrains concepts' (Cameron, 1999: 18) and suggests the possibilities and limitations of metaphor analysis for evaluating social policy.

Introduction

'Modern society will be a learning society' announces the European Commission (European Commission, 1996b: para. 143). And in this 'self-perpetuating Learning Society', says the Kennedy Report on Further Education in the UK, 'the pace of change in the economy, and in society more widely, is such that we will all need to develop and add to our work skills. The ability to learn is the most important skill and the central thrust of public policy for learning should be the development of the capacity to learn throughout life' (Further Education Funding Council, 1997: 23).

Here we have two of many thousands of official comments on the learning society, a concept and now a whole discourse of very recent formation. The British government has announced a raft of initiatives such as the National Grid for Learning and the University for Industry (UfI) and set up a whole web site of lifelong learning policies and reports (Department for Education and Employment, 1999), while the European Parliament designated 1996 as the European Year of Lifelong Learning (European Commission, 1996a) which produced a similar flurry of reports (see European Union, 1999). Commentary and critique too is being produced on a similar scale (e.g. Dohmen, 1996; Economic and Social Research Council, 1997; Smith & Spurling, 1999). As linguists we have much to understand about how such new concepts and discourses emerge. How do they become stable and taken for granted, or what kind of internal contradictions exist which undermine this stability? How do they contribute to and evolve from understandings of social life, in the case of our study from contemporary perceptions of change and risk?

Of the many possible answers to these questions, in this paper we pursue the issue of metaphor. After some brief comments on social theories of change and risk and on the notion of metaphor itself, we carry out a preliminary analysis of some keywords in the discourse of the learning society from which we then identify a range of metaphors associated with change and with learning. In the light of these, we examine the notion of 'generative metaphor' (Schön, 1993) and theoretical claims that 'metaphor constructs, motivates and constrains concepts' (Cameron, 1999: 18). Finally we consider the possibilities and limitations of metaphor as a stabilising influence on a discourse and the potential offered by metaphor analysis in evaluating social policy.

In recent work on the learning society (Piper, in press 2000a,b), Piper has explored two of Stubbs's claims concerning the development of discourses of culture, politics and social life. The first is that such discourses are 'characterised by debate around a relatively small set of key words which frequently occur' and which 'gain stability when they fit into a schema' (Stubbs, 1996: 159, 162); the second is that by studying such recurrent wordings circulating in the social world, we can 'glimpse how linguistic categories become social categories' (ibid: 194). Through corpus-based analysis of the collocational behaviour of *learning* and of two of its key participants – *individuals* and *people* – it was possible to demonstrate the reiterative power of such keywords in constructing the institutionalised concept of 'the learning society' and to situate it within theoretical models of late modernism such as human and social capital, individualism, consumption, risk and reflexivity.

One of the public tips of this iceberg-like phenomenon of cultural production is 'The Third Way', a political concept which includes the notions of change and risk which are the topics of this paper.[2] 'The Third Way' is both a book by the British Prime Minister's allegedly favourite sociologist (Giddens, 1998) and the denotation of a 'new' principle of the centre-left, a political grouping manifested in Britain as New Labour. It has also cynically been described by a well-known journalist as inhabiting 'some vacant space between the Fourth Dimension and the Second Coming' (Francis Wheen, no reference available). The book describes 'the overall aim of third way politics' as being 'to help citizens pilot their way through the major revolutions of our time: *globalisation, transformations in personal life* and our *relationship to nature*' (Giddens, 1998: 64, original italics). It explicates risk as a double-sided property of change, which draws attention not only to the dangers we face 'but also to the opportunities that go along with them'. Thus it is 'not just a negative phenomenon – something to be avoided or minimized. It is at the same time the energizing principle of a society that has broken away from tradition and nature' (Giddens, 1998: 62–3). So where we have official policy-makers proposing a learning society of change and opportunity, sociologists present 'the risk society' (Beck, 1992), a place both of uninsurable and uncontrollable manufactured dangers of a nuclear, genetic and ecological kind and also of heavily marketed insurance and security arrangements. In this combination risk is a typically reflexive product of late modernity. 'Avoidance imperatives' may dominate the risk society but their effect is not to minimise danger but to produce a perpetual revision of what constitutes it. 'Risks are infinitely reproducible', so that 'the expansion and heightening of the intention of control ultimately ends up producing the opposite' (Beck, 1994: 9).

Metaphor and the Learning Society

All these explications of the learning society, of change and risk and of the Third Way were chosen to introduce this paper because they provide brief and representative accounts, not because they include particular metaphors. However the world which they embody is represented as a shifting metaphorical place of containers, pathways, movements and natural forces. These are the kind of metaphors we shall be tracking, following a cognitive approach which sees 'the sources of metaphor' as lying in image schemas, frames and scripts, which arise from the interaction of bodily and cultural experience' (Chilton, 1996: 73; Lakoff, 1993; and particularly Lakoff & Johnson, 1980).

Chilton's major study of 'security metaphors' and the Cold War has been a strong influence on our current project. In presenting a detailed interpretation of metaphors, particularly of containment, in the international relations of the period, he demonstrates the ways in which metaphor can play both a cognitive and an interactive role in policy making and diplomacy and how the concept of security changed as it was mediated through political discourse. His emphasis on the social, cultural and political dimensions of concept formation, not well integrated into more cognitive approaches (ibid: 47), is evidence that 'metaphor is a part of discourse, and discourse is a part of the process of forming and changing concepts' in a way which is linked to recurrent human experiences (ibid: 73–4). Metaphors can thus act as a stabilising framework within which change can take place.

Such recursive and constructivist theories of late modernism are also reflected in Schön's study of 'generative metaphor' (Schön, 1993). He examines how housing problems were metaphorised in different decades by 'naming and framing' (ibid: 146) a few salient features and relations for attention – 'blight and renewal' in the 1950s (a disease which must be cured) and 'a dislocated natural community' in the 1960s (something natural must be protected/restored). These descriptively coherent 'stories' were then used to set the direction for transformation. However, problematising 'A as B' sets in train a potential conflict of means and ends, 'disanalogies' which may derive as much from the problem setting process as from the original situation itself (ibid: 144). The resulting transformations can then be highly unproductive.

How Chilton and Schön theorise metaphor as a means of understanding specific political and social contexts is highly relevant to understanding the contemporary development of the discourse of the learning society. In such a short paper as this, however, our aim will be to identify metaphors in the form in which they are produced by writers rather than to analyse them in terms of how they are actually used and understood by other participants in the discourse. Thus we set out to determine metaphoricity at what Cameron describes as the 'theory level' (identification and categorisation) rather than at the 'processing level' (concept activation or modification by the user) (Cameron, 1999: 7), seeking to establish what metaphors of the 'bodily and cultural' type appear particularly salient in the discourse. The outcomes of the study can then act as a basis for further work in exploring their pragmatic significance.

Hypotheses, Data and Method

Our initial assumption was that, in line with the results of the earlier work on *individuals* and *people*, we would find that in the official texts of the *learning* society learning would be linked with social and cultural change, upheaval and risk. Our questions were how far and in what ways this association would be manifested metaphorically, and to what extent any such metaphors might be said to stabilise this new discourse. In order to ensure comprehensive coverage of these official texts, we used a corpus of 850,000 words, all of which, except for the Kennedy Report (Further Education Funding Council, 1997), was down-loaded from the internet in July 1999. Most of the material was taken from the Department for Education and Employment's lifelong learning site (Department for Education and Employment, 1999), and included major government and quasi government policy documents, reports of research or 'learning projects', and more informal matter such as on-line newsletters; some was obtained via the search facility of the European Union website (European Union, 1999). We manipulated the data using *Wordsmith Tools* (Scott, 1997), particularly the con-cordancing facility. This allows searches of words in the context of other words and presents collocations of node words; unless we indicate otherwise, we examined collocations within five words either side of the node. The analysis was carried out through personal interpretation of the processed data.

Change and Learning

Before examining *change* in the discourse of the learning society as a whole, we explore how it operates in the context of the word *learning*. We look first at some statistics, then at the collocational behaviour of the two lemmas, and finally at patterns in which change and learning occur close together in examples of text.

Table 1 shows the relative frequency of the various forms of the 1,154 occur-rences of the lemma change in the lifelong learning corpus.

Table 1 Occurrences of *change* in the lifelong learning corpus (total = 1,154)

Noun	
• change	389
• changes	391
Verb	
• change	98
• changes	8
• changing	73
• changed	42
Adjective	
• changing	148
• changed	5

In examining metaphors associating *change* with *learning*, we initially looked at the different forms separately but found no substantial difference between them in their metaphorical meanings.

As a recurring theme in the corpus, *change* is in the top 25 lexical words of the 15,500 total word types. The most common lexical word, unsurprisingly, is *learning*, which occurs 8426 times and represents 0.97 per cent of the total words. *Change*, however, comes far down the list of its collocates, after more than 250 other lexical words. The top ten lexical collocates of the lemma *change* are *work, learning, economic, education, social, technological, need, society, world, time*. While the high position of *learning* is only to be expected, the presence of the classifying adjectives in this list, although they are commonplace enough, is more significant, suggesting that the discourse situates changes in *learning* and *education* within a scenario that is comprehensively socio-economic and/or technological. In terms of the relationship between *change* and *learning*, however, this turns out to be uni-directional: *learning* is an important collocate of *change* but not the other way round. If we explore this association a little further, it is interesting to note that, while *change* has *work* as its top collocate – where it affects its *pattern, organisation, nature, content, structures, processes* and *activities* – this is not true in reverse: *work*'s top five collocates are *learning, training, education, skills, experience*, with *change* much further down the list. If we then look at *work* in the environment of *learning*, it turns out to be *learning*'s fifth top lexical collocate, providing evidence for a bi-directional relationship between *learning* and *work* and suggesting that this is an important axis around which the learning society is (supposed to be?) taking shape. The second feature of the relationship between *change* and *learning* thus turns out to be their strong respective collocations with *work*, shown diagrammatically in Figure 1, where arrows indicate a strong collocation and its direction.

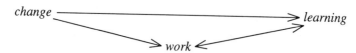

Figure 1 Collocational relationships between *change*, *learning* and *work*

Turning to textual patterns of *learning* and *change* in the corpus, *learning* occurs 69 times within seven words before the lemma *change*, and 77 times in the same word span after it. This is not often given its nearly 8,500 occurrences. When *learning* precedes *change*, it tends to refer to an instrumental activity carried out by implied human actors in response to or as a means of coping with something changing. Usually this is social or work-associated change. This pattern also operates across sentence boundaries, with change coming after a comment or title about learning.

- *Why Learning Direct?*
  The world of work is changing.

- *Teamwork and collaborative learning.*
  Changing skill mixes ... may require skilled workers to work more intensively with others.

- *The Learning City ... needs to learn about the context of change.*

- *lifelong learning, work and citizenship in a rapidly changing world*

- *learning builds capacity to respond to this change*

When *change* precedes *learning*, it tends syntactically to govern the process of learning. It happens in response to the needs of learners, affects the behaviour or attitudes of learners, or changes the way learning is delivered.

- *changing the way we think about learning*

- *the University for Industry:*
  Changing the Way we see Learning

- *changes that are needed to make learning easier*

- *permanent change to allow for adaptability, innovation, learning*

- *sea-change in the public attitude to learning*

- *central to achieving these changes will be the new Institute for Learning and Teaching*

Change when associated with learning thus seems to have two meanings. Rapid changes in society can be dealt with through learning – learning as the answer – but since attitudes to learning and its means of delivery need to be changed in order for it to provide this answer, learning is also a problem, or at any rate an issue. Or put another way, the hoped-for effect is also the precondition. This ambiguity suggests the first of several instabilities in the discourse.

Change and Changes

Is the broad social change which can be solved by learning the same as the process which also needs to be applied to learning? How is change in its ontological sense conceptualised and is this the same for its instrumental sense? To answer these questions we now examine a series of metaphors associated with change, which we identify with motion, with structure, with relative location and with action, all of which we found represented across the whole corpus.

At first sight the most obvious metaphors for *change* relate to MOTION, conceptualised as SPEED and FORCE. This motion, shown by underlining in the following examples, is either an agentless force of nature or something mechanical, even railwaylike.

- *knowledge and skills, which <u>keep pace with</u> change*
- *the <u>speed</u> of change is far greater than it was*
- *<u>accelerating</u> change in many dimensions of life*
- *the <u>scramble to keep up with</u> changing labour market demands*
- *respond creatively to the <u>forces</u> of change*
- *bringing a <u>wind</u> of change*
- *<u>spurred on by</u> the changing world of work*
- *change <u>generates</u> problems*
- *the <u>driving force</u> behind economic change*
- *a <u>mechanism</u> for change*
- *a <u>lever</u> for change*
- *a <u>signal</u> of cultural change*
- *tutors ... provided a kind of '<u>buffer</u>' between rapid educational change ... and the ... experience of the students*

These conceptual frameworks of speed, force and mechanics derive from an underlying schema of change as a Newtonian law of the physical universe. In this metaphor, change is nature and thus outside human control. It is as though governments, financial systems and commercial institutions have no agentive existence in bringing about the learning society.

However, the change as motion schema, while a familiar one, is in fact not very common in the corpus. Far more frequent are the metaphorised propositions which describe responses to change, since change is rarely ignored and invariably stimulates human physical or cognitive engagement. Some responses are embodied processes of control and orientation, such as

- *adapt flexibly to a changing environment, adjust to change, handle change, look at change, the change we face.*

Most of these responses involve mental or verbal control, which seem more like scripts in which human actors are the managers of a bureaucratised institution:

- *bring about changes, targets aimed at changing..., proposals for detailed changes, agenda for change, legislating for change, options for change, implement change, proposed change, choosing to change.*

Change as a law of nature suggests that change is OUTSIDE whatever it is represented as affecting. In the bureaucracy schema, however, change can be subjected to human agency, suggesting that it is INSIDE. In fact we were surprised by the widespread association of change in the corpus with INSIDE, particularly inside a STRUCTURE. Initially we noted structural metaphors of width, depth and solidity, although the following very specific examples are actually rare:

- *profound socio-economic changes, in a time of fundamental change, change should build on ..., a substantial change, structural change, radical change.*

Most often the evidence for change being INSIDE comes from its collocation with *in*, its second most frequent grammatical collocate after *the*. In a concordance of the 389 instances of *change* as a singular noun, 73 of these consisted of *change* in; for a similar number of *changes* in the plural, the number was more than twice this (159). There is *change* or *changes* in

- institutions or practices
  central government initiatives, communication and information systems, pay, price competitiveness, supply and demand, the composition of the populations involved, the distribution of funds, the definition of unemployment, the public attitude to learning, the worlds of work and leisure

- individual human actors
  aspects of their practice, attitudes, career direction.

What emerges is a metaphorical picture of change which has several interacting perspectives. Firstly, change can be INSIDE or OUTSIDE or operating at the boundary between the two. Secondly, change is MOTION, either a FORCE OF NATURE or an ACTION. In this it resembles Lakoff's 'time passing is MOTION', which manifests a duality of metaphorical constructions in which time is both LOCATION (the observer moves in relation to time) and MOVING OBJECT (time moves in relation to the observer) (Lakoff, 1993: 219). While these usually occur separately, they can also be present together, as in his example *within the coming weeks*. How we understand this is explained by Lakoff in terms of his hypothesised Invariance Principle, which allows more than one feature of the source domain of the metaphor to be mapped simultaneously on to corresponding features of the target domain. Thus the two mappings with *change* – INSIDE/OUTSIDE and FORCE OF NATURE/ACTION – can be present together as well as separately. We find this in examples such as

- *equipping him or her to deal with changes* (FORCE OF NATURE) *in the way we live and work* (INSIDE),

- *an orientation towards* (BOUNDARY) *change* (FORCE OF NATURE),

- *legislating for change* (ACTION/INSIDE).

However we disagree with Lakoff in his characterisation of 'changes' as movements 'into or out of bounded regions' (ibid: 220), since our data suggests that change is a movement that may remain INSIDE.

The extensive metaphorisation of change as INSIDE and as ACTION can partly be explained by the socio-economic nature of the corpus; in a meteorological or geological corpus, dominant metaphors of change would probably be expressed as MOTION and OUTSIDE. However the very rationality of the phenomena which change is 'IN' suggest an Enlightenment ideology of ever continuing progress and development which is so long established and so culturally embedded in the system that we fail to notice it.

Curiously for theorists of late modernity, Beck and Giddens rarely refer to change in so many words, even though their writings are concerned with all kinds of nominalised and implied changes like globalisation or individualisation, and generic terms like revolution or transformation. Perhaps the metaphorical containment of change we have just noted means that only the lay person and the policy writer need the word in their script, while the expert social analyst merely dissects its manifestations. Nevertheless in an unusually explicit reference, Giddens uses, in quick succession, several of the metaphors that we have identified: MOTION as FORCE OF NATURE, change INSIDE a structure, the embodied response to change OUTSIDE, MOTION as MECHANICAL FORCE. Talking of change being engendered by globalisation, he talks of 'the sheer sense of being caught up in massive waves of global transformation'. 'Such change' is 'intensive' so that 'it reaches through to the very grounds of individual activity and the constitution of the self ', and 'achieving control over change, in respect of lifestyle, demands an engagement with the outer social world'. At which point he moves on to 'understanding the juggernaut-like nature of modernity' with its constant crises (Giddens, 1991: 183–4). This is a good example of Lakoff's 'simultaneous mappings', very commonly found in poetry (Lakoff, 1993: 219) and almost poetically represented here as a drama of primal forces pitted against the individual psyche.

Risk

It is Giddens who provides the metaphor in our title (Giddens, 1999). In this case, however, it is risk rather than change which is conceptualised as MOTION, in its subdomain of MECHANICAL FORCE. There are only 118 occurrences of *risk* in our corpus, of which the majority are the singular noun, plus a number of instances of particular types of plural *risks* such as *personal* or *financial*. *Risk*, designated as such, plays almost no part in the learning society. In so far as its does and in so far as we can draw conclusions on the basis of so little data, the risk which is most commonly adduced is that of social exclusion and its associated phenomena:

- *a risk of a social rift,* (re evening classes) *a general reluctance on the part of residents to leave their homes owing to the high risk of burglary*

Risk in Giddens's sense of a double-sided property of change in the form of both danger and opportunity only features explicitly once in the corpus. However, singular and plural *opportunity* is a major collocate of *learning* in the corpus, and *learning*, as we have seen, is implied as the solution to problems of both change and social exclusion. The collocational behaviour of *opportunity* thus suggests some implicit entailment-based overlap between the policy makers' 'learning society' and the theorists' 'risk society'.

Learning

Turning now to *learning*, we find that it presents a number of metaphorical faces, some better developed than others. We analysed all forms of *learn* in the corpus: 8,540 instances of *learning* (almost all adjectival nouns or nouns), 1,026 of *learner(s)*, 438 of *learn* and 118 of *learned*. The first three of these proved the most fruitful in terms of their association with metaphor.

The major collocations of *learning* (for a fuller account of which see Piper, in press 2000b) establish it as the purpose of a social or cultural group, particularly a physically located one, as in

- *the learning society, Learning Partnerships, learning organisations, family learning, the Learning City, Learning Centre, Learning Town, learning community,*

where the textual focus is on processes of developing and managing these new institutional formations as much as on the learning itself. These formations most obviously metaphorise themselves as containers, in which learning happens or exists. *Opportunity/opportunities, new,* and *work* are also within the top ten collocations of *learning*, and in the case of *work*, one in three instances consists of the 'contained' concept of *work-based learning* or *learning at work*.

Piper's earlier study, by linking lifelong learning with human capital, showed learning to be represented as a socio-economic activity, an outcome which suggested that learning as MONEY or a SOURCE OF MONEY might turn out to be an important metaphor in our corpus. However this was not the case. Certain texts make frequent use of *individual learning accounts,* and there are variations on *the value of learning, invest in their own learning,* and *the market for learning but this is about all.*

Learning initially looks like an OBJECT OF DESIRE. About 60 concordance lines of *learn* consist of collocations with the infinitive *to learn* such as

• *(the) need, willing(ness), seek(ing), motivated/motivation, commitment, desire, resolution, efforts, choice/choose, strives*

and there is *attracted to learning, a thirst for learning, crave learning opportunities, enthusiasm for learning* and *disenchanted with learning.* It is also a recursive desire contained within itself, so that we have about 40 instances of *learning (how) to learn* plus other variations, culminating in the Chinese box of *the importance of developing in learners learning to learn skills.*

In a corpus with a noticeable absence of health and disease metaphors, learning is also metaphorised in terms of ability and disability. For learning as an ABILITY, we have around 30 instances of *ability to, able to* and *can learn.* 'Not learning', a property of 'non-learners', is a DISABILITY which more powerful agents have a repeated duty to help its possessors to overcome:

• *make it easier for people to learn, enabling people to learn, providing people with opportunities to learn, helping people to learn.*

Support and *need* are the third and fourth highest lexical collocates of *learners.*

However, the most powerful and elaborated metaphor of learning in the corpus is of a JOURNEY, which is particularly associated with the important collocation of *learning* with *new* and *opportunity.* This accords with Lakoff's proposal that, in the event structure metaphor, long term, purposeful activities are journeys (Lakoff, 1993: 220). Here are a few of many examples of the frames and scripts which enrich the metaphor.

• Pathways, networks and routes
learning takes place along *a new learning pathway* linked *through a new learning network across (the UK)*; there will be *diverse and accessible routes for learning* and *clear progression routes.*

• Starting points and departures
there will be *new access points, Learning Information Points, a variety of first steps ... for learners* and a *secure point of entry into learning,* although *learners may leave programmes*; there are *important gateways into learning* and *information gateways for Ufl.*

- Maps and guidance
  regional partnerships ... can point learners to real opportunities; learners will be able to chart their learning gain; local communities will need *a 'learning opportunities' route map.*

- Movements
  learners can approach colleges, UfI will put learners first, the flow of successful learners; (learners will) *return to education, companies... are exploring new ways of expanding learning opportunities.*

- Obstacles
  current barriers which stop people learning, very real obstacles to participation in learning, the impediments hampering lifelong learning, social security ... can inhibit ... learning.

- Reaching the destination
  (opportunities for learners to) *progress to their full potential, to successfully stay the courses*; there will be *new national learning targets* which will *make learning everyone's goal.*

These scripts provide a rich set of entailments for the learning as a JOURNEY metaphor.

Conclusions

Metaphor and the stability of a discourse

It is somehow counterintuitive that, faced with Giddens's tsunamis and juggernauts, the most appropriate response is to go on a journey. This might be the case in the sense of getting the hell out of here, but escape is not an entailment of our particular journey schema. Our implied traveller in the learning society is in pursuit of a metaphorised object of desire, although in the absence of any clear specification for this object, the journey is more a quest for some grail-like entity which, viewed through the perspective of another keyword in the discourse, *lifelong learning*, is idealised as a lifetime's commitment.

However, this begs the question as to whether congruence between different metaphors is a factor in stabilising a discourse. As analysts we find the dissonance rather unsettling, whereas the ordinary reader perhaps would not have noticed. And since we have not engaged in any research on the reception of these metaphors by participants in the learning society, we have no evidence either way. Nevertheless it leaves open an interesting question for further research.

Stubbs proposes that ideas gain stability when they fit into a schema, his definition of which is a system of meaning where, for example, particular vocabulary is used and particular things are taken for granted or allowed (1996: 162). For his account of how linguistic categories become social categories, Stubbs relies particularly on Giddens's structure/agency duality, whereby social systems such as language are both the medium and the outcome of the practices that constitute them, practices that are continually produced and reproduced by human agents (Giddens, 1979: 69). This recursivity helps to account for the discourse building effects of repetition, such as keywords and their collocations.

However, repetition is only one of those 'micro-processes of discourse coherence' which 'explains the stability of discourses over time' and makes it possible to speak of specific discourses such as those of the Cold War (Chilton, 1996: 412), or the learning society. Other factors which link coherence and stability are provided by pragmatic and cognitive processes. As Chilton shows, there is pragmatic pressure for stabilisation in that, even in highly conflictual interactions, there is an expectation of co-operation which encourages the continuing replication of meanings. And there is cognitive pressure in that 'many metaphors derive from cognitive frames, scripts and image schemas that are relatively stable' (ibid: 34). Chilton's notion of 'schema' is a model based on the human experience of having a body, acting as an overarching concept like motion or container which other writers on metaphor often call a 'domain' (ibid: 48). Such a domain can provide coherence not just textually but also through its entailments. Metaphorical entailment, though, also offers great scope for imagination and creativity, and can potentially produce a highly volatile discourse, or in the case of Chilton's 'runaway metaphors', one which progresses far beyond an original author's intentions. However, if sufficiently constrained by pragmatic and cognitive considerations, entailment actually gives metaphor an additional claim to a stabilising effect over and above the repetitional and collocational properties of keywords.

It is the tension between creativity and stability which gives metaphor its capacity to be 'generative'. But there are two conditions for such generativity, these being that the metaphor is both textually and pragmatically salient, in other words that it gets taken up, mediated and developed by its participating audience. It is not clear to us how salient are the metaphors we have identified in our corpus. We have already noted that the earlier study of *learning* (Piper, in press 2000b), based on a quantitative approach to its collocational behaviour, revealed an uncompromising socio-economic agenda running through the discourse of the learning society. Yet the learning is MONEY metaphor is a rare occurrence and on its own would not have provided evidence for so comprehensive a conclusion. On the other hand the presence of the learning is a JOURNEY metaphor is much more obvious, although not repeated on anything like the scale of its socio-economic collocations. Nevertheless, it was only obvious when we came to look; the *learning* study did not pick it up. This suggests that any claims about metaphor constructing, motivating and constraining concepts is conditional on pragmatic and contextual factors. It also raises another question about stability: if this is partly an issue of salience in the discourse, is stability maintained in cases where one dimension of textuality, metaphor say, is incongruent with another, in this case extensive and all-pervading repeated collocational patterns, as long as the former is less perceptible?

What the earlier study did pick up was that the idea of the learning society is a response to change. And as Fairclough has said, 'relationships between discursive, social and cultural change are typically not transparent for the people involved' (Fairclough, 1992: 9). If we conjure up an entailment of Fairclough's understanding is SEEING metaphor, it is therefore only to be expected that the metaphors in the discourse of the learning society will be of varying visibility. Learning as a JOURNEY, for example, is probably a very old metaphor, 'dead' even, except that its place in our corpus and its many supporting entailments suggests that it is one of those 'metaphors we live by'. In this case the metaphor is produced without anyone noticing either its existence or its incongruity in the face of change as a FORCE OF NATURE. Since new ideas for learning in the face of social and cultural upheaval are well documented – in the work of Durkheim, in the history of literacy and state schooling, in reflections on new technology – it would be interesting to investigate this metaphor on a historical basis; indeed the JOURNEY metaphor certainly has a long and classical European history in its association with life itself. It would also be important to compare the findings about *change* and *learning* from our own corpus with evidence from a very large reference corpus such as the Bank of English, and having not done so is a limitation of our study. Regarding learning as a JOURNEY therefore, on the evidence available to us we can only suggest that, however incongruous its juxtaposition with change, its very familiarity is a stabilising factor in the reception of (or indifference to?) concepts of a learning society.

Metaphor and the evaluation of social policy

Finally, how do we, as researchers interested in metaphor, evaluate the social policies we have been examining? Although, as we have said, we recognise that in quantitative terms metaphor is a relatively minor contributor to the discursive formation of the learning society, we have a number of concluding observations to offer.

Initially we note that presenting change as a FORCE occludes all considerations of political power by writing out of the text all mention of human or institutional agency. This is true whether the force is natural or mechanical, elemental as in Giddens or imperceptible as in Beck, who curiously describes 'the reflexive modernization of industrial society' as proceeding 'on cats' paws' (on tiptoe?) (Beck, 1994: 3). Similarly with change as OUTSIDE or INSIDE, when implied human actors are required to respond to some unspecified agent. If change is natural or institutional, who can be called to account? And if familiar metaphors of forces and journeys are available, why go to the trouble of recasting the issues in different language? So what 'generative metaphor' generates is politically expedient discourses and intellectual inertia just as much as Schön's 'disanalogies'.

The required response, whether as an individual learner or as some kind of provider, is to exert bodily or cognitive control over change or to act as a change agent him/herself (change as ACTION). A less explicit response is to learn, or to deliver learning to other people, and this is presented through a series of frames and scripts associated with the concept of a JOURNEY. The domains of both metaphors are presented as positive and achievable, implying that the problems entailed by change can be solved by learning. The journey, however, is not straightforward in that its objective is idealised but unclear, and, as close reading of some of the project reports in the corpus reveals, many people seem reluctant to make it on the terms required or even at all.

An underlying concern of the policy makers is the risk of non-learners as the socially excluded, another INSIDE/OUTSIDE metaphor. Under the heading of 'Difficult Questions', one European Commission report bluntly comments on 'the ever-smaller numbers of pupils required by the labour market' and the fact that 'personal development, which is at the very heart of the educational mission, means questioning most of our initial assumptions, the very foundation that gives many people their feeling of belonging to society' (European Commission, 1996b: para. 170). The paradox of how individual social actors are supposed to respond to both the socio-economic agenda of the learning society and to unavoidable 'natural' forces of change by going on a learning JOURNEY is focused by many more metaphors of insideness and outsideness in our corpus than we have been able to examine. Perhaps, given the long historical pedigree of packing troublemakers off on a journey, these represent subconscious wishful thinking on the part of the policy makers.

Relative to engaging on the ground with the intractable and complex problems of social life, it is easy to sit back and deconstruct a discourse and leave it at that. We end therefore by suggesting that a linguistic activity like metaphor analysis has value over and above critique in identifying confusions of which policy makers are insufficiently conscious or issues which they may be unaware of not addressing. Put less charitably, of course, metaphor may represent a preference for maintaining existing or preferred scenarios rather than addressing fundamental problems, and thus in this sense, metaphor may be what gives the game away. However, the promulgators of the learning society can hardly be accused of intentions of a conscious malignity, nor, as in our final quotation, of failing to recognise that there are conflicting policy and personal agendas. Here is what *Creating learning cultures: Next steps in achieving the learning age* has to say about lifelong learning:

> *As yet, the expression has not fired the imagination of the population at large, especially those not yet engaged in learning beyond school – at work, in the community, in their homes and families and in their leisure and recreational lives. To some people, the notion of 'lifelong' learning sounds more like a penal sentence or endurance test than an invitation to pleasure, achievement and progress*
>
> (National Advisory Group for Continuing Education and Lifelong Learning, 1999: para. 3.12)

Once again we find journeys good and bad, institutionalised containers, objects of desire, and now even fire. The National Advisory Group can clearly marshal a splendid mix of metaphors, after which they immediately go on to 'offer one contribution to developing a suitable and more inspiring definition of lifelong learning'. But it does make you wonder just precisely what might be on offer, and how, and why.

Acknowledgements

We are grateful to the Arts and Humanities Research Board for small grant *SG-AN5231/APN8401* in support of this work. Also to Professor Bob Fryer for helpful material.

Notes

1. Giddens, 1999; summary p. 2.
2. Since the time of writing, Fairclough has contributed an important sociolinguistic analysis of some of these core concepts of the New Labour project (Fairclough 2000).

References

Beck, U. (1992) *Risk Society: Towards a new modernity.* London: Sage Publications.

Beck, U. (1994) The reinvention of politics: towards a theory of reflexive modernization. In U. Beck, A. Giddens and S. Lash (eds). *Reflexive Modernization: politics, tradition and aesthetics in the modern social order.* Cambridge: Polity Press.

Cameron, L. (1999) Operationalising 'metaphor' for applied linguistic research. In L. Cameron and G. Lowe (eds) *Researching and Applying Metaphor.* Cambridge: Cambridge University Press.

Chilton, P. A. (1996) *Security Metaphors: Cold war discourse from containment to common house.* NY: Peter Lang.

Department for Education and Employment (1999) *UK Lifelong Learning.* London: Department for Education and Employment. http: //www.lifelonglearning.co.uk.

168 CHANGE AND CONTINUITY IN APPLIED LINGUISTICS

Dohmen, G. (1996) *Lifelong Learning: Guidelines for a modern education policy.* Bonn: Federal Ministry of Education, Science, Research and Technology.

Economic and Social Research Council (1997) *The Learning Society: Knowledge and skills for employment.* University of Newcastle, Department of Education. http: //www.ncl.ac.uk/~nfjc/index.html.

European Commission (1996a) *1996 The European Year of Lifelong Learning.* European Commission DGXXII. http: //europa.eu.int/en/comm/dg22/eyinet.html#2.

European Commission (1996b) *Accomplishing Europe Through Education and Training: Study group on education and training report.* Brussels: European Commission DGXXII. http: //europa.eu.int/en/comm/dg22/reflex/en/homeen.html.

European Union (1999) *Europa Home Page.* http: //europa.eu.int/index-en.htm.

Fairclough, N. (1992) *Discourse and Social Change.* Cambridge: Polity Press.

Fairclough, N. (2000) *New Labour, New Language?* London: Taylor & Francis Books Ltd, Routledge.

Further Education Funding Council (1997) *Learning Works: Widening participation in further education (The Kennedy Report).* Coventry: Further Education Funding Council.

Giddens, A. (1979) *Central Problems in Social Theory.* London: Macmillan.

Giddens, A. (1991) *Modernity and Self-identity: Self and society in the late modern age.* Cambridge: Polity.

Giddens, A. (1998) *The Third Way: The renewal of social democracy.* Cambridge: Polity.

Giddens, A. (1999) *Risk.* No. 2 of the BBC Reith Lectures 1999. London: British Broadcasting Corporation. http: //www.bbc.co.uk/reith99.

Lakoff, G. (1993) The contemporary theory of metaphor. In A. Ortony (ed.) *Metaphor and Thought.* Cambridge: Cambridge University Press.

Lakoff, G. and Johnson, M. (1980) *Metaphors We Live By.* Chicago: University of Chicago Press.

National Advisory Group for Continuing Education and Lifelong Learning (1999) *Creating Learning Cultures: Next steps in achieving the learning age.* National Advisory Group for Continuing Education and Lifelong Learning. http: //www.lifelong learning.co.uk/nagcell2/index.htm.

Piper, A. (in press 2000a) Some have credit cards and others have giro cheques: A corpus study of 'individuals' and 'people' as lifelong learners in late modernity. *Discourse and Society.*

Piper, A. (in press 2000b) Lifelong learning, human capital, and the soundbite. *Text.*

Schön, D. A. (1993) Generative metaphor: A perspective on problem-setting in social policy. In A. Ortony (ed.). *Metaphor and Thought.* Cambridge: Cambridge University Press.

Scott, M. (1997) *Wordsmith Tools.* Oxford: Oxford University Press.

Smith, J and Spurling, A. (1999) *Lifelong Learning: Riding the tiger.* London: Cassell.

Stubbs, M. (1996) *Text and Corpus Analysis: Computer-assisted studies of language and culture.* Oxford: Blackwell.

11 The Role of Idioms in Negotiating Workplace Encounters

ALMUT JOSEPHA KOESTER
University of Nottingham

Abstract

This paper examines the discourse function of idioms in naturally-occurring face-to-face office communication. In the data examined, idioms were found to be used in the performance of a number of different discourse functions: (1) summarising and closing off encounters, (2) evaluating and (3) signalling problem–solution patterns. These functions are presented and discussed using examples from a corpus of British and American workplace talk. It was also found that idioms occurred more frequently in some genres than in others. It is suggested in this paper that the use of idioms in workplace discourse may reflect speakers' orientation either to a transactional goal in accomplishing a workplace task, or to an interpersonal goal linked to the developing or maintaining of relationships with co-workers.

Introduction

The findings reported in this paper are based on research currently being carried out on a corpus of approximately 34,000 words consisting of naturally-occurring office conversations in a variety of settings in Britain and the US.[1] The conversations involve mainly different workplace tasks (e.g. giving instructions, briefing, going through work, deciding on a course of action, problem-solving), but also talk which is not task-oriented, such as office gossip or small talk about the weekend.

In workplace conversations, speakers are continuously orienting towards the dual goals of achieving certain tasks and negotiating role relationships with their co-workers, and this is reflected in the lexical choices made. Certain lexical items seemed to play an important role in the structuring and development of the discourse. Other lexical choices showed that speakers were paying attention to the interpersonal aspect of the encounter, for example in choosing a more indirect way of expressing something, or using vague rather than specific words. In fact, as we shall see, some lexical choices seemed to function on the transactional and the relational level simultaneously. This paper will focus on one particular group of lexical items, idioms, and will examine how the use of idioms reflects speakers' orientations to these two types of goals.

Defining Idioms

But first it is necessary to specify what kinds of items are referred to here as idioms, as it is possible to take a fairly narrow or a broader definition. The term 'idiom' is sometimes used to refer only to fixed phrases made up of completely opaque frozen metaphors, usually consisting of verb + complement, e.g. *have a chip on your shoulder,* or prepositional phrases, e.g. *over the moon.* But there is no clear dividing line between such so-called 'classic' or 'pure' idioms and other types of more transparent metaphors, such as *to bad-mouth (someone)* or *get the drift (of something).* In addition, there are a number of phrases and expressions that can be considered to be idiomatic because they are grammatically anomalous, e.g. *every once in a while* or *rumour has it.* According to Flavell (1992), idioms are anomalous grammatically and/or semantically. Moon (1998), who provides a corpus-based classification of a large number of fixed expressions and idioms, takes three factors into account in defining such items:

(1) Institutionalisation: the degree to which a string of words has become conventionalised

(2) Lexico-grammatical fixedness, e.g. restrictions on inflections or word order

(3) Opacity/non-compositionality: the degree to which an expression is figurative and non-literal.

My classification of idioms is based largely on these three criteria, although I did not include all the types of items Moon (ibid) examined. The defining criterion in my classification was that the item should be figurative and non-literal, at least to some degree; therefore I did not include conversational routines, such as *excuse me* or discourse-organising phrases and prefabs, such as *by the way* or *the thing/point is* …. I did include metaphors, even if they occurred as single words, as these have non-literal meanings and (at least in speech) are usually conventionalised and not original. In addition, the same item often occurred either on its own or in a fairly fixed collocation (e.g. *a pain* or *a bit of a pain*), and it therefore made sense to include both types of items.

The three criteria listed above for defining idioms yield the following broad categories of idiomatic expressions (based on Moon, 1998). The list below also shows the types of items found in my corpus within each category, with examples given for each type:

(1) Formulae (institutionalisation):

- Cultural allusions: proverbs, maxims, catch phrases:
  That's life (isn't it), Murphy's Law
- Idiomatic prefabricated clauses: *What's the story? The good news is ...*

(2) Lexico-grammatically anomalous strings: Anomalous collocations and prepositional expressions: *every once in a while, neither here nor there, on the off-chance*

(3) Metaphors (non-compositionality):

- 'Classic' idioms: extended opaque frozen metaphors:
  get in under the wire, clear the deck
- Extended spatial/motion metaphors: *You know where you stand, get it moving*
- Idiomatic phrasal verbs: *foul up, trickle down*
- Other metaphors and metaphorical collocations:
  to have a word (with someone), a mad dash

Another reason for taking a fairly broad definition of idioms in this study is that, statistically speaking, idioms occur relatively infrequently. Moon (1997) found that 70% of the idioms she examined had frequencies of less than one per million words. In addition, she found that, contrary to common perception, most idioms were less frequent in the spoken data than the written texts she examined (Moon, 1998). Strässler (1982), who examined idioms in spoken data, found such items occurring on average only once every 1,150 words. As my corpus is quite small, taking a broader definition of idioms allowed me to examine more items.

Discourse Function of Idioms

There is a large body of research in the field of idiomatology, which will not even be touched upon here, but only a few studies have looked at the use of idioms in naturally-occurring discourse (see Drew & Holt, 1998; McCarthy, 1998; Moon, 1992, 1997, 1998; Strässler, 1982). Building on these studies, I was interested in investigating whether, in my data, idioms occurred at particular places, and performed particular functions in the discourse, and whether they were more frequent in certain types of discourse than others.

I will be looking at three different discourse functions that I found idioms to be performing in my data, and also at the relative frequency of idioms in different genres in my corpus.

Summarizing/Closing Function of Idioms

A number of conversations in my data had no idioms at all, and many had only one or two, but there did seem to be a tendency for idioms to occur at particular junctures in conversations (this was particularly noticeable in conversations with few idioms). Consider how the following workplace encounter is closed off. The two speakers, Don and John, have just made arrangements for a part of the building to be cleaned.

(1) Arranging Cleaning[2]
Don: That- that uh... (is like a little insurance)
John: Yeah. /Oh yeah it's easy /to get all these-
Don: (Keep it straight) Yeah.
John: (/Yeah/)
[1: John moves towards door]
John: You get confused enough around here.
Don: Heheheh [1] Especially this stuff. [1] ↑This- you know... this *job*.
         Of all the *jobs*. This is the one where the↑*least* little error ↓ will **come**
         back to haunt you.
John: Uh-huh?
Don: (/Yeah/)
(author's data)

The encounter is closed off in the two turns following the production of the highlighted idiom, which summarises the whole encounter. In addition, another non-literal expression (*keep it straight*) is used in the preceding discourse.

Drew & Holt (1998) observed a similar phenomenon in the way idioms were used in informal telephone conversations. They found that idioms tended to occur at topic transitions: they were often used to summarise the current topic, followed by both speakers collaboratively closing down the topic, before opening a new topic.

As my own data involved, for the most part, task-oriented workplace talk, this kind of fluid movement of conversations from topic to topic was not common. However, as in example (1) above, idioms were used to summarise previous discourse, and either move towards closure of the encounter or to section off a particular phase of the talk. Below are some further examples of this. Each extract shows the use of one or several idioms (shown highlighted) at or towards the end of an encounter.

(2)
(a) Training a new employee:
Sam: ↑hhh Okay, [sighs]
Ben: All right, but you're sort of- **getting the... getting the drift of it** yeah,=
Sam: ⌊/I'm off/
Sam: =Yeah.
Ben: =↓Yeah
Sam: =↓All right yeah.

(b) Explaining a procedure:
Hugh: Yeah I will do. Yeah. That's great. Mm.
Liz: Uh... Yeah. **Takes a bit of digesting,**
Hugh: It will do. Yes.
Liz: /Still try it/ Hehehe!
Hugh: You got it, Hehehe

(c) Small talk about people who are ill or in hospital:
Jane: Right. So that's today's **doom and gloom,**
Liz: There's plenty of it isn't there

(d) Assistant briefing boss after return from a business trip:
Beth: I just wanted to like **clear the deck,**
Carol: Mhm,
Beth: and so at least I know what I'm... **hittin' the ground with** next week,
Carol: Mhm,
Beth: ⌊when I come in. you know,
Carol: Okay, Okay, Well it sounds like uh...
Beth: ⌊**Get moving.**
Carol: everything's gone very well.
Beth: Yes. **The fort has been held down.** Hehehehehe

(a–c author's data, d © Cambridge University Press)

In the last example (d), a whole cluster of idioms is produced mainly by one speaker. McCarthy (1998) noted a similar clustering of idioms in narratives: after completion of a story, speakers and listeners often produced a series of idioms to comment on and evaluate the story. Evaluation also plays a role in the above examples: as well as summarising the preceding discourse, these idioms function to evaluate the whole encounter. In (2d) idioms such as *clear the deck* and *the fort has been held down* seem to express the judgement that a great deal has been accomplished by having the meeting and that things have gone well in the boss's absence. Similarly, the idiomatic expressions used in example (1) express a positive evaluation of the arrangements for cleaning that have just been made, as well as hinting at possible negative consequences if such arrangements are neglected:

keep it straight

the least little error will come back to haunt you.

The idioms used to close off these encounters thus are performing a double work load. On the one hand, they perform the transactional job of summarising and closing the encounter, and simultaneously they function on an interpersonal level by positively evaluating the encounter. This allows the participants to feel good about themselves and what they have accomplished, and thereby reinforces solidarity and common ground between them. Even in example (2c), where the idiom *doom and gloom* summarises the encounter as having been about negative things, solidarity is created, as the idiom provides a locus for speakers jointly to interpret the preceding discourse. Liz's response shows that she concurs with Jane's evaluation of their talk:

Jane: Right. So that's today's **doom and gloom,**

Liz: There's plenty of it isn't there

Evaluative Function of Idioms

Other studies looking at the use of idioms in naturally-occurring spoken discourse (Moon, 1992, 1998; Powell, 1992; Strässler, 1982) also showed that idioms often have an evaluative function. The following complete conversation shows a number of very clear examples of idioms performing such an evaluative discourse function. In this conversation, the two speakers who work for a paper supplier, are discussing an order they have lost (idioms are highlighted).

(3) Lost order
Paul: Office Manager
Mark: Sales Rep

1. **Mark:** We lost that one... that /??/ one,
2. **Paul:** ↑Did we?
3. **Mark:** Yeah. Someone quoted seven hundred pound a ton,
4. **Paul:** On what.
5. **Mark:** ⌊/Didn't say,/ Well... say equivalent sheet. but... as far as *I* was aware, we was the only ones who could get hold of [name of paper].
6. **Paul:** No. various mills... various merchants can get hold of it,
7. **Mark:** Just... they call it something else. yeah.
8. **Paul:** Yeah. [name of paper] or whatever
9. **Mark:** (Yeah)
10. **Paul:** That's **a bit of a *pain***, isn't it.
11. **Mark:** Yeah. So... so-
12. **Paul:** ⌊Remember that next time

13. **Mark:** I said to him uh... let us know next time you know... what... prices
      you're getting in and we'll always see if we can better... that /?/.
14. **Paul:** Well you'll know it for next time,
15. **Mark:** Mm
16. **Paul:** [funny voice] Trying to be too greedy,
      [2]
17. **Mark:** Mm
18. **Paul:** ⌊Well I m- we won't- y' know **don't know do yous**
19. **Mark: You don't know**
      [3]
20. **Mark:** Well it's /annoying/ that he's got an order in if you think about it at
      forty pound a ton or whatever,
      [...]
21. **Paul:** Mm
22. **Mark:** It's not exactly like not getting an order at all /though/
23. **Paul:**   ⌊Annoying, isn't it
      [3]
24. **Mark:** (/That would have been quite nice/)
25. **Paul:** Oh well,
      [11]
26. **Paul: It's a pain**, isn't it.
27. **Mark:** Mm
      [1.5]
28. **Paul: Can't win 'em all,**
      [9]
29. **Paul:** About a *grand* that, isn't it.
      [...]
30. **Mark:** Yeah
31. **Paul:** Oh well,
      [4]
32. **Paul: Win some you lose some**. /so/ [1.5] We coulda made seven hundred
      quid out of it, couldn't we.
      [1]
33. **Mark:** (Mm)
34. **Paul:** Oh well
      [2.5]
35. **Paul:** It's an*noy*in' though, isn't. hhh

From about turn 16 onwards, Mark and Paul's talk consists entirely of
negative evaluations of what has happened, as if they cannot stop expressing
their annoyance. The discourse seems to get stuck in a rut: unlike in the previous
examples, the speakers do not move towards closure after production of evalua-

tive statements (in the form of idioms), but, after pauses of several seconds, keep reopening the topic with further comments. This frustration about the lost order is sometimes expressed with direct evaluative statements (*annoying* – turn 20, 23 and 35 and *that would've been quite nice* – 24), but frequently also with the use of maxims, metaphor or other idiomatic phrases:

10.   That's a bit of a pain
18. **Paul:**   don't know do yous
19. **Mark:** You don't know
26.   It's a pain isn't it
28.   Can't win 'em all
32.   Win some lose some.

The function of all these idioms is clearly to evaluate this negative turn of events.

The question is why the speakers here should so frequently choose to use idioms for this purpose instead of more direct evaluative language. Moon (1992; 1998) suggests that idioms reduce the interpersonal risk of evaluation, because they are generalising statements referring to culturally-accepted truths and values, and therefore allow speakers to 'shelter behind shared values' (1992: 24). Low (1988: 128) attributes a similar function to metaphor: it can be used as a kind of distancing device, which allows speakers to discuss emotionally charged subjects or avoid committing themselves.

The conversation shown in (3) involves a particularly delicate situation, where a subordinate (Mark) has admitted to a mistake. The use of idioms allows his boss (Paul) to express his displeasure without actually directly blaming Mark, thereby allowing Mark to save his face. The only direct reference to what the sales rep may have done wrong is spoken with a 'funny' voice, thus distancing the speaker from what he is saying: *trying to be too greedy* (16). But for the most part, evaluations are expressed indirectly through idioms and metaphors. The appeal to shared values is especially evident in the repeated use (by Paul) of maxims, which, like proverbs, invoke generally accepted folk wisdom:

28. Can't win 'em all
32. Win some lose some.

McCarthy (1998: 145) notes that proverbs are direct cultural allusions, and therefore 'express cultural and social solidarity' even more than other idioms.

This encounter shows idioms performing a particular and vital function in face to face workplace discourse. In delicate situations like this, where a mistake has been made, idioms and metaphors can play an important role in delivering negative evaluation, whilst at the same time preserving the working relationship.

Idioms in Problem–Solution Pattern

The use of idioms for negative evaluation was in fact very common in my data. A number of conversations in my corpus involve the discussion of problems, and here speakers used a relatively large number of idioms. Many of these conversations followed a problem–solution pattern, as identified by Hoey (1983 and 1994) in different kinds of expository text. It is interesting that such a textual pattern, originally found in planned and highly structured and expository prose, should also occur in unplanned spoken discourse.

The phases of the problem–solution pattern as identified by Hoey are:

Situation → Problem → Response/Solution → Evaluation

The textual pattern begins with a situation in which a problem is identified. The next step is a response or possible solution to the problem, which is then evaluated in terms of how successful it was. If the evaluation is positive, the pattern is complete; if negative, other responses become necessary – the pattern is thus recursive.

The different phases of this pattern can be identified in a variety of ways, but often they are signalled lexically through the use of certain key words. I found that a number of the signal words identified by Hoey were used by speakers in my data to signal the different phases of the pattern, e.g.:

- Problem: *problem, difficult*

- Response/Solution: *response, result, figure out*

- Evaluation: *work, good.*

But what I also found was that idioms and metaphors were frequently used as signals, especially for the problem phase, e.g.:

> *a (bit of a) pain, a killer, a real headache, struggle, a bloomer, kinks (to work out), foul up, screw up, piss (somebody) off, goin' crazy, hangin' over our heads, (be) an arm and a leg, rough day(s)*

The above list also includes items used for negative evaluation of a response (e.g. *be an arm and a leg* – i.e. the proposed solution is too expensive), which starts the problem–solution cycle over again.

There were also a number of idioms used in the response/solution phase, e.g.:

come up with, sit down (together) (and talk/think about), wrack our brains,
get it moving, get it sorted, straightened out, make it stick, get a focus on

The first item, the idiomatic phrasal verb *come up with*, is in fact one of the
lexical items identified by Hoey as a signal for the response phase. The second
item occurred in several conversations with a few variations: *sit down (together)*
(and talk/think about.) This may not at first sight seem idiomatic, but it is
noticeable that this expression was always used when people were discussing
solutions to a problem. It seems therefore to have become pragmatically specialised as a signal of the response phase in the problem–solution pattern, and to
have lost some of its literal meaning of 'sitting down'.

And finally, idioms were also used in evaluating responses and solutions to
problems:

dead easy, it's not that big a deal, it never hurts, makes sense, works for me,
that's where we stand, par for the course

Most of these are positive evaluations, but some are more non-committal, e.g.
that's where we stand, par for the course.

The following extract shows how some of these lexical signals, both literal
and idiomatic, are actually used in a conversation where problems are being
discussed:

(4) Discussing Computer Problems
Chris: President
Joe: Sales manager

1. **Chris:** Haven't seen much in the way of *sales* the last half of the week.
2. **Joe:**   .hh Well, a lot of the media, the- the orders have been *very* **difficult**
    getting out. Stuff is- is **jammed.**
3. **Chris:** Oh they didn't go out?
4. **Joe:**   *Yeah.* Anne's orders are *clog*ged. And... trying to get out heheh
5. **Chris:**   ⌊Heheh   ⌊**clogged** orders!
6. **Joe:**   **Clogged** orders! .hh they can't get out o' the s_ystem.
7. **Chris:** ⌊Oh no!
8. **Chris:** Well, hh Okay-
9. **Joe:**   ⌊*I've* got uh...
10. **Chris:** John's- (Well-)
11. **Joe:**   Well, uh he's been ***work*ing** on 'em to get 'em out, but she's been →
12. **Chris:**   ⌊/Really/
13. **Joe:**   **goin' *crazy* trying to** get- she's- she's written... four or five *or*ders
    this week. An' uh they haven't gone out, .hh I had **problems** too...

(author's data)

In turn 1 a negative situation is identified: sales have been low. Turns 2–9 then contain a number of signals of the problem phase: *difficult, jammed, clogged,* two of which are metaphorical. One of these is in fact a creative metaphor: *clogged orders* (this is unusual in my data – most metaphors are conventional). It is probably because of its novelty that it is responded to by laughter and repeated three times. In turns 11–13 different responses to the problem are reported using signal words (*he's been **working** on 'em, she's been **goin' crazy trying** to ...*), but they are evaluated negatively (*they haven't gone out*), and further *problems* are mentioned in 13. These signal words are often spoken with emphatic stress (shown in italics in example), which is a further indication that they are key items in the discourse. The rest of conversation (not shown here) then goes through the phases of the problem–solution pattern, using some of the following lexical signals:

- Response: *good response, result, handled*
- Positive Evaluation: *look pretty good, that's good, hoping*

In this extract, as in a number of conversations involving problem-solving, there is a clustering of signal words, a number of which are metaphorical. Such a clustering of semantically related lexical items creates a network of lexical cohesion, which contributes to the structuring of the discourse into the different phases of the problem–solution pattern.

These examples show that idioms and metaphors play an important role as lexical signals in problem-solving discourse and thereby contribute to the structuring of the discourse, even in spontaneous dialogue. But the structure of unplanned spoken discourse must of course be seen differently from the structure of a planned written text. Discourse patterns such as problem–solution are emergent here and negotiated between the participants: there is much more switching back and forth between the different phases, and the pattern is often incomplete. Some conversations also have an additional phase to do with assigning blame or responsibility, something which is usually absent from neutral written prose.

But it is not only in terms of discourse structure that idioms can play a role in problem-solving discourse. As mentioned at the beginning of this section, idioms and metaphors were used particularly frequently to talk about problems and make negative evaluations. Evidence that this is not just a chance finding is provided by Moon's (1998) investigation of idioms. She found that in her (much larger) corpus idioms were used for negative evaluations twice as frequently as for positive ones. She suggests that this may be because of the role idioms play as politeness and face-saving devices. The last section showed examples of idioms being used in this way (for negative evaluation), and indeed the large number of idioms and metaphors used in talking about problems may well

perform a similar function in negotiating interpersonal relationships and reducing threats to face.

Idioms in Different Genres

Finally, I was interested in seeing whether idioms occurred more frequently in
certain genres or discourse types in my corpus than others. Table 1 shows how
frequently idioms occurred in four different genres: the second column shows
the total number of words in each genre, the third column shows the total
number of idioms that occurred and the figures in the last column give an
average idiom frequency in 1,000 words of speech.

Table 1 Frequency of idioms by genre

Genre	Total word count	No. of idioms	Average frequency per 1000 words
1. Decision-making/ Problem-solving	8,782	97	11
2. Reporting/Recounting	2,324	22	9.5
3. Information provision/ Briefing	3,524	9	2.5
4. Procedures/Instructions (Training)	5,195	11	2

As the results in the table show very clearly, idioms were most frequent in
discourse which involved decision-making/problem-solving and reporting, with
on average at least nine idioms occurring every 1,000 words. Idioms occurred
much less frequently in discourse dealing with procedures/instructions and
information provision: here there were only about two idioms in 1,000 words of
speech.

Why should there be such a marked difference in idiom frequency between
the first and the second two genres? I suggest the explanation may lie in the
evaluative function of idioms discussed earlier, and in the role they play in
negotiating interpersonal relationships. Giving instructions, explaining pro-
cedures and giving information are fairly straightforward activities, where the
focus is on the transfer of information, rather than on evaluating and making
judgements. In these genres, idioms often occurred only at the end of the

encounter or to close off phases within the encounter, performing the summarising function illustrated in examples (1) and (2).

Decision-making and problem-solving involve much more personal involvement on the part of the participants in performing such discourse acts as giving opinions, evaluating the situation, suggesting solutions, agreeing, disagreeing, justifying or defending. Idioms and metaphors can play an important role here in softening judgements and negative evaluations and reducing potential threats to face.

Although reporting/recounting is similar to information provision and procedural discourse in that it involves the transfer of information, speakers who recount something also have to evaluate the events reported and often justify their own actions. This is particularly the case in workplace discourse where (as in my data) the speakers often report to a superior. Furthermore, in my corpus speakers often reported problematic events, and, as we have seen, idioms are frequently used in talking about problems.

In examining the evaluative function of idioms, a distinction can be made between evaluations which reinforce solidarity between the participants and those that threaten common ground or the other speaker's face. As we saw earlier, idioms that perform a discourse-summarising function also usually evaluate the encounter positively, thus creating a bond of solidarity between the speakers. But the comparison of idioms in the different genres shows that they are used much more frequently in discourse dealing with problematic situations. Therefore although idioms are in fact used both for positive and negative evaluation, it seems that they play a particularly important role in negative evaluation.

These results suggest that idiom use can vary considerably from genre to genre. Moon (1998) found differences in idiom frequency between the different types of written texts she examined, and, as already mentioned, found that overall idioms were less frequent in spoken than in written discourse. My findings seem to indicate there may be significant differences in idiom frequency between different spoken genres as well.

Conclusion

In this paper, I have investigated three different discourse functions of idioms in my data:

(1) the use of idioms to summarise and close off a section of the discourse or the entire encounter,

(2) the use of idioms in making evaluations and judgements – here idioms allow participants to negotiate delicate workplace situations, as idioms invoke shared values, and thus reduce potential threats to face,

(3) the role of idioms and metaphors as signal words in a problem–solution pattern.

Finally, I examined the overall frequency of idioms in different spoken genres, and found some striking differences here, which can be linked to the different discourse goals in each genre and the different types of discourse acts the participants perform.

The findings presented indicate that although idioms may not be frequent in spoken discourse, they do perform important functions. These functions and the frequency of idiom use may differ considerably from genre to genre. In examining the role of idioms in different conversational genres (narratives and observation–comment), McCarthy (1998) found that they tended to occur in particular genres and at specific junctures. My findings seem to confirm that there is indeed a link between genre and idiom use. I found that whereas idioms were infrequent and were used mainly as summarising devices in procedural discourse and information provision, they occurred much more frequently in decision-making/problem-solving discourse and reporting, where they played an important role in performing evaluations (particularly negative ones). In these genres, idioms and metaphors were also frequently used to signal the different phases of a problem–solution pattern.

The use of idioms in the naturally-occurring conversations presented here clearly shows that, contrary to common perception, idioms are not just colourful alternatives to more literal lexical choices, but that they perform important discourse functions. This paper has focused specifically on workplace talk, and here idioms may be used by speakers for transactional purposes in accomplishing a workplace task, or for interpersonal goals in maintaining or building working relationships. They play an important role in terms of transactional goals in the joint structuring of talk by participants, for example in summarising and closing off encounters (or sections of the discourse) or in signalling where the discourse is going and what the key elements are, for example in signalling a problem–solution pattern. But perhaps even more importantly, idioms can also play a crucial role in making evaluations and judgements in situations where decisions have to be made or where problems are discussed. In these situations issues such as assigning responsibility or blame may pose a serious threat to face, and here idioms can perform an important function in the delicate negotiation of roles and relationships between co-workers.

Notes

1. The corpus was collected and transcribed by the author as part of a PhD research project in progress at the University of Nottingham, School of English Studies
2. The following transcription conventions are used:
   - ,   slightly rising intonation at end of tone unit
   - ?   high rising intonation at end of tone unit
   - .   falling intonation at end of tone unit
   - !   animated intonation
   - ...   noticeable pause or break of less than 1 second
   - [ ]   longer pauses: 1 second or more (number of seconds is given) and other non-linguistic information, e.g. speakers' gestures or actions
   - -   sound abruptly cut off, e.g. false starts
   - *italics:* emphatic stress
   - / /   uncertain transcription
   - /?/   inaudible utterances
   - ⌊   overlapping or simultaneous speech
   - ⌊ ⌋   interjected utterances within another speaker's turn
   - ↑   a step up in intonation (high key)
   - ↓   a shift down in intonation (lower key)
   - ( )   utterances spoken 'sotto voce'
   - =   latching: no perceptible inter-turn pause
   - .hh   inhalation (audible intake of breath)

References

Drew, P. and Holt, E. (1998) Figures of speech: Figurative expressions and the management of topic transition in conversation. *Language in Society* 27 (4), 495–522.

Flavell, F. (1992) *Dictionary of Idioms and Their Origins.* London: Kyle Cathie.

Hoey, M. (1983) *On the Surface of Discourse.* London: Allen & Unwin.

Hoey, M. (1994) Signalling in discourse: A functional analysis of a common discourse pattern in written and spoken English. In R. M. Coulthard (ed.) *Advances in Written Text Analysis* (pp. 26–45). London: Routledge.

Low, G. (1988) On teaching metaphor. *Applied Linguistics* 9 (2), 125–47.

McCarthy, M. (1998) *Spoken Language and Applied Linguistics* (Chap. 7: Idioms in use: A discourse-based re-examination of a traditional area of language teaching, pp. 129–49). Cambridge: Cambridge University Press.

Moon, R. (1992) Textual aspects of fixed expressions in learners' dictionaries. In P. Arnaud and H. Béjoint (eds) *Vocabulary and Applied Linguistics* (pp. 13–27). London: Macmillan.

Moon, R. (1997) Vocabulary connections: Multi-word items in English. In N. Schmitt and M. McCarthy (eds) *Vocabulary: Description, acquisition and pedagogy* (pp. 40–63). Cambridge: Cambridge University Press.

Moon, R. (1998) *Fixed Expressions and Idioms in English: A corpus-based approach.* Oxford: Clarendon Press.

Powell, M. J. (1992) Semantic/pragmatic regularities in informal lexis: British speakers in spontaneous conversational settings. *Text* 12 (1), 19–58.

Strässler, J. (1982) *Idioms in English: A pragmatic analysis.* Tübingen: Günther-Narr-Verlag.

12 Looking at Changes from the Learner's Point of View: An analysis of group interaction patterns in cross-cultural settings

TAN BEE TIN
Centre for International Education and Management, University College Chichester

Abstract

In this paper, I discuss the view of learning and knowledge construction reflected in group interaction tasks in academic settings. The data used here are the transcripts of group discussion tasks involving overseas students on British undergraduate programmes in both intra – and inter-cultural settings. Within the paradigm of progressive educational ideology, several educational issues such as independent learning, peer/group interaction, group work have been adopted in British higher-educational programmes and ELT with the assumption that group interaction has a role in engaging learners in the process of negotiating meaning, or constructing knowledge collectively; but the effectiveness and appropriateness of these for learners with different educational, cultural and ideological backgrounds have rarely been examined. The analysis of group interaction patterns of students from different cultural and learning backgrounds can throw some light on the way in which they view learning and knowledge; and this in turn will help us justify the effectiveness of a particular educational practice, ideology or innovation, and implement it more successfully. This paper will bring attention to the importance of looking at educational changes from the learners' point of view, taking into consideration their views and beliefs about learning and knowledge.

Introduction

Over the years, we have seen many changes in both ELT and education in general in response to changes in various sectors and disciplines such as research, society, the economy and technology. For instance, changing views on language and learning resulting from research findings, the demands made by a rapidly changing and increasingly complex society, and changes in educational policy and ideology have all led to changes and reforms in teaching. There are also cases where changes in teaching have gradually been driven by the types of textbooks and teaching materials that are available on the market and are exported and promoted by publishers and materials writers. Moreover, as we have seen in the recent years, rapidly changing technological advance has led to the use of computer-assisted learning and the Internet in ELT and education.

So, what are these changes for? And why do we need to change so much? Although changes in education and ELT are claimed to be in the interest of the learners (or disguised to be so), they are also in the interest of people other than the learners, such as professionals, policy makers, and research communities, who need the stimulus of innovations and make changes, not for their own sake, but for the sake of demonstrating that 'we are still dynamic' (in Widdowson's (1998: 705) words).

Although the assumption and the claim behind these changes is that they will significantly improve the quality of learning and lead to higher educational standards for students, changes have very often been discussed from the perspective of the practitioners, or the teachers (e.g. How do the changes relate to teachers' understanding of their work? How do teachers respond to/or resist changes? (e.g. Louden, 1991)); and have very rarely been looked at from the perspective of the students, in whose name and interest, changes are often implemented.

Thus, the aim of this paper is to highlight the need to look at changes from the learners' point of view. That is, if changes are meant to be in the best interest of the learners, as we claim they are, we need to look at changes from the learners' point of view, by which I mean:

• How do the changes relate to the learners' (unconscious and conscious) perceptions of learning?

• How are the changes viewed, implemented and responded to by learners?

• Are the changes implemented and exported appropriate to a particular group of learners?

• How does a particular pedagogical innovation 'work' for a particular group of learners?

One 'popular' change in ELT and education in recent years has been the change from the teacher-centred classroom to the learner-centred classroom; from the emphasis on teacher talk to one on student talk. Under this paradigm of the learner-centred approach, or progressive educational ideology, the use of group work and student talk has been promoted and widely used in education and in EFL classrooms. Many studies on the role of 'talk' and 'group interaction' in learning have been conducted in the fields of both ELT (e.g. Allwright, 1984; Boulima, 1999; Day, 1986; Long, 1981, 1983) and education (e.g. Barnes & Todd, 1977; Edwards & Mercer, 1987; Edwards & Westgate, 1994; Mercer, 1995; Vygotsky, 1978, 1997; Wood et al., 1976). The findings of these studies suggest that group interaction has a role in engaging learners in the process of negotiating meaning, or constructing knowledge jointly, and in the process of learning. In other words, it (group interaction) works.

However, many of these studies, especially those educational studies on the role of talk in learning, have been mainly based in primary or secondary school settings and in Western contexts, i.e. the studies have been carried out using primary/ secondary students from Western cultural and educational backgrounds (e.g. British students and American students). Thus, we need to consider whether the way group work works in these settings is the same as in other settings (higher education settings and other cultural contexts); and whether the findings and ideas arising from these research findings are appropriate to students from other cultural and educational backgrounds; or how these findings can be made appropriate to students from different backgrounds. This in turn highlights the need to investigate these educational issues (in this case, the role of group interaction in learning), focusing on students from different cultural and educa-tional backgrounds.

In this paper, I will look at the way group work 'works' for a group of over-seas Malaysian students on a British undergraduate programme, as part of learning and knowledge construction; or the way group work is perceived and implemented by those students for learning and knowledge construction.

In order to investigate how group work 'works' in the process of learning and knowledge construction, it is first necessary to define what knowledge is and how it is constructed through the use of language in interaction. In the next section, I will, therefore, briefly discuss some theoretical issues which underpin my study of the way group work works in learning and knowledge construction.

Defining Knowledge and Idea Framing

Knowledge, viewed from a psychological perspective, is represented as a propositional network in memory which is made up of nodes (propositions or ideas) and links (associations between the ideas) (e.g. see Anderson, 1980). An idea is defined as 'a separate assertion, i.e. the smallest unit about which it makes sense to make the judgement true or false' (Anderson, 1980: 101–2) or 'a content that is complete enough to be true or false' (Hofmann, 1993: 7). Moreover, an idea, in Bakhtin's (1986) and Lotman's (1988) view, has a dual function of not only conveying information but also generating other ideas. That is, once an idea is uttered, it can stimulate the thinking process, making one think backward (reflect on old ideas); and think forward (generate new ideas).

This view of knowledge and ideas suggests the significance of studying the links between ideas in order to understand the way we construct knowledge. In terms of group interaction in academic settings, this suggests that in order to understand how knowledge is constructed collectively and individually, we need to study not only the type of ideas (or propositions that represent knowledge) that are constructed but the link between them as well.

The term 'framing' is used in my study to indicate not only a link between ideas but also the flow of ideas in a larger context, in other words, a series of links between ideas. 'Framing' thus is a much broader term than 'linking' when referring to the association between ideas. It refers not only to a retrospective link but also to a prospective link between ideas. Hence, 'idea framing' will be used to refer to the way ideas are developed and linked with each other both prospectively and retrospectively.

On the other hand, knowledge, viewed from a sociological perspective, is not given but socially constructed and, in the case of academic knowledge, it is constructed by the members of an academic discourse community (e.g. Tuyay *et al.,* 1995; Young, 1971). According to this view, what counts as valuable educational knowledge can vary from one socio-cultural educational setting to another. Education, according to sociologists, is the process of socialisation into a view of knowledge (Olsher, 1996), and this process of socialisation is carried out through three message systems (curriculum, pedagogy and evaluation) (Bernstein, 1971). Group interaction, which is part of the second message system, pedagogy, can thus be seen as a process of socialising students into a view of knowledge. Alternatively the group interaction patterns, or the patterns of idea framing in group work, will reflect the view of knowledge into which students have been unconsciously or consciously socialised through their previous and present educational experience.

Taking both these psychological and sociological views of knowledge into consideration, the issue which will be investigated in this paper is:

What do the different patterns of idea framing tell us about the students' (unconscious or conscious) view of knowledge or what counts as valuable knowledge for them; and about the way group work is perceived and implemented by the students in the process of learning and knowledge construction? In other words, what do they tell us about the way group work works for students from different socio-cultural educational backgrounds in learning and knowledge construction? And what does this in turn tell us about the process of implementing a pedagogical change involving the use of group work?

Background to Data

There are different ways of looking at the role of group work from the learners' point of view. Among them, one is to interview the students concerning their view of the role of group work in learning; and another is to observe their actual performance during group work. The students I interviewed acknowledged that they had experienced more group work in the UK than back home (Malaysia), and many of them spoke favourably of group work, using a very handy cliché: 'it works'. What they meant by 'it works', though, may not be the same as the institutional definition of 'it works'. As many researchers have noted, however, what people believe they do and what they actually do are not always the same. Thus, it is important to examine the actual behaviour of the students during group work, in other words, their group interaction patterns during group work.

The main source of data for the study is the naturally occurring data of group interaction recorded during academic group discussion tasks in classroom settings, using overseas Malaysian students following modules as part of their studies on a BEd programme with the Centre for International Education and Management at University College Chichester.[1] A number of recordings of student–student group interaction were made in various modules which Malaysian undergraduate students on the BEd programme study. The modules the students have to take on the programme are of two kinds: TESOL modules (major modules) and arts modules (elective modules). While TESOL modules are usually mono-national (i.e. there are only Malaysian students), elective modules are bi-national (i.e. the Malaysian students study alongside with the British undergraduate students). The findings from this data have also been triangulated with other data such as field notes, interview data, and written data collected from the same group of informants.

Framing of Ideas in Group Interaction

From the analysis of the data, I have developed a taxonomy of idea framing, with two major types of idea framing (Additive framing and Reactive framing), their subcategories, and the linguistic features (lexical and syntactic features) which mediate the process of knowledge construction and idea framing.

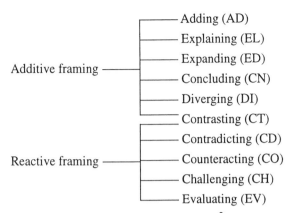

Figure 1 Framing of ideas (A taxonomy)[2]

A brief summary of the taxonomy's subcategories is given in Appendix 1. As the focus of this paper is not on the framing of ideas itself (how ideas are framed in association with each other) (which I have presented elsewhere at the 1999 Lancaster Applied Linguistics Conference, July) but on what the patterns of idea framing observed in group interaction tasks tell us about the way group work 'works' for learning, I will not go into detail about each category in this paper.

When the above taxonomy of idea framing is applied to various group interaction tasks recorded in both mono-national settings (where there are only Malaysian students) and bi-national settings (where there are both Malaysian and British students), several interesting insights emerge. Differences in the way ideas are framed appear both at the group level and at the individual level.

In order to illustrate this, I will here refer to two particular tasks (AR200 and RW2). The first task (AR200) was recorded in an arts module in a bi-national setting. There were three British students, all female, (LIZ, LIN, R) and two Malaysian students (Y, male) and (L, female). The task was 'Discuss the advantages and disadvantages of doing seminar presentations and writing essays.' The second task (RW2) was recorded in a TESOL module in a mono-national setting. There were six Malaysian students engaged in the task (Y, RI (male); S, C, E, L (female)). The task was 'Discuss the advantages and disadvantages of reading aloud.' The students Y and L appear in both tasks (AR200 and RW2). These two tasks are chosen for comparison as their nature is very similar. I will first discuss the framing of ideas in these two tasks (i.e. the types of links between ideas). Then I will look at the types of ideas contributed by the students to the requirement of the tasks.

First, one interesting finding that emerges from the comparison of idea framing at the group level in these two tasks is the way Additive framing and Reactive framing occur in the tasks. The following is an example of the framing of ideas in the two tasks. The actual texts for these frames are given in Appendix 2.

Table 1 Framing of ideas in AR200 and RW2

AR200

	Y[T]	LIZ[Y]	LIN[LIZ]/[Y]	Y[LIN]							LIZ[Y]	Y[LIZ]	LIN[Y]
	↑	→	→/↓	↑	↑	↑	↑	↑	↑	↑	→	↑	→
172-270	ED-- EL-- CT:C-- EL== CO--	ED==	AD/-- CT:O	EL==	ED--	EL---	EL--	EL---	CN--	EL==	CD==	RE==	CO==

RW2

	S[T]	E[S]	C[+]	RI[C]	L[RI+]	S[L]	RI[S]	S[S]	RI[S]	L[S,RI]	RI[S+]	Y[L]	Y[Y]/[L]	L[Y]	Y[Y]/[L]
	↑	↑	↑	↑	↑	↑	↑	↑	↑	↑	→	→	→/↓	→/↓	
13-76	ED== RE== AD==	RE==	AD==	RE---	EL==	ED==	RE==	EV==	AD==	CT:O==	CD---	EL/CD=	CT:O==	CO==	RE/CD ==

== indicates a change of speaker;   -- indicates the same speaker

→ indicates Additive framing;   ↓ indicates Reactive framing

Y[LIZ] indicates the orientation: the idea uttered by Y is linked with its preceding idea uttered by LIZ

+ ...... indicates 'all the preceding ideas uttered by various speakers'

T ...... indicates 'Task/Task question'

As can be seen from the above frames, there is a difference in the way Additive and Reactive framing are used in the two tasks. In AR200, Additive framing and Reactive framing are used alternately, and spread out across the task. Additive framing is followed by Reactive framing or vice versa. In RW2, Additive framing and Reactive framing are clustered together. That is, there is a cluster of Additive framing and a cluster of Reactive framing across the task. In other words, the students add or react together in RW2.

Differences in the choice of the type of idea framing can also be seen at the individual level. For example, if we compare the framing of ideas by Y with LIZ in AR200 (lines 172–270), we can see that Y's way of participating in that particular task is through Additive framing. He adds to what other people are saying and to what he is saying himself. On the other hand, LIZ uses Reactive framing as the starting point for her contribution, which is then followed by Additive framing. For her, Reactive framing is immediate whereas Additive framing is delayed.

In addition to the difference in idea framing, interesting issues emerge when we look at the types of ideas themselves which are framed and contributed by the students in these two tasks. The following is the summary of the ideas framed by two students (Y and R in AR200).

Table 2 Y's ideas in AR200

			Task			
			Speaking/Seminar Presentations		Writing/Writing Essays and Assignments	
Line no.	Framing	Orientation	Advantages (+)	Disadvantages (−)	Advantages (+)	Disadvantages (−)
18–19 19–26	H EL	Y[T] Y[Y]	Things like: talking, fluent when I talk ...			
65–68	ED	Y[LIN]	I just put my points and talk.			
79–82	CT:C	Y[Y]				It needs accurate references (who, what, when, etc.)
82–85	CT:C	Y[Y]	I don't have to think much about references, etc.			

Table 2 Y's ideas in AR200 *cont.*

			Task			
			Speaking/Seminar Presentations		Writing/Writing Essays and Assignments	
Line no.	Framing	Orienta-tation	Advantages (+)	Disadvantages (–)	Advantages (+)	Disadvantages (–)
172–175	DI	Y[+]				I lost confidence because of the need for detailed references.
175–178	EL	Y[Y]				
222–236	ED	Y[LIN]	Handouts given to the audience.			
240–243	EL	Y[Y]	If I mix up my points, the audience will remind me.			
243–244	CN	Y[Y]	Audience can prompt me and help me out.			
272–273	AD	Y[Y]	It is a good way to start a discussion, a way to get direction.			
277–278	AD	Y[Y]				
279–285	CT:C	Y[Y]		I don't know whether your'e doing the right thing (no prompt)		
431–433	CT:O	Y[Y]	Seminar is ok.	Background reading is the problem.		
514–516	RE	Y[Y-old]	I prefer seminar.			
516–519	EL		I became better marked.			
707–709	DI	Y[+]	I can gain knowledge from others (can sees and listen's to others' presentations as well) It helps me understand more.			There is no chance to read other people's essays.
726–733	CT:C	Y[Y]				
750–751	CN	Y[Y]				

Orientation ....   indicates the speaker of the preceding idea with which a given idea is linked
(e.g. Y[LIZ] ....   the idea uttered by Y is linked with its preceding idea uttered by LIZ)
+ ......   indicates 'all the preceding ideas uttered by various speakers'
T ......   indicates 'Task/Task question'

Table 3 R's ideas in AR200

Line no.	Framing	Orientation	Speaking/Seminar Presentations — Advantages (+)	Disadvantages (−)	Writing/Writing Essays and Assignments — Advantages (+)	Disadvantages (−)
118	CN	R[LIN]		There is only one chance.	You have one load of chance (of changing)	
123	CT:C	R[R]				
127–129	CT:C	R[R]		It's like a coursework or		
135–136	EL	R[R]		exam. Once done you can't change it.		
142–143	CT:O	R[R]	But that is a benefit in some way (knowing that you can't do more to it)			
143–145	EL	R[R]				
145–148	CT:C	R[R]				You keep changing and feel bad and not necessarily (improving your work).
320–322	CO	R[LIZ]			Conscientious markers can spend a long time marking essays (so can see how your mind works).	
322–323	CN/CT:	R[R]/R	so tutors may			
323–325	O	[LIN28	prefer seminar			
	EL	7]	as they've			
		R[R]	only got to pay instant attention.			
351–353	DI	R[+]			The skills you	
353–362	ED	R[R]			learn from writing essays are important ...	

Differences can be seen in the types of ideas contributed by Y and R. The ideas contributed by Y are related to the advantages of speaking. He thinks favourably of speaking. On the other hand, R's ideas are related to both the advantages and disadvantages of speaking and writing. She switches from talking about the advantages of speaking to its disadvantages, from the advantages of writing to its disadvantages. She thinks both positively and negatively about the same topic under discussion.

Idea Framing, View of Knowledge and How Group Work 'Works'

What do these different patterns of idea framing tell us about the way group work works and the way knowledge is constructed?

First, the difference in the choice of Additive and Reactive framing suggests two different views of knowledge and learning into which students may have been unconsciously or consciously socialised through their previous sociocultural educational experience. On one hand, there are students who may have been socialised into a view of learning or knowledge construction as more additive than reactive. For them knowledge is to be added to and they will probably keep quiet when they have nothing new to add to. On the other hand, there are also students who may have been trained to view learning or knowledge construction as more reactive than additive. For them knowledge is to be reacted to and they will probably keep quiet when they do not have anything to react to.

Second, the difference in the types of ideas that are generated and framed in accordance with the requirement of the task can also reflect two different ways of thinking: thinking either positively or negatively of a piece of given knowledge vs. thinking both positively and negatively of a piece of given knowledge.

In many of the group interaction tasks I recorded in mono-national settings where there were only Malaysian students, they tended to frame their ideas in more additive ways. For them, it was apparently more important to complete the whole task, and to go through all the sub-questions in the discussion task in additive ways. On the other hand, the framing of ideas was more reactive in the tasks I recorded in bi-national settings, using both British and Malaysian students; and reactive framing was usually used by the British students in the group as their starting point for taking part in the discussion. It did not seem very important for the British students to go through all the questions in the discussion task. Instead, they were quite willing to spend more time on one particular task question and frame their ideas in reactive ways. When I interviewed the Malaysian students after such group work in bi-national settings, they often expressed their dissatisfaction with not completing the whole task and with getting distracted by too much argument on one particular task question.

This kind of Additive and Reactive framing is also observed in the way students interact in other situations. For example, in lectures where the discussion was led by the teacher and the interaction was between the teacher and the class, it was noticed that the majority of the Malaysian students would very often interrupt the teacher when they wanted some information or when they had something to add to what the teacher was saying whereas the British students tended to interrupt the teacher when they had something to react to and when they did not agree with the teacher. In bi-national classes, where both Malaysian and British students attended together, when the teacher asked a question to the class to test their knowledge about a particular subject area (display question), the Malaysian students were the ones who usually volunteered information, and very often such voluntary information was given collectively in chorus (adding together). In such instances, the British students were usually quiet and the collective response to the teacher's display question in chorus was not at all common among the British students. While the British students were actively engaged in reacting to the teacher's lecture (evaluating, contrasting, etc.), the Malaysian students were quiet. By remaining quiet when they had nothing to add to, or by talking when they wanted the teacher to add to what they were not clear about, the Malaysian students let the teacher continue with his/her pre-planned lecture notes, or complete his/her pre-planned lesson (completing the whole task). On the other hand, by engaging in Reactive framing with the teacher's lecture, the British students did not sometimes let the teacher get through his/her pre-planned lecture notes. At times the reactive framing could take over the teacher's lecture, and the teacher's pre-planned lecture notes were only half delivered.

These interaction patterns suggest that there seems to be a difference in the British and Malaysian students' view of what counts as valuable educational knowledge. For Malaysian students, what counts as valuable knowledge is knowledge that is framed in more additive ways; knowledge is to be added to. For British students, what counts as valuable knowledge is knowledge that is framed in more reactive ways; knowledge is to be reacted to. For them, it is not that 'I know something you don't know' which matters, but 'I know how to react to something you know' seems to be more important.

Conclusion

Referring back to the main theme of this paper 'looking at changes from the learner's point of view', what do these patterns of idea framing and the students' unconscious or conscious perceptions of knowledge and learning reflected in these patterns tell us about the way a particular pedagogical innovation, in this case group work, should be implemented?

The unconscious and conscious view of knowledge and learning into which students have been socialised as part of their previous socio-cultural educational experience needs to be considered when implementing educational innovations. Just getting students to work in groups, and just seeing students engaging actively in discussions and talking actively does not mean that a particular educational change will successfully be implemented. How group work 'works' might not be the same for different contexts and different learning groups. What students mean by 'it works' may not be what the teacher and the institution perceive as 'it works'.

As professionals involved in the process of educational innovations, we need to look at changes with reference to the student's previous experience. If a particular change is desirable and requires to be implemented, one needs to be aware of ways of implementing it not at the superficial level but more importantly at the deeper ideological level. It is important to relate the changes not only to the teacher's ideology and belief but more importantly to the students' especially when the changes are originated and promoted by a professional or institutional community (including researchers, practitioners, policy makers, etc.) whose socio-cultural and educational background is not the same as the students'.

We need to be aware of the importance of the power of the past (not only the teachers' but also the students') in shaping the future. Louden (1991: xiv), in a discussion of looking at changes from the teacher's perspective, says: 'Until those of us who look for improvement and change in education learn to approach teachers with more respect for the power of continuity in their work, we are likely to continue to be disappointed with the progress of educational reform.' Applying this to the student's perspective, one may wonder 'Isn't it also important to approach students with respect for the power of continuity in their study when implementing a pedagogical change?'.

This view may sound too 'democratic' with too much empowering of students. However, it is quite in tune with the paradigm shift from the teacher-centred to the learner-centred approach, from the emphasis on teacher talk to student talk, from lecture-based teaching to the use of group work, which implies, to some extent, a shift of power and responsibility from teachers to learners. Thus, it may well be reasonable to say that changes should be looked at from the learner's point of view, relating the changes to the students' past experience, in other words, recognising the role of the students' past in the process of a particular educational innovation/change.

Acknowledgements

I am grateful to the University College Chichester for funding my research. Also many thanks to the lecturers and the students who helped me with my data collection.

Notes

1. An initial pilot study was first undertaken by Dr Mick Randall and Sue Lavender. The pilot study examined the effects that task type, cultural background and individual factors played in interaction patterns when learners were engaged in group discussions on different undergraduate modules (see Randall & Lavender 1998).
2. The taxonomy and the scheme used here for data analysis have been developed as part of my doctoral study.

References

Allwright, R. L. (1984) The importance of interaction in classroom language learning. *Applied Linguistics* 5, 156–71.

Anderson, J. R. (1980) *Cognitive Psychology and its Implications* (2nd edn). NY: W. H. Freeman and Company.

Bakhtin, M. M. (1986) *Speech Genres and Other Late Essays*. Austin: University of Texas Press.

Barnes, D. and Todd, F. (1977) *Communication and Learning in Small Groups*. London: Routledge & Kegan Paul.

Bernstein, B. (1971) On the classification and framing of educational knowledge. In M. F. D. Young (ed.) *Knowledge and Control (New directions for the sociology of education)* (pp. 47–69). London: Collin Macmillan.

Boulima, J. (1999) *Negotiated Interaction in Target Language Classroom Discourse*. Amsterdam/ Philadelphia: John Benjamins Publishing Company.

Day, R. R. (ed.) (1986) *Talking to Learn: Conversation in second language acquisition*. Rowley, MA: Newbury House.

Edwards, A. D. and Westgate, D. P. G. (1994) *Investigating Classroom Talk* (2nd edn). London and Washington DC: The Falmer Press.

Edwards, D. and Mercer, N. (1987) *Common Knowledge (The development of understanding in classroom)*. London and New York: Routledge.

Hofmann, Th. R. (1993) *Realms of Meaning (An introduction to semantics)*. London: Longman.

Long, M. H. (1981) Input, interaction and second language acquisition. Paper presented at the New York Academy of Sciences Conference on Native and Foreign Language Acquisition.

Long, M. H. (1983) Native speaker/nonnative speaker conversation in the second language classroom. In M. A. Clarke and J. Handscombe (eds) *On TESOL '82: Pacific perspectives on language learning and teaching*. Washington, DC: TESOL.

Lotman, Yu. M. (1988) Text within a text. *Soviet Psychology* 26 (3), 32–51.

Louden, W. (1991) *Understanding Teaching: Continuity and change in teacher's knowledge*. New York: Cassell.

Mercer, N. (1995) *The Guided Construction of Knowledge (Talk amongst teachers and learners)*. Clevedon: Multilingual Matters.

Olsher, D. (1996) Some issues in analyzing classroom interaction: An interview with Deborah Poole. *Issues in Applied Linguistics* 7 (2), 297–307.

Randall, M. and Lavender, S. (1998) Task, personality or culture. In *Proceedings of the Cross-cultural Capability Conference* (pp. 263–70). Leeds Metropolitan University.

Tin, T. B. (1999) Analysing group interaction patterns in academic settings: Group interaction, knowledge construction, and idea framing. Paper presented at the 1999 Lancaster Applied Linguistics Conference (Discourses and learning: Theoretical and applied perspectives), July.

Tuyay, S., Jennings, L. and Dixon, C. (1995) Classroom discourse and opportunities to learn: An ethnographic study of knowledge construction in a bilingual third-grade classroom. *Discourse Processes* 19, 75–110.

Vygotsky, Lev. (1978) Mind in society. Cambridge MA: Harvard University Press.

Vygotsky, Lev. (1997) (10th printing) *Thought and Language* (newly revised and edited by Alex Kozulin). London: The MIT Press.

Widdowson, H. G. (1998) Context, community, and authentic language. *TESOL* 32 (4), 705–16.

Wood, D. J., Bruner, J. S. and Ross, G. (1976) The role of tutoring in problem solving. *Journal of Child Psychology and Psychiatry* 17 (2), 89–100.

Young, M. F. D. (1971) An approach to the study of curricula as socially organized knowledge. In M. F. D. Young (ed.) *Knowledge and Control (New directions for the sociology of education)* (pp. 19-46). London: Collier Macmillan.

Appendix 1

Additive Framing:

When two ideas have an additive link, the second idea is an addition to the first idea without judgement or evaluation or comment on the quality, or truthfulness, or validity of the propositional content of the first idea. The second idea can be an addition to the first idea in many different ways.

Adding   'Adding' is an addition of a similar new idea to the head-idea or the list of ideas preceding it. In terms of lexical links, the two ideas have a co-hyponymous and near-synonymous link. In terms of syntactic links, the two ideas often have a similar syntactic pattern. These syntactic and lexical links mediate the process of generating the second idea (Y) in relation to the first idea (X). In terms of cognitive load, this type of idea framing does not seem to be as demanding as other types of idea framing as it follows a similar pattern of thinking mediated through the use of a similar pattern of lexical and syntactic items.

Explaining   The second idea is an explanation of the first idea. It can be a reason to justify the first idea (answering the 'why' question) or it can be a paraphrase of the first idea (explaining the meaning of the first idea in other words). The second idea can also be a consequence of the first idea. In terms of lexical link, there is a causal relationship (showing the cause-effect relationship) or a temporal relationship (showing the sequential relationship). This type of idea framing is often indicated by such syntactic markers as 'because', 'so', 'I mean ...' etc.

Expanding   The second idea is an elaboration on a part or the whole of the first idea. It is an addition of more specific information to the part or whole of the preceding general idea. In terms of lexical link, there is a general-specific (superordinate-hyponymous) link between the two ideas. In terms of syntactic link, there is often a shift from the present simple tense (which indicates the general status of the information) to other verb forms such as past tense, future tense, present continuous tense, etc. (which refer to specific cases or examples).

Concluding	While expanding is adding more specific information to the preceding general information, concluding is an addition of a generalised idea to a part or the whole of the preceding specific idea(s). In terms of lexical link, there is a specific-general (hyponymous-superordinate) link. In terms of syntactic link, there is a shift from such verb forms as present continuous, past tense, etc. to the present simple tense; and the use of such syntactic markers as 'so', 'usually' can also be found.
Diverging	Diverging is an addition of a different idea to the preceding ideas. This type of link indicates the kind of thinking, diverging from the flow of thinking preceding it, or a change in the direction of thinking to something different. The second idea Y is a different idea to the preceding ideas, initiating a switch from the flow of its preceding ideas. In terms of lexical link, there is a lexical shift (from a set of co-hyponymous lexical items in the preceding idea(s) (X) to a new different lexical item in the second idea (Y)).

Reactive Framing:

When two ideas have a reactive link, the second idea is an addition to the first idea, with the speaker's judgement or evaluation on the truthfulness, validity or value of the first idea. There are several kinds of reactive framing.

Contradicting	The second idea contradicts the validity or truthfulness of the first idea, indicating that the first idea is not true. In terms of lexical/syntactic link, there is a link of negation between the two ideas.
Counteracting	The second idea reduces the validity or truthfulness of the first idea, indicating that the validity or truthfulness of the first idea is reduced under certain conditions or does not apply in certain conditions. In terms of lexical link, there is an antonymous (opposite) link as well as a general-specific link between the two ideas. This type of idea framing is often indicated by such syntactic patterns as 'if-pattern', 'but'.

Challenging	The second idea questions the validity or truthfulness of the first idea. In terms of syntactic link, the second idea is often in the form of a question, challenging the validity or truthfulness of the first idea rather than checking or asking for information.
Evaluating	The second idea is an evaluation of the quality, truthfulness or validity of the first idea. The second idea is an evaluative comment such as 'That's good', 'That's interesting', etc. judging the quality of the first idea, by using evaluative adjectives (e.g. 'interesting', 'good'). In terms of lexical and syntactic links, the use of evaluative adjectives and the syntactic pattern of 'It/That is + Adjective' or 'It/That is + Adjective + Noun' can be found.
Contrasting	'Contrasting' is an addition of an opposite or different idea to the preceding idea or ideas. It can be an addition of an opposite idea which does not question the truthfulness or validity of the preceding idea itself, just to show two sides of the coin. The addition of an opposite idea can, however, also be seen as affecting the truthfulness or validity of the preceding idea. Thus, 'contrasting' will be considered as a category which falls between both Additive Framing and Reactive Framing as shown in Figure 1. In terms of lexical link, there is an antonymous link. This type of idea framing is often indicated by such syntactic markers as 'but', 'anyway'.

Appendix 2

Text for Frame 1: AR200 (172–270)

Framing	Orientation	Text	
ED	Y [T]	Y: /for one thing.. when I'm writing	172
		an essay because I have ..I've lost	173
		confidence when I have to write..	174
		read...write an essay/because...	175
EL	Y [Y]	there's book to be referred to ...as I	176
		was writing and...'is that true?'look	177
CT:C	Y [Y]	at book./whereas for speaking yeah	178
		most of the time I just took points	179
EL	Y [Y]	and I speak it up/.. because most of	180
		the time it's there.../	181
		:	
		:	
CT:O	LIZ [Y]	LIZ: /Yeh but you're lucky there are	188
		a lot of people .. can't do that.you	189
		know/ =	190

		Y: yea. I know	192
ED	LIZ[LIZ]	LIZ: =/they they freeze up. =	194
		R: mhm	196
		LIN: it's true.	198
		LIZ: = unless they have so much to	200
		refer to.. um../	201
		LIN: yes. and ..	203
		Y: I guess I have(xx)	205
AD/	LIN[LIZ]/	LIN: /and on certain circumstances you	207
CT:O	LIN[Y179]	need to hand out some...	208
		LIZ: yeah.	210
		LIN: written information, wouldn't	212
		you? to people that were attending./	213
		Y: most of [the time is]....	215
EL	LIN[LIN]	LIN: /[so they could] go to books and	217
		I mean because.. yea./	218
		L: yeah.	220
ED	Y[LIN]	Y: /... ah most of the time what I	222
		do is get a piece of paper./put some	223
EL	Y[Y]	of my points what I will talk about	224
		on it. but I don't have that much =	225
		LIN: right.	227
EL	Y[Y]	Y: = that much./actually just that	229
		piece of paper will go to the	230
		audience./	231

```
                              LIN:  right.                         233


EL      Y[Y]                  Y:   /and they carry it as I talk     235
                              along./                               236


                              LIN:  right.                          238


EL      Y[Y]                  Y:   /so .. sudden.. suddenly I just  240
                              mix up my point. sometimes the        241
                              audience will say umm 'so you've      242
CN      Y[Y]                  missed that point'/... so it's a way  243
                              of  the ... audience  to prompt me./  244


                              LIN:  yes.                            246


                              R:         yeah.                      248


EL      Y[Y]                  Y:   /that way I don't have to keep   250
RE      Y[Y-243]              looking at my notes./so  it's the     251
                              audience helping me  out./the         252
RE      Y[Y-240]              audience is  actually saying  'that   253
                              is my next point. that's my next      254
                              point. that's my next point'./        255


                              LIN:  right.                          257


CD      LIZ[Y]                LIZ: /you can't rely on the audience. 259
                              [they're not there. can you?]/        260


RE      Y[LIZ]                Y:   [yea, most of the time you can't 262
                              rely] on the audience but             263
                              [[sometimes]]                         264


CO      LIN[Y]                LIN: /[[unless you]] ask questions and 266
                              get the discussion going or           267
                              something./                           268


                              R:     umm                            270
```

Text for Frame 2: RW2 (13–76)

Framing	Orientation	Text	
		E: /(laugh) ok. advantages?	4
		RI: what are the possible	6
		advantages?	7
		S: reading aloud?/	9
		RI: if you read aloud.	11
ED	S[T]	S: /yeah. .... you ..... pronounce	13
		the [....vocabulary...]/	14
RE	E[S]	E: /[pronunciation]./	16
AD	C[+]	C: /help to pronounce.../	18
RE	RI[C]	RI: /help the pronunciation/=	20
		:	
		:	
AD	L[RI+]	L: /[and also] your word projection	25
		too./	26
		E: mhm.. helps...	28
RE	S[L]	S: /yeah. it does ....actually./	30
		:	
		:	
EL	S[L]	S: /[you learn how to]... yes. you	35
		learn how to speak clearly...if you	36
		[are reading]/	37
ED	RI[S]	RI: /[especially when] you're reading	39
		dialogues./	40
RE?	S[S]	S: /yeah. [(your pronunciation is]	42
		so much tightened)/	43

EV	RI [S]	RI: /[yeah. I think there is a point	45
		there.]/	46
AD	L [S,RI]	L: /intonation..../	48
CT:O	RI [S+]	RI: /[but usually it's quite	50
		difficult for you to read and	51
		understand at the same time./you	52
		should better]....	53
CD	Y [L]	Y: /[but intonation doesn't go in	55
EL/CD	Y [Y]/Y [L]	you know/.. if you're reading	56
		aloud.... you never...] you do not	57
		follow intonation. right./	58
CO	L [Y]	L: /[but what if ...you're...you're	60
		reading stories?]/	61
		:	
		:	
RE/CD	Y [Y-old]/Y [L]	Y: /[[[sorry it's not intonation./	74
		...when reading story ... if students	75
		read the most... they don't]]] /	76

Contributors

Gillian Brown began her career teaching English Language in the University College of Cape Coast, Ghana. She became lecturer in Phonetics at the University of Edinburgh in 1965, and Reader in Linguistics in 1981. In 1983 she moved to the University of Essex as Professor of Applied Linguistics, and in 1988 to Cambridge as Professor of English as an International Language and Director of the Research Centre for English and Applied Linguistics. She is currently working on how listeners construct the context within which a spoken message makes sense. She has written or co-written 15 books and some 50 papers including *Phonological Rules and Dialect Variation* (CUP 1971), *Listening to Spoken English* (Longman 1977, 2nd edn 1990), *Discourse Analysis* and *Teaching the Spoken Language* (with George Yule, CUP 1983), *Speakers, Listeners and Communication* (CUP 1995), *Phonics for Reading* (with Kate Ruttle, CUP 1999).

Michael Stubbs is Professor of English Linguistics at the University of Trier, Germany, and Senior Honorary Research Fellow, University of Birmingham, UK. He was previously Professor of English, Institute of Education, University of London, 1985–90; and Lecturer in Linguistics, University of Nottingham, 1974–85. He has published widely on educational linguistics and discourse analysis. His most recent book is *Text and Corpus Analysis* (1996 Blackwell); in preparation is a book entitled *Words and Phrases: Studies in Corpus Semantics*. He was Chair of BAAL 1988–91.

Malcolm Benson is a Professor at Hiroshima Shudo University, Japan, where he has taught English, Applied Linguistics, and Culture courses since 1987. Prior to that he taught in Zambia, England, Kenya, and Saudi Arabia, before getting a PhD at Florida State University. His current interest in the history of language teaching in part derives from these varied language teaching experiences.

Susan Gass is University Distinguished Professor in the Department of English at Michigan State University. She is the Director of the English Language Center and Co-Director of the Center for Language Education and Research. She has published widely in the field of Second Language Acquisition in a number of different areas. Her most recent books are *Stimulated Recall Methodology in Second Language Research* (published by Erlbaum, with Alison Mackey), *Input,*

Interaction, and the Second Language Learner (published by Erlbaum), and *Second Language Acquisition: An Introduction* (published by Erlbaum, with Larry Selinker). She is the winner of Michigan State University's Distinguished Faculty Award.

Florence Myles is Head of Linguistics in the School of Modern Languages at the University of Southampton. Her research interests are in Second Language Acquisition, especially of French. Her recent work has focused on the interaction between linguistic theory and language processing in SLA, the acquisition of interrogative constructions in French, and the role played by formulaic language in the construction of linguistic knowledge. She is co-author of *Second Language Learning Theories* (Arnold 1998, with Rosamond Mitchell).

Ben Rampton is a Reader in the School of Education, King's College London. He does socio- and applied linguistic research, with particular emphasis on ethnography and interactional discourse analysis, and his interests cover urban multilingualism, ethnicity, youth, and education. He was author of *Crossing: Language and Ethnicity among Adolescents* (Longman 1995), a co-author of *Researching Language: Issues of Power and Method* (Routledge 1992), and he recently guest-edited a special issue of the *Journal of Sociolinguistics* entitled *Styling the Other* (Volume 3/4 1999).

Mairian Corker is currently a visiting Senior Research Fellow in the School of Education, Kings College London, where she is developing research relating to disability discourse. She is author and editor of numerous publications, including *Deaf Transitions* (Jessica Kingsley), *Deaf and Disabled or Deafness Disabled?* (Open University Press), *Disability Discourse* (Open University Press) with Sally French, and the forthcoming *Disabling Language* (Routledge). She is an Executive Editor of the foremost journal in disability studies, *Disability and Society*.

Bernard McKenna lectures in the School of Communication, Faculty of Business at Queensland University of Technology. As a communication specialist, he has extensive research publications and consultancies in business, technical, and scientific writing. However, his most recent work includes studies of political communication. His recently completed doctoral thesis critically analysed the ideological shift during the Hawke-Keating years. He has also published on the Hanson and One Nation phenomena. He is currently co-authoring a book that identifies the political sea-change occurring during this globalised hyper-capitalist era.

Alison Piper is a Senior Lecturer in the School of Modern Languages at the University of Southampton. Her involvement with the University's learning and teaching strategy and the widening participation agenda led her to focus her research as a sociolinguist on the discourses of UK government policy on lifelong learning, and she has papers in press on the commodification of learning and the role of the individual in the learning society. She is currently extending this research to investigate health policy, and to explore the interplay between linguistics and social theory in analysing social policy in general.

Charmian Kenner is based at the Institute of Education in London with the Culture Communication & Societies Academic Group, where she is director of a two year ESRC research project on five year olds learning to write in more than one script system. She is also a Research Fellow with the Language and Culture group in the Educational Studies Department at Goldsmiths' College. Her publications include *Home Pages: Literacy Links for Bilingual Children* (Trentham Books, 2000).

Almut Josepha Koester is a PhD student and part-time lecturer at the University of Nottingham in the School of English Studies doing research on spoken discourse in office settings. She has an MA in Applied English Linguistics from the University of Birmingham and has extensive experience as an EFL teacher and teacher trainer in France and Germany. Her last position was as Director of Studies in the English Department of the Munich College of Adult Education. She has worked on projects of the Council of Europe and the British-German Academic Research Collaboration to develop materials for teacher training in the areas of Business English and Language Awareness.

Tan Bee Tin comes from Burma and she is currently undertaking her doctoral study at the Centre for International Education and Management, University College Chichester, UK. She worked as an English language teacher at the Rangoon University, Burma, and then at the British Council, Burma. Her main research interests are cross-cultural sociolinguistic studies and educational linguistic analyses of academic discourse.

Martin Gill is a lecturer in the Department of English at Åbo Akademi University, Finland, where he teaches sociolinguistics and British cultural studies. His PhD (University of Edinburgh, 1998) was concerned with the role of reading in second language learning, and his current research interests include literacy studies, the social history of reading, and the development of a sociocultural approach to learning and cognition.